HOW WE TALKED

and

COMMON FOLKS

HOW WE TALKED

and

COMMON FOLKS

Verna Mae Slone

Illustrations by Len Slone

THE UNIVERSITY PRESS OF KENTUCKY

Scholarly publisher for the Commonwealth,
serving Bellarmine University, Berea College, Centre College of Kentucky, Eastern
Kentucky University, The Filson Historical Society, Georgetown College, Kentucky
Historical Society, Kentucky State University, Morehead State University, Murray
State University, Northern Kentucky University, Transylvania University, University
of Kentucky, University of Louisville, and Western Kentucky University.
All rights reserved.

Editorial and Sales Offices: The University Press of Kentucky
663 South Limestone Street, Lexington, Kentucky 40508-4008
www.kentuckypress.com

Library of Congress Cataloging-in-Publication Data

Slone, Verna Mae, 1914–
   How we talked ; and, Common folks / Verna Mae Slone ; foreword for How We
Talked by Michael B. Montgomery ; foreword for Common Folks by Sidney Saylor
Farr ; illustrations by Len Slone.
      p. cm.
   First work originally published: Pippa Passes, Ky. : Pippa Valley Printing, 1982; 2nd
work originally published: Pippa Passes, Ky. : Writers and the Appalachian Learning
Laboratory, Alice Lloyd College, 1979.
   ISBN 978-0-8131-9209-3 (pbk. : alk. paper)
   1. Knott County (Ky.) — Biography. 2. Knott County (Ky.) — Social life and customs.
3. English language — Provincialisms — Kentucky. 4. Pippa Passes (Ky.) — Biography.
5. Pippa Passes (Ky.) — Social life and customs. I. Slone, Len. II. Slone, Verna Mae,
1914– Common folks. III. Title. IV. Title: Common folks.
   F457.K5S57 2009
   976.9'165 — dc22   2009007432

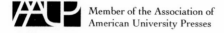

CONTENTS

HOW WE TALKED

To Brandon, Justin, and Kari
my three great-grandchildren

"May their tribe increase."
They are the twelfth generation of Slones
that have lived on Caney.

ACKNOWLEDGMENTS

In no way have I tried to list all the peculiar words and phrases used by my people. Also, many that I have included are universal—used by other people from another locality with a different background; but every word seen here in this book was used by us, so maybe that just goes to show we were just like folks everywhere.

The following people helped me to gather the information to write *How We Talked*:

The late Herbert Slone
Armatha Inmon
Mary Sparkman
Edna Pratt
"Dock" John Whesley Hall and his wife, Bertha
Lurainia Watson Hall
Jimmie Smith

FOREWORD

The remarkable circumstances of how a memoir, written by a
native of a small rural community in Knott County, Kentucky,
became an Appalachian classic are unique to the annals of American literature. Critics and readers alike wondered how Verna Mae
Slone, a grandmother who did not devote herself to writing until
well into her sixties, could emerge to produce such a striking,
compelling account of life in the Kentucky mountains. Given her
plainspokenness, she probably would have told an interviewer
something like, "I wrote when I was ready to write." Indeed,
she was prompted first to write for her descendants, to preserve
the memories of her struggles and redeeming joys. This private
audience, however, soon shared her work with others. But in a
more profound sense I suspect that she was ready to write after
a lifetime persuaded her to become an apologist and defender of
such mountain values as unpretentiousness, closeness of family,
endurance in trial, respect and consideration for others, dignity,
and pride tempered by modesty. By presenting her story as one
that could have been told by any ordinary woman in Caney Creek,
What My Heart Wants to Tell gained the universal appeal that con-
tinues to give it a special place in the hearts of those who have read
it and recommended it to friends. What more effective antidote
for the demeaning stereotypes of Appalachian people than the

account that is *What My Heart Wants to Tell?* The story of Slone's life, so touchingly and powerfully rendered, makes each of us reflect on our own lives.

How We Talked is in many ways a sequel to *What My Heart Wants to Tell.* Produced by a tiny publisher in Pippa Passes in 1982, it too is meant as a testimony to lifeways rapidly fading. The book is part glossary and part memoir; it catalogs usages and expressions mainly by subject matter (medicine, superstitions, food, school, etc.), often with accompanying anecdotes from episodes and patterns of Appalachian family life. The arrangement is never alphabetical — one cannot simply "look up" a term — but is ramshackledty and seemingly based on loose association. This fluid organization permits comparison with terms never or rarely used (as by only men or women) and the inclusion of other types of information not usually found in conventional glossaries.

The reader quickly learns that the author aims not to compile language so much as to reveal how language was the essential glue of mountain life. Slone explains not just the forms of language that were used in certain situations to mean certain things (although there is, to be sure, plenty of insight into the nuances of mountain vocabulary), but, more important, the implicit rules governing language use in the mountains. One of my favorite examples is found on page 29, where Slone recounts her son's experience with a bus driver in Gary, Indiana, where he worked. When her son asked a question, he pronounced *light* in his downhome way as *laht,* eliciting a sneer from the driver: "'What part of the South are you from, boy? Haven't you been up here long enough to learn how to talk?' 'I hope that I never lose my way of talking,' my son replied. 'If and when I do, I am going home. If I forgot how my mother taught me to talk, I might forget what she taught me, and one of the first things she taught me was to be kind to strangers.'"

I don't reckon that bus driver argued with that boy much for teaching such a universal lesson. Slone has a typical Appalachian sense of insider/outsider duality, but she wants less to take pleasure in the tables being turned on a "foreigner" than to affirm the integrity of mountain speechways and behavior, and the values communicated, such as a highly refined sense of propriety. *How We Talked* is thus about much more than talking. It's about the entire range of communicative behavior witnessed by the author during her early adulthood—how people related to one another and how communities functioned. The rules of interaction are finely nuanced; often what is not said is as important as what is actually spoken. Slone is a keen, lifelong observer of the intimate language that encapsulates the mores, customs, beliefs, humor, attitudes, empathy, and wisdom of generations of mountain people.

This book is a fine blend of sharply personal narrative and typical Appalachian life. People from other communities (and perhaps the rare anthropologist who learns the insider's world) will have to judge how typical Caney Creek speech and customs are, but the material in this book comes from a sharp lifelong observer of her community, and is a chronicle of mountain life made all the more precious by the gradual passing of that life. *How We Talked* stands virtually alone as a testament by an insider to what many mountain people will recognize as an accurate, sensitive, and unvarnished presentation of a way of life they once knew and that, though receding, is too deeply ingrained, too vital a part of what makes mountain people who they are, to disappear in a generation or two. It should be read closely by sociologists, anthropologists, social workers, educators, and many other specialists. *How We Talked* will teach or remind all of us how "talk" makes mountain society work.

Michael B. Montgomery

A NOTE ON THE TEXT

This book presents Appalachian language as it was spoken during Verna Mae Slone's formative years, nearly a century ago, and it includes some language that modern readers might find offensive. After serious consideration, the publisher decided to retain that language in the interests of authenticity and preserving the historic record. This book offers insight into the development of modern mountain life, and censoring it would provide an inaccurate picture of the heritage of Appalachian language.

OUR OLD SAYINGS

The beautiful language of our people is slowly fading into the past. Impossible to capture on paper, hard to understand or learn, it cannot be imitated: even on tape it loses something. Yet it's never forgotten or lost by someone born into it. I have seen and heard folks come back to the hills after being away, Ph.D's to their credit, slip back into our dialect in a manner of hours. Yet I have heard professional actors that speak several languages fluently think they were talking "like a hillbilly": to us it sounds so unreal it would be pathetic if it were not so laughable.

I have heard the words "deep twangy" used to describe our voices, which is correct as far as it goes, but its musical, soft, low murmuring sound is hard to describe. The memory of its beauty has been tarnished by outsiders, ridiculed and demeaned by its exaggeration. Our language belongs only to us people of Appalachian Mountains. It may vary from state to state; small but distinct differences in the pronouncing of a word, use of an expression; even families living only a few miles apart are found to have some words used only by them. For example, when we mean to say "I don't know if I will," I say "I don't know where I will or not." My husband says, "I don't know what I will." We do not talk the same to outsiders as we do among ourselves. My husband can tell when I am on the phone if I am talking to "one of us" or an outsider. I am proud of our way of talking. I wish to retain it, I want to preserve its memory. I hope to accomplish more than just a list of words and their meaning; the expressions, the thoughts behind them, how they were used...thus capturing the way mountain people think and believe, their customs, traditions, way of life.

The softness of our voices causes us to drop the "g" in words ending in "ing," then "laughing" becomes "laughin'"; "morning" becomes "mornin'"; "smiling" becomes "smilin'." We slur two syllables together, then "chestnut" becomes "chesnet." Sometimes two or three words become one, the greeting "how do you do" turns to "howdy"; "how are you" — "harrie."

We do not talk as our fathers and mothers did. As the outsiders moved in, our language was absorbed into theirs. Our children have lost more, the grandchildren have only a small trace of it left, as they get more educated. I know it's something that must be folded and put away, as the clothes worn by our dead ancestors, but it must not be forgotten, but preserved, taken out now and again, admired for its beauty, accepted for its wisdom, and remembered with pride by those to whom it belongs.

Some of my sayings belong to the Slone family, some just to the community of Caney Creek here in Knott County of Eastern Kentucky—but most were used by all hill people of Appalachia.

I will not try to keep them alphabetically, but group them as food, work, medicine, school, religion, superstitions, etc.

Some words or expressions are a little "off color" and as a Christian I am reluctant to use them, but as they were a part of our language, I feel I must include them. I have tried to make this as interesting as I can so it will not be too boresome to read. Some parts are amusing, some perplexing, all educational. Some words are still used. Most are forgotten by the grandchildren of the people that once used this form of communication. Yet it will bring back memories to others of another place and time. It's not my intention to ridicule or criticize in any derogatory manner these, my people. I love and respect them. I am one of them.

To call these, our people, ignorant is the highest act of ignorance that could be imposed by anyone. There is a great difference between being ignorant and illiterate. The ingenuity they used to accomplish some of the things they did shows wisdom. That the results were sometimes crude and simple does not mean a lack of intelligence, just that they had less to work with. People that obtain their education from books are only learning what someone else learned before them; our folks learned out of need and necessity. Like learning to tell time by the sun, the seasons and the stars; how to measure by using the length of the fingers, hands, arm spread, or walking stride; weather prediction by watching the formation of the clouds, how the smoke rose from the chimney, actions of the animals. Sure it was spiced with superstition, but among the chaff were kernels of truth. To remember which were the short months and which were the long ones, they counted the knuckles on the fist, each knuckle counting one, the space between one; beginning with January for the first knuckle, the space between the first and second finger as February, the second finger March, etc., the last one July, then back to the beginning with August. All the knuckles were long months, the spaces between the short ones.

All our sayings had a different meaning when they originated. Some were first used for the first time as late as the last fifty or sixty years, some are so old no one knows when they began — based on a real event, the incident forgotten, the expression still used because so much can be implied in a few words when both parties know the meaning of an expression, yet so useless and misunderstood by others with a different background. Some phrases have lost their meaning and are now used humorously.

— When someone knocks on the door he might hear a voice from inside say, "Come in if your nose is clean." Long ago people were not welcome if they had some contagious disease. An unclean or runny nose might be a sign of sickness, a clean nose meant a healthy and welcome person. We now use this phrase just as a joke and only as long as we know to whom we are speaking.

— Lots of older people on Caney still say, "Now I guess you know how Humpy stands it." This means, "Now that you are having the same trouble that I have been having for some time you can now sympathize with me." When Mrs. Lloyd first established a school on Caney in Knott County of Eastern Kentucky, which later became the Alice Lloyd College, she used coal for fuel. Abisha Johnson was hired to attend the fires in all the buildings connected with the school. The coal was bought from and delivered by other residents of Caney. As the houses were built high on the sides of the hills, the coal had to be carried from the coal house, where it had been dumped, to each house. Abisha carried it, one sackful at a time, on his back. It's very uncomfortable to carry coal this way; the edges of the coal are sharp. It's also very dirty. To make things worse, Abisha had a hunchback that had given him the nickname "Humpy." One day he met my father in the road leading through the campus. (My father was also employed by the college, to make chairs.) This time my father also had a sack of coal on his back. Looking at him with sympathy and humor, Abisha said, "Now I guess you know how Humpy stands (endures) it."

— Another: "It's strictly understood that old dry don't count" means, "Don't bring up anything from the past although it is relevant to the present situation. We must only use the present evidence as bearing on the case." A small boy was helping my father make molasses, getting into more trouble than helping, when he almost fell into the pan of boiling molasses, frightening everyone, as well as himself. My father said to him, "I bet you a quarter that you got so scared you nastied your britches (pants)." The boy took him up on the bet. "There's only one way to prove it, you must pull down your clothes and show me." As the little fellow began to remove his pants he said, "Now, it's strictly understood that old dry don't count." Needless to say, he got the quarter.

—Another one: "The peanuts are coming up awful pretty," belongs only to our family and oddly enough means, "Let's change the subject. This talk is going to hurt someone that's listening and cause us all to be sad." When my children were very small, my husband was away from home a lot of the time. The children and I were alone. We had no close neighbors. There was only one bedroom, which was also the living room. After we had gone to bed we would talk for a while. I would not let them bring up any subject that might cause us to be sad, just before we went to sleep. If it was something that needed to be discussed, it could wait until the next day. One night something had bothered them and they kept on again and again referring to it, as I kept trying to talk away from it. At last, in desperation, I said, "Can't you all think of anything else to talk about?" My oldest son answered, "Mom, our peanuts are coming up awful pretty." The laugh that followed chased away all the gloom and we went to sleep in a happy mood.

—"Being paid by Grant" means you are working without wanting or expecting any pay. Grant was the name of a man who drove around with his wife in a buggy, staying with first one person, a relative or friend, then another, having no home of their own. Going the same route, they usually visited Caney once a year. One day some men were playing horseshoes. A neighbor asked them, "When do you expect to get paid for this hard work?" One of the men answered, "Oh, Grant will pay us on his next trip around."

— The words "Nigh to me" can mean "We are close kin," but it means a lot more than just that. If you hear someone say of another person, "He is nigh to me," it represents a closeness, a belonging to each other, that no one nor anything can come between, not even death. This is only found in the mountains, and not understood by outsiders. Some man might jokingly say of his wife, "I have lived with her so long that she has begun to feel nigh to me."

— The word "love" is not used very much by a hill person except when he is talking about the love he has for God. The word love is held too sacred to be used lightly, if at all. "I think a lot of that person" means I like them a lot. Some respected man of the community in a high position is said to be "Well thought of" and a woman or man that shows love for their spouse or children is said to be "a fool about them." Young people beginning to show interest in someone of the opposite sex are said to "be claiming each other"; the feeling has not progressed quite far enough along for a date. Then, when they begin to date, they are "going with each other." The real dating was "sparking." This word "sparkin'" got its beginning because the couple's only way to get to talk to each other was to sit side by side in two straight-backed chairs (homemade split bottoms) before the fire, after the family had gone to bed in the same room. Whispering to each other, sparks rising from the chimney told the neighbors that someone was up later than the usual bedtime. During the daytime they might do their sparking lying across the bed, side by side, while the family went in and out of the same room. Not much privacy, huh? Maybe that's why they did not spark very long before they got married and "set up a housekeeping." Yet most often they lived with their parents for the first months, until they got together enough "house plunder." Some parents had a small, one-room house close by where the newlyweds first lived, while waiting to build a house of their own. This house was called "a weening house" and was used over and over again as each child got married. The term meaning sexual intercourse was "fooling around with a woman." A man would boast of his faithfulness to his wife by saying, "I never fooled with any woman in my life but her." Rape was "mistreating a woman" and the man involved was dealt with very harshly—sometimes hanged. Using obscene language was "blackguarding." One of the first lessons taught to a boy by his father was "Never talk bad to a good girl and never fool with a mean girl under age. Never talk bad in front of your women kinfolks." A man could be indicted for asking a woman for a sexual favor unless he could prove she had "thrown herself at him" (showing undue friendship)—even as small an act as asking for a cigarette, as smoking was "unbecoming to women." Incest and homosexuality were seldom heard of. The few times it was suspected it was unbelieved, talked about in whispers. The man was hated, shunned, called a "brute," sometimes beat up or flogged, and even hanged.

— "We'uns will pay you's": when these words were used, with a handshake by a mountain man, it was more binding than any contract drawn up by a lawyer, or a treaty between countries. On these words were based the very essence of mountain philosophy. Even death could not break this promise. It did not just mean, "I will pay you," but, "If for some reason I cannot pay you, some of my family or kinfolks will see that you are paid. If for some reason you can't receive it, then it will be paid to some of your family or kin." The cash money would be paid only once, but the favor remembered and paid again and again, over and over, generation after generation. A grudge (resentment for an insult or injury) was repaid the same way, thus resulting in the family feuds. Almost all local elections were either lost or gained by this custom. A man could lose or gain votes for something done by his grandfather. Another well-known custom: if you asked a price for something, and someone offered to give you what you had asked, you must take this price, even if you had later changed your mind and did not want to sell at that price. It was counted very shameful if you did not, and was called "ruing back." Also, when trading with someone, you might ask for something else thrown in "for boot." Like, "I will give you my horse for yours if you will throw in the saddle to boot."

— "Laying a child to someone" meant to tell who the father was. This phrase had its beginning before our folks left the "old country." Many times a poor girl, pretty enough to catch the eye of a rich neighbor, found herself pregnant and deserted. When the girl's father learned of it, he would take the baby and leave it at the door of the rich man. The guilty man would raise the baby as his own, never telling anyone that it really was his; she was "laying the baby to him."

Once a middle-aged man, a resident of Caney, had been indiscreet with his neighbor's wife, whose husband had been gone from home for some time. The affair progressed long enough for the woman to get pregnant. The man knew the woman would soon be showing and the news would soon become common knowledge, and his wife would hear it. Thinking that it would be better if she heard it from him, one night he said to her, "Well, you know that baby our neighbor is going to have, well she is laying it to us."

— Our folks did not mind being joked about their looks. If they had a long nose, big ears, large feet, or were cross-eyed, it was treated and accepted as something to laugh about. As long as it was not meant to be an insult it was accepted as a joke, as long as it was by kinfolks. You did not talk about a person if they were not your people (relative). My father was always telling one of my cousins, whom he loved very much, that he had a face "that would scare a dog to death." One night my cousin came home and found his old dog lying before the fire. He was very old and apparently dying. He pushed the dog and told him to move. When

16

the dog did not move quickly enough, he took him by the ears, meaning to put him out of the house. The dog took one look at him and "dropped dead." "Well," he said, "Uncle Kitteneye has always told me that I had a face that would scare a dog to death, now I've went and done it."

— The word "mind" was used many ways and had different meanings — If I have to mind a child, and it don't mind me, I might have a mind to whip it. I don't think its parents would mind, for I was out of my mind to agree to mind it.

a) mind - take care of a child
b) mind - to obey
c) mind - not care
d) mind - to have a mind; to think
e) mind - to not mind; not care
f) mind - "out of your mind"; crazy
g) mind - out of your mind
h) mind - bring back to mind; remember
i) mind - "Do you mind that time"; do you remember
j) mind - "Pay that no never mind"; don't let that bother you
k) mind - "I have a half a mind"; undecided
l) mind - "give him a piece of my mind"; tell him what you think
m) mind - "I don't mind if I do"; sure, I would love to
n) mind - "I don't mind my children going swimming"; I don't care.
o) mind - "Just put that out of your mind"; forget it
p) mind - "It came to my mind"; I remembered
q) mind - "out of his mind"; delirious; sick with fever
r) mind - "out of sight, out of mind"; quickly forgotten
s) mind - "lost his mind"; gone crazy

— TURN
a) turn - personality; "He has a good turn." "She has a friendly turn."

17

b) turn - "a turn of meal"; a sackful. When folks took their corn to be ground into meal, it was first come, first served, so each waited his turn.

c) turn - to turn a post; in making a chair the post was formed on a turning lay (a large wooden wheel made to go around by a foot pedal, causing a smaller wheel to turn the piece of wood so it could be cut and formed by a sharp chisel.

d) turn - "He won't turn a hand to help me." He won't do anything.

e) turn - "Turn and turn about is fair play"; You help me and I will help you; one good turn deserves another.

f) turn - for milk to turn, or a turn of milk; milk was put in a crock or churn and set before the fire or in the sun so the warmth would cause it to ferment, or become sour, so it could be churned and made into butter. When the process first began it was said to "blinky," also called "blue John," then "clabbered."

Once, when an old woman that I will call Aunt Rue sat her churn before the fire, her dog Fido came into the house and used the side of the churn for his own purpose. When Aunt Rue saw this she screamed, "Oh, now I will have to strain my milk all over again, because Fido has - - - - - - in it." Now we use this phrase when we are going to do some job over, although we know it's useless.

g) turn - "a turn for the better"; also, "on the mend", meaning for a sick person to start to recover, or a person to change his habits - someone that has decided to become a Christian.

—Nater (nature) also means personality. "It's just not my nature to lie," or, "She is natured just like her mother."

—Takes atter (after) - to act like someone or inherit their looks or personality. "He takes after his father." Someone might say, "He took after his father, only his father took everything before he came along."

18

—Favor - looks like; "She favors her mother."

—"To Daddy itself or oneself" - an illegitimate child that looked like its father was said to daddy itself.

—"A sprout of a boy" or "a young sprout" also meant a young boy. From the word sprout (the young plants that came up from the roots when a tree was cut down).

—"If the house was to catch a-fire, the water bucket would be the first thing to burn," meaning the water bucket was empty, won't someone please go get some water? Some folks had wells dug. A hole in the ground about twenty feet deep and about two or three feet wide was "walled up" with creek rocks. Some had a chain and pully to make it easy to get water out. Some had a well sweep (a long pole that turned on a swivel) but all water used for cooking, cleaning and drinking had to be "drawn up" in a water bucket. A piece of iron (maybe an old horseshoe) was tied to one side of the bail to make it sink when dropped into the well. Others had a "spring," a natural spring of underground water that had found its way to the surface. A "sprang house" was built over it, and inside milk and food were kept fresh and cool.

—"The creek is so dry, if the fire got out it would be the first thing to burn up." Lots of times the fire got out of control when they were burning off the pastures of sage grass or when they were burning the brush left over when they cut the trees for to make their houses or to make room for the crops. Of course the creek could not burn. That was their way of saying it was a real dry time and they needed a rain.

—Purty (pretty) was used different ways:

a) purty - a play thing or toy
b) purty - real, like "purty good"
c) purty - awful, like "purty ugly"
d) purty near - almost
e) purty apt - almost sure

If you told someone that they were pretty they might answer you, "Yes, I am pretty ugly and pretty apt to stay that way a pretty long time, if I don't change pretty quick."

— "I got a dread on me" - a lonesome feeling, a forewarning of a coming disaster. Many people believed they were warned of their death or the death of a loved one.

— "Take that old gray mule up at the house." An expression used when we are going to change the subject of conversation and bring it back to the subject that we know we have already said too much about. There was an old man that had never had a mule of his own in his life. Here in the mountains a mule, at that time, was almost a necessity for survival. Finally, at last, this old man managed to buy a mule. He was so proud of that mule he brought it up in everything he talked about, no matter how or what the conversation, he managed to say something about his mule, beginning by saying, "Take that old gray mule up at the house."

— "Countin' in your head" or "countin' on your fingers" - Many of our folks, although they had no education, were experts at counting in their heads from memory. They learned to add, multiply, and divide simple problems just from memory by using a method they invented by themselves for their own use.

— "Nubbin" - an ear of corn that is very small, but that did mature. Usually fed to the cows or calves with the shuck or husk attached. Phrase: "This good weather is going to spile (spoil) my nubbin crop, it's making big ears out of them."

— "Shucking someone's corn" - being unfaithful with his wife.

— "Shucking someone in a trade" - getting the best of them or the best end of the deal.

— "Shucking someone" - getting them to believe a ridiculous story.

— "Planting the crop before building the fence" - getting pregnant before getting married, yet getting married before the baby is born.

— A real poor horse or cow was sometimes said to look like

it would make a good set of quilting frames (four narrow pieces of wood hung from the ceiling with strings, on which quilts were made).

—"Gettin' mashed up in the mines" - a mining accident that resulted in death or a bad injury.

—A coal bank - a small opening not as large as coal mines, where people dug coal for their own use.

—"I hain't nigh doon" - I haven't finished.

—"There will be all hell to pay" - There will be real trouble.

—"We tore down the house and put it up in the loft." - We made a big disturbance. All houses had a loft in which was kept all the extras that there was not room for in the bottom of the house, and sometimes an extra room for the young children.

—"What the caze fer?" - What cause did you have for doing that?

—"Died in the shell" - some project or job that was begun but never finished, from the little birds and chickens that died before they hatched.

—"I feel like I been mauling rails" - meaning I am real tired. Fence rails were made from logs by splitting them with a fro [iron tool], with a wooden maul; very hard work.

—"I hain't got a penny to my name" - I am broke.

—"Getting washed off"- to have your house or property or self be destroyed by high waters or overflowing creeks or rivers caused by rain.

—"Beholding" to someone - be obligated to someone for a past favor, or to have to depend on someone for help. Mountain people were very independent and proud, they did not like to be beholden to anyone.

—"Chunk up the fire" - to stir the fire with a long poker. From the work "chunk" (a piece of root or log); also could mean a large piece of something, like a chunk of bread or meat.

—"For who laid the chunk" - to favor the best one in a competition.

21

—"Going to the bull hole" - when a man lost in an election (political); from the term used in playing marbles. A hole was made in the ground, the object of the game was to see who could knock one marble into this hole by striking it with another, flipped with the finger and thumb from a distance along the ground.

—"Milk tastin' of the weeds" - Cows ate more weeds than grass and it gave the milk a bad taste, especially wild onions. Adding a small pinch of baking soda sometimes helped to remove this taste.

—We did not use the word lunch, the three meals were break-fast, dinner, and supper, in that order. Dinner and supper were both large meals and breakfast was almost as large, only a little different, such as hot biscuits while there was cornbread for the other meals.

—"Goin' the second mile" - When someone was too sick to ride a horse or in a wagon or sled, and had to be moved for many miles to a doctor, the neighbors carried them on a stretcher made of blankets or quilts. Some member of the family went along with them. The folks along the route took turns helping. When one man had gone for a mile or two and came to a house where another man would take over his place, the first one went back home. The second one went on until he, in turn, gave his place to another neighbor along the way, and so on to the end of the journey. No one ever refused to help if he was able to. If someone went over his share of miles, he was said to be going the second mile, as spoken of in the Bible. Corpses were carried this way also, if the route was where there was no road.

—To "soft soap" someone - Be nice to them so as to get them to do a favor for you. Sometimes when making soap it did not get as hard as it should, and remained soft. It then had to be dipped and rubbed onto the clothes or body. Sometimes soap was made from potash (lye made from ashes by putting them in a barrel, covered with water and allowed to drip through a small hole in the bottom of the barrel). This always made soft soap. A soap gourd was an extra large gourd used as a container for soft soap and hung on the wall near where the washing took place.

—"To whup (whip) the devil around the stump" - to pretend to be honest about something, while all the time you were not; or, doing one thing to hide the real reason why you are doing another.

—"Your feet are so dirty they look as if you have been grinding coffee and the grounds have settled" - Our coffee came to us in one-hundred pound bags, green. We browned it by roasting it in a large pan in the oven of the stove, ground it in a coffee mill, boiled it in a coffee "biler" (pot), poured it into the cups and allowed it to settle. Some folks claimed to be able to read fortunes by looking at these grounds. The grounds were also used to pour around where ants came into the house, to kill them.

—"Someone must have scraped the bottom of the barrel to come up with him." We bought our flour in one-hundred pound barrels. By the time we used this much, what was in the bottom was no good, so to say you had found someone at the bottom of the barrel was to say they were no good.

—"Fireboard" or "mantle" - sometimes just a long plank nailed over the fireplace to form a shelf, a necessity for most everyone. It was a nice place to keep anything warm: a string or line was stretched across just below, where wet clothes could be dried, socks or baby clothes warmed.

—"His ears are so thin you could sun bees through them" - There were a lot of wild bees with their nests and wild honey in hollow trees or between rocks in high cliffs. Folks loved to find them, get the honey, and sometimes capture the bees. They would try to find where the bees were "watering" (getting water from the creek), then watch what direction they flew. This helped them to locate the bee tree. As the bees were so small, and one can't look directly toward the sun, a piece of glass, slightly darkened with soot from the fireplace, or a very thin piece of cloth, was used to protect the eyes, allowing them to sight the bees.

—To "chivoree" someone - On the night of a wedding, all the neighbors and friends of the newlyweds got together and marched around where the bride and groom were, beating on pans, singing, shouting, playing musical instruments, and just making noise in general. Sometimes they would ride the groom on a rail. (Sit him astride a fence rail, with two men holding each end of the rail high enough that his legs could not touch the ground, and carry him. It was very uncomfortable. The bride was ridden in a washtub. The groom would give them whiskey if they would spare them from this treatment.)

—Our use of double negatives is very misleading and confusing. Try these:

a) I hain't never been to no sech place no how.
b) I don't want to hear nary 'nother word out of ary one of you all.
c) I guess I had not aught to better do that.
d) He did not have no cause to do that no how.
e) I hain't never seed (saw) no such goin' ons and I hain't never heard of no such.

—We add "one" on to a personal pronoun to show possession; like, "his one" or "her one." Then, we slur them together, and it becomes her'n and his'n, your'n.

—I said - seez me; she said, seez her; he said, seez he; you said, seez ye.

My uncle was once telling about a polecat (skunk) that had gotten under his floor among the chickens that were roosting there. While his wife held the lantern for him to see, he prepared to shoot. Suddenly, he thought, "That just might be my house cat." Afterwards he was telling about it, and he said, "Seez me, 'That might be my cat,' and seez her, 'Shoot him anyhow.'"

—"Me" was used in the place of "my." My stepmother was married to two men by the same name, Isom Slone. Once she

24

was telling something that her first husband had done or said. My father heard her and remarked, "I don't recollect that," and she said, "Oh, that was when me had me other Isom."

My uncle was "dodgin'" the law. His wife was staying with his father one night. My uncle decided he would slip into the house for a visit with his wife. Knowing where she was, he just quietly got into the bed. My aunt awoke and screamed, "There is someone in the bed with me, a man." My grandfather shouted back, "Just hold him till me gets me gun."

—A friend was talking about his dog catching a groundhog. "The fust 'un he ever cotched, he nailed him right ar, (pointing to his nose) as he went in after him and out he fotched him."

—"He is mean enough to steal the nickels off of his dead mother's eyes" - Our hill people were their own undertakers. They buried their own dead. When a body was being prepared for burial, nickels or some other coin were placed on the eyes to hold them together. After the body became stiff, the coins were removed, kept as something sacred, never used again except for the same purpose when another death occurred in the family.

—"Look where you are going" - Once my son was at a ball game. As he was going through the door, another boy was coming from the other side. Both stepped to the right, then both to the left, then to the right again, then both stopped, then both started on. I am sure everyone has had this happen to them at one time or another. In anger the other boy said, "Why don't you look where you are going?" As my son looked up, he saw that the other boy was cross-eyed, and he answered, saying, "Why don't you go where you are looking?"

—To say someone was "common," that meant he was down-to-earth, a very friendly, sociable person, not thinking himself better than anyone else. To call anyone "common" was a nice compliment.

—"Gettin' above your raising" - Hill people saw no wrong

in a person wanting to make something out of themselves, make money, improve their way of living, as long as they did not become ashamed of their parents and how they grew up. This was "getting above your raising."

—"Getting in a hard place," or "gettin' hard up" - in need of food or money; "a scarcity" of the necessities of life. If a person or family got in a hard place because of sickness or misfortune, his friends and neighbors always came to the rescue and helped him out, all knowing that he would do the same when and if they ever needed help.

—"Pint" - point. "When I pint my finger at you, you had better jump." Also meant a high point at the top of the hill — around the ridge and over the point.

—"I got a tail hold and a down-hill drag" - meaning, "I have everything under control, and it's going to be easy." Anything was easier "drug" downhill. Once some young boys were out hunting and found where a mother bear had some young ones, back in a hole under a cliff. The mother bear was not at home. The boys could hear the baby bears. They decided for one of them to go back into the hole to get one of them, while the other one waited on the outside and watched for the big bear. Suddenly, the mother bear returned. The boy on the outside caught her by the tail just as she entered the hole. The boy on the inside yelled, "What darken the hole out there, brother?" His brother answered, "Tail hold slip and you will see what darken the hole."

—When a mountain person began to tell a rumor he had heard, he would begin, "They say such and such." Then someone would remind him, "Don't you know that 'they say' is the biggest liar that ever lived?"

—If someone was wearing a new hat of which they were very proud, a friend might say, "I wish I had two of those hats." "Why two?" he would be asked. "Well, one to use as a slop jar (an indoor outhouse), the other one to cover it over with."

—"Dwinnel" (dwindle) - A person losing weight was said to

be "dwinnelin' away to nothing," or a sick person that was not getting any better or worse was said to be just "dwinnelin' along." A hen that kept setting on the nest of eggs that never hatched was "dwinnelin' on the nest."

— Something "brought on" was anything coming from outside the hills. Anything not made at home was called "brought on." Anyone coming from outside the hills was a "brought on" person. For a long time they were feared and hated. Our folks were very skeptical of outsiders. They had been mistreated, misjudged, misunderstood, and mistrusted. There is more understanding now, and outsiders are being accepted.

— The word "awful" is used many ways, many "warped" and confusing:

a) awful pretty - real pretty
b) awful good - real good
c) awfulest crowd
d) awfulest meeting (church service) meaning good, or wonderful
e) awfulest storm - large

— Children were often asked, when they had a hole in the end of their shoe, "Did your toe come out to see if it was spring, and find snow on the ground?" One pair of shoes a year was all the kids got. They went barefoot during the summer. One pair was usually well-worn by spring. Each fall the father would measure each one's foot by cutting a stick the right length, and would take these to the store for the shoes. They were just as happy to get these new shoes then as they were to discard them in the spring. Every family had an iron last on which the shoes were "half-soled" or mended. Worn-out strings were replaced with a small strip of "groundhog hide" made soft by rubbing it with sheep's tallow, (this also made it more pliable) and drawing it backwards and forwards over the back of a chair. Tallow was also rubbed into the leather of the shoes as polish, making them soft, waterproof, and prolonging their lives.

— "There are only two people that will take the back off of a watch" was another saying. The answer: a fool and a watch tinker. In every community there was one man that could repair or fix watches and clocks. He was called a watch tinker. Very few folks had a "time piece." They learned to tell time by the sun, by watching the shadow cast by a familiar tree or rock.

— "Gettin' settled in for the winter" - putting away food for the family; also called laying up for the winter. Preparing fuel, coal and wood for heat and cooling, was also done. How pleased they were when winter found them with shelves full of canned fruits and vegetables, holes full of potatoes, two or three hogs to kill, three or four dozen hens to lay eggs, two or three hundred bushel of coal, a large stack of wood; they were as rich as they wanted to be, what more could they ask for?

— "Scrouge" - to place close together; to sleep too close. Joke: "What did one tonsil say to the other?" Answer: "Move over, you are scrouging me."

— "Sent his saddle home" - A wife might say this if she meant she was going to divorce her husband, or if she had reason to break up their relationship. When a man was killed while in the army, his saddle was sent home to his wife. Also, if a man was found dead too far away from home, his saddle was sent home to his wife. If it was too far away to send the body to her, he was buried and just the saddle sent home. Another way of using this expression was, "I sent his saddle home," meaning, "I made him understand I was not to be pushed around."

— A hickory stick, a long limb from the hickory nut tree, was cut and used as a means of measurement, to measure a corpse when making a coffin. A phrase someone might use when very angry: "If he fools with me, they will be cutting a hickory stick for him soon." Or a teacher might say to her students, "I will straighten you out with a hickory stick," meaning, "I will punish you by whipping you."

—"I don't care if I do," means, "Sure," in answer to the question, "Do you want or will you have some?" This different way of expressing ourselves has been the cause of more misunderstanding than any other one. Once a real nice fellow from the west coast was visiting Caney for the first time. He moved into a building close to my brother's chair shop, where my brother and his son were making chairs. The newcomer was very anxious to make a good impression and make friends. Each morning he came into the shop drinking a cup of coffee. "Would you care for a cup of coffee?" he would ask. "I don't care if I do," my nephew would answer him. The other man would stand there and finish his coffee and leave. When this had happened for the third time, my nephew became angry. "Listen sir, if you give me a cup of coffee or not, that's your concern. But if you ask me if I want one, and I tell you that I do, you had better be ready, for man, I will push that cup down your throat."

—We say "lite" for "light." Once, when one of my sons was working in Gary, Indiana, he was riding to work on the bus. "Will you let me off at the first red lite?" he asked the bus driver. "What part of the south are you from, boy? Haven't you been up here long enough to learn to talk?" "I hope that I never lose my way of talking," my son replied. "If and when I do, I am going home. If I forgot how my mother taught me to talk, I might forget what she taught me, and one of the first things she taught me was to be kind to strangers."

—"Get a lout; do a lout eat corn bread or die?" To get without; to do without means, if you have used up all you have and have no chance of obtaining any more, then you just have to die, a possibility hill people of long ago faced daily.

—A "make do" - there is a lot of meaning in these words. Mountain custom and philosophy of mountain life is based on learning to "make do," expecting and accepting to make the best of whatever you have, knowing that God does not ask more of us. To "make do" also means to substitute one thing

29

for another: to make something last longer by repairing it again and again.

— To borrow: Mountain people borrowed everything from each other, from a few matches, a pinch of soda or black pepper, to a horse to ride, even clothes. It was no shame to borrow, if you were faithful to pay back, and also willing to loan. But woe to the person who refused to loan to his neighbor.

— In the winter the gatherin' place for the family was before the fire in the grate. They sat in chairs in a circle around the fire, the small ones in someone's lap. If someone stood too long in front of another, he might be told, "When you get warm, I will turn around." It was very important that the door be kept closed as much as possible. If someone left it open too long he was asked, "Where were you raised? In a barn where the door opened and shut itself?"

— We don't say that we "met" someone, but that we "learned" them. "Have you learned the new girl at school? I learned her brother last year."

— "Nary" (not any) and "hain't" (have not) are the most misused words. "I hain't got nary pencil." A teacher asked her student one day if he was going to go on the picnic the next day. He answered, "No, I hain't goin'." The teacher said, "No, John, that's not right. You should say, "I am not going, she's not going, he is not going, they are not going, you are not going, we are not going. Now do you understand?" And he answered, "Yeah, looks like they hain't going to be nary picnic, cause they hain't nobody goin'."

— A "gnat smoke" - In summer, when folks wanted to sit in the yard of an evening after supper, in the cool before going to bed, they would make a slow-burning fire from old rags - preferably woolen. This smoke kept away gnats and mosquitoes.

— "Doing up the work" or "getting the work done" - doing evening chores; bringing in coal, wood, and water into the house, feeding the animals, hunting and milking the cow, gathering the eggs, seeing that all the gates and doors were closed, small chickens were fastened inside so rats could not catch them. These jobs were usually done by the children of the family. They also had to do the same each morning before going to school.

— "Petticoat government" - a man that was bossed by his wife was said to be living under a "petticoat government." A petticoat was an underskirt or slip worn by women. It was thought disgraceful for a man to let his wife be the boss of the family, even a sin. Yet all family life centered around the woman.

— If someone was in a hurry to leave, he would be asked, "What did you come for, a shovelful of fire?" Without matches it was very difficult to start a fire. Sometimes a child would be sent to a neighbor's house to get some burning coals, which they would bring back home in a shovel.

— "To dance in the hog trough" - When a boy or girl got married, having older brothers or sisters at home still single, the older ones were supposed to dance in the hog trough at the wedding as punishment for letting the younger get married first. This trough was where the hogs were fed. It was made from one-half of a split log, hollowed out. It was a difficult and nasty place to have to dance.

— The "here-to-yander people" - folks that had no home of their own, but just stayed a few days or weeks with one family, then another, then go on to another. Some had a certain route they traveled, making the circuit each and every year. They were not thought of as bums or tramps, but were respected by everyone. They helped with the work and brought all the news, earning their board and keep. Some were great storytellers. Once a here-to-yander man by the name of Combs stopped to spend the night with my husband and me, when we were first married. He was a stranger to us, and we were to him. My cousin had told him where we lived and that he would be welcome. Just as we were going to bed, my husband remembered that he had forgotten to chop kindlin' wood for the morning fire. It was now dark outside and he could not see. He brought in the axe, meaning to chop some kindlin' from a larger stick, by the light of the fire. He set the axe down in the corner. When old Mr. Combs saw that axe, he became so frightened, thinking that my husband was planning on chopping him in his sleep. We could not change his mind and he left in a run. We never saw him again.

—"To throw up wet or dry" - Just like tossing a coin for heads or tails, our folks used a small stone. They made one side wet by spitting on it. Leaving the other side dry, they tossed it up in the air to see which side came up on top, the dry or the wet.

—A "puncheon floor" - The log cabin floors were made from split logs lain side by side, the split side up, and hued to a smoothness with a broad axe. It was scrubbed with a scrub broom and sand (made from pounded creek rocks).

—"Scrub brooms" - made from hickory, a pole cut the desired length, about fourteen inches in diameter. With a drawing knife, long shavings were cut almost the length, left attached about one foot from the end. When the pole is small enough to fit the hand, turn the shavings back over the end, tie into a bunch with a splint of white oak made pliable by soaking in warm water.

—We grew broom corn, a species of the cane family of plants, for our sweeping brooms. After cutting the tops containing the seed pods, let dry. Remove the seed by raking a dull knife over the straws, boil them in hot water or soak in hot water until pliable. Tie to a hickory stick, braid together with a small strip of groundhog hide or leather. It took a lot of skill to make a broom that was durable. Made right, they would last for two or three years of normal use.

—A "battlin' board" - a long, shallow, hollowed half of a split log, used to wash clothes. One end was left flat, a place to lay soaked clothes one at a time to beat out the dirt with a "battlin' stick." The hollow end was to hold the water. A battlin' stick was a long-handled paddle used to beat the clothes, to get out the excess water and dirt.

—A "gritter" - from the word "grater." Made by punching holes in a piece of tin (an empty peach can), nailing it to a board, the sharp sides of the holes outward. Used to change corn into meal by rubbing the ears of corn over the sharp holes. Corn could be used when in milk stage (when a white liquid would appear when grains were pierced with the finger) or until it was dry enough to shell.

—To "scour" or "scrub" - We used sand rocks pounded into sand with a hammer, sprinkled over the floor and scrubbed with a scrub broom. Sometimes more sand was sprinkled over the floor to hasten it to dry. This also kept it clean longer by absorbing things later spilled, then swept up.

—"I don't know what went with it" - It means, "I don't know where something is," or "I have lost it."

—"It never hope it" - It did not help it. "Hope" was used as the past tense of the word "help."

—A person said to be "smart" means he is wise; also means he loves to work.

—If a woman or girl is called "honest," it does not mean she will not steal, but that she has high moral values. If she is not honest, she is a "mean woman."

—"Whup" - whip; "I'll whup the sock off of you."

—"Off yander" - could mean just a few yards, like "I am getting so that I can't see off yander," or a long distance - "He comes from off yander," meaning another state.

—"Are you from around here?" - Do you live in this community or neighborhood?

—"You look like something the cat drug in" - Used humorously to a child or close friend, meaning you don't look so good, as cats would sometimes bring in animals they had killed.

—"Scarce as hen's teeth" - rare; hens have no teeth.

— "Foggy hair" - unbrushed or not combed. "Your hair is all foggy and your clothes don't fit you right."

— "Noggen" - your head, maybe from the meaning of a small mug. "You may fall and crack your noggen."

— "Never darken my door" - Don't ever return.

— "Again' dark" - By the time it gets dark.

— "The last button on Gabe's coat" - All there is. I am sure that at some time there was a man named Gabe, and for some reason this phrase got to be used; the reason lost in the past, the saying still used.

— "I'll pay you back if I ever do" - humorously said when borrowing something.

— "I will pay you with the first dollar that I find rolling up the hill" - never.

— "Where is the balance of them?" - Where is everyone else?

— If more than one person was working together, after they had rested, one might remind them that it was time to go back to work by saying, "Well, this is not making the baby's dress, nor sleeping with its daddy either."

— A stingy person was described as:

a) As tight as Gabe's hatband.
b) Tight as the bark on a tree.
c) So tight he screws his socks on.
d) So tight he screaks when he walks.

— "Do me a favor and I will dance at your funeral and throw rocks at your grave" - humorously said.

— "My dog is so fast, he walks on three legs to keep from running himself to death" - another humorous phrase.

— "A horse so poor, he looks like a set of quilting frames."

a) He looks like he's been fed wind all winter.

—"I will be behind you in a fight." - I'll stand at your back until they beat your belly blue.

—"The still hog gets the slop" - (slop - leftovers from the table, added to the dishwater and fed to the hogs).

—"She was leaving the pasture gate open" - said about a woman when she was showing too much attention to a man.

—"One man won't stop to mend another man's fence unless he sees the gap down." - Meaning, a man won't show attention to another one's wife unless she shows him by her actions that she wants him to. (A gap was a place in the fence where the rails could be removed and replaced, as an opening.)

—"She must have known something bad about herself, to have married him" - She married someone ugly or below her station in life.

—Bugger:

a) a ghost
b) the devil or Satan
c) the dried mucus in your nose
d) small lice living in your hair or on your body

—"Poke fun" - to laugh at someone, to belittle or demean them by saying disrespectful things about them.

a) poke - a paper bag
b) poke - push

—"I hain't got a penny to my name" - broke

—"Pon-my-onor" - upon my honor. Used to back up a statement, as "pon-my-onor it's true."

—"Ridden up the house" - making it ready for company. The daily chores; sweeping, dusting, making the beds.

—"Ginning"; also, "ginning around" - doing odd jobs. Might

be used as an expression to tell someone to hurry. "You better gin around and get this job done."

a) a "gin hand" - one who helps someone that has a more important job.

—"Mosing around" - walking or moving slow. "Just mosing around doing pert nigh nothen'."

—Foxfire - fluorescent wood said to be used as a light by the foxes.

—"Across the big waters" - across the ocean.

—A "warsh out" - flood waters. When rain caused the creeks to rise and overflow their banks.

—Someone telling about a quarrel: "She let loose and talked mean to me. I helt back and took it."

—"I went and took" - meaning, "I began."

—An "ill" person - a mean temper; he is hard to get along with.

—"You fool with me, and I will turn you ever which way but loose."

—"Some people are like a cow that gives a big bucket of milk, and then kicks it over."

—"I am going to lick you; I am going to make a greasy spot on the floor out of you and then lick it up with my tongue."

—A "fer piece" - a long distance.

—"In hollering distance" - close enough to hear a voice yelling.

—To "holler" at someone - to call loud. You call to someone, but you holler at them. The expression "to holler," because the hands were placed on each side of the mouth in order to send the voice further, thus causing a resemblance of a holler (hollow), the space between two hills. It was very needful for the people of the hills to communicate by yelling to each other: to call the men from work for dinner, to know where the children were, to keep from getting lost, to warn of approaching strangers that might be "law men."

—"Just a whoop and a holler away" - not far.

—Grub:

a) grub - food
b) grubs - the small, young sprouts that grew up from the roots and around the stumps of trees or small bushes
c) to grub - cutting and digging up these grubs
d) a grub worm - the larva stage of the "tumble bug," a beetle that lay its eggs in manure balls and were very destructive to cabbage

—"Pervidin'" - if; "I will go, pervidin' it don't rain."

—"Well, it's a new spoon or a ruined horn" - meaning, "It is a failure or success, it's too late to do anything about it now. Spoons and combs were made from horn of deer and cattle.

—A "reddin' comb" - a large comb, as in comparison to a fine comb. Fine comb was spoken as one word (finecomb). A "reddin' comb" was of larger teeth or prongs. It was used to get the tangles from the hair, while the fine comb was used to get bugs from the hair.

—Sometimes a small stick was used as a button, when the real one got lost. Two small holes were cut in the garment close together, and the stick pushed through. The button hole could then be fastened over this.

—Question: "Did you know that there were enough bones in a pig's foot to place one at every man's door in the county?" Answer: "Put one in the door of the courthouse, it belongs to everyone in the county."

—"Pam of your hand" - palm. Phrase: "It's just as plain as the pam of your hand."

—"Riding shanks mare" - walking.

—A "lumber stretcher" - an imaginary tool used to stretch lumber when a board has been cut too short. A greenhorn or someone new at the job was always sent to borrow a lumber stretcher.

— "An inch short and a foot behind" - being defrauded or disillusioned; to get the small end of a deal. "Everything I have to do with him, I come up one inch short and a foot behind."

— "Out of hearing, out of mind" - easily forgotten.

— "Out of hearing and around the bend" - gone. Our hills are so close together and intertwined that the roads are very crooked, with a lot of bends and curves. One can't see very far. You could be very close and yet, if you were around the bend in the road, you could not see the other person.

— "To my way of thinking, I never laid eyes on him in my life" - I never saw him before.

— "Eating someone out of house and home" - staying too long, wearing out your welcome. Mountain people visited one another a lot, and no one ever thought about not keeping their kinfolks, even if they had become a burden.

— "Gom" - dirt. To make a mess. "You have made a messy gom of this house." "You have gom all over your face."

— "Blood kin" - everyone that was related to each other by birth. If you were blood kin, you were honor-bound to love, respect, protect, and uphold each other. A closeness of family ties, hard to understand or explain, taught to us long before we could remember being taught. As much a part of our being as life itself.

— Grudge - to hold a resentment. To begrudge someone something was to not be willing for them to have it. If someone was eating something and they dropped it, then it was said that someone must have been begrudging them.

— "Slap your hands" - cheer someone.

— "Under the leak of the house" - under the edge of the roof, where the rain ran off. Tubs or barrels were set here to catch rain water.

— Doing something "for looks" - for pride. True, our hill people did not care if they dressed themselves in style. It was not that they lacked pride; to do something "fer looks" was thought of as sinful.

—"Warsh day, snack day" - to do the family wash or laundry took all day, also the use of the kitchen and the stove. So, the family knew they would have to eat leftovers on wash day, sometimes cold corn bread and milk.

—"Making fun" of someone - to belittle or demean them by saying derogatory remarks. Someone might say, "You are making fun of me," and the person so addressed would answer, "No, the fun is already made. All I have to do is hump my shoulders and laugh."

—"Just around the bend" - just out of sight along the path or road. Our roads are so crooked as they wind along following the creek, you can't see very far.

—"Got him in a log, both ends stopped up" - meaning, got him in my power, no way he can escape. Animals were caught sometimes by stopping them up in a log.

—"Got any to spare?" - Do you have more than you need? Everyone always was more than pleased to have something they could share with their neighbors. When saving seeds for next year, they always wanted to have "a plenty and some to spare." They always used the words "a plenty," not just the word "plenty" by itself.

—"To get the best berries, you have to go through the most briars" - To get what you want, you must be willing to work for it. Everyone picked berries. They were a very essential part of our diet. They grew wild all over the sides of the hills.

—"Racking my brain" - trying to think.

—"Enough grub to feed a working" - a large amount of food.

—A "working" - when neighbors got together to share work. If someone was not able to work because they were sick, or if they were in a hurry to get a job done, like when they got their house burned down, or if it was a job that took more than one person to do by himself, then they all got together and helped each other out. This was called a working. The women made a real good dinner.

—"Heading for high ground" - running away; leaving the scene.

—"Just a drap in the bucket" - very small; too little to be of any use.

—"Up fer grabs" - for whoever wanted it, and got there first.

—A "wash bench" - a long, backless bench set along one side of the kitchen wall, where the wash bowl and pitcher were kept, and everyone washed their faces and hands. There was also another long bench set along the back side of the dining room table. Here the small children sat to eat, like crows on a fence.

—"Settin' room" - living room, which was often the bedroom also.

—"I have a crow to pick with you" - I have something to talk over with you. A crow was very hard to pick the feathers off.

—"She went all to pieces" - lost control of herself.

—"In all my born days" - all my life.

—"She will never amount to nary thing" - never succeed at anything.

—"More than a plenty" - enough.

—To "arn" (iron) clothes, we used big, heavy, flat irons, heated on the stove or grate.

—"In a hard place" - in need of the essentials for living; food and shelter.

—"Ball the jack" - hurry, make speed. From the word used by people that worked on the railroads, a term meaning to let the train go through.

—"You are telling a bare-faced lie" - to lie without any emotion showing on your face.

—"Don't whip the devil around the stump" - to pretend to be honest about something, while all the time you are not, or to use one excuse for doing something, yet you really have another cause for doing it.

—"Bawling her head off" - crying.

—"He needs to be brought down a notch" - have his ego deflated. Notches or nicks were cut into a stick and used as a measuring device.

—"Bet your bottom dollar" - bet all you have.

—"Brand spanking new" - just bought, with the brand still attached.

—"He is not bringing up his children just right" - not teaching them the right way to live.

—For a horse to "curry double" - two people ride at the same time.

—"I never seed such carrying on" - I never saw anything happen like that.

—"Carrying on" over someone dead - showing how hurt you are by crying.

—"Your people" - relatives, family, clan.

—"The spitting image" - to look just like someone.

—To "patch things up" between two people - make peace between them.

—"Toll dish" - a small wooden box used by the miller to measure wheat or corn, to determine his portion as payment for grinding the grain.

—A "comb case" - a small pocket made of stiff paper, sometimes decorated with corn beads (Job's tears), hung on the wall to keep the comb used by all the family.

—"We just allus (always) done it that way" - When asked why they did something a certain way, they always gave that answer. Just the way they had been taught, and, although shown a better way, they were very hard to be convinced, and would not change. Not just stubborn, they just would not change. "If it's good enough for my father, then it's good enough for me," they would sometimes say.

—"Sot in his way" - stubborn

—"Looks like there's no show for him" - He is terminally sick.

—"It did not make me mad (angry), it just hurt my feelin's" - caused me to feel bad.

—"Got a worm in his tail" - upset. From the way a cow acted when it got a worm in its tail, which sometimes happened.

—"Try to get a word in edge-wise" - try to interrupt someone.

—To "get rid of someone" - cause them to leave, or not bother you any more.

—To "wool" a baby - to fondle or handle gently a baby; to play with it.

—"Staying in the house with someone" - making their home yours.

—To "send somebody word" - to let them know, send a message by someone.

—If someone was very slow doing something, he was told, "I would hate to have to send you to the granny (midwife)."

—"Granny race" - when the midwife came to someone's home for to deliver a baby.

—If a man was waiting for his wife to have a baby, he was said to be "sleeping with his shoes on."

—Being "saving" - It was very important for a girl to have learned to be "savin'" (thrifty) before becoming a wife and, if she had, she was thought to be a much better wife. Any woman that was wasteful was despised by her neighbors, and they would say of her, "She can throw more out through the back door with a teaspoon than her husband can shovel in through the front door with a shovel."

—After a child died the word "Little" was always added to its name when talking about it, like "Little Sarah," "Little Bob," etc. When an animal that was loved died, the word "old" was added to its name, like "Old Pide," "Old Barney," "Old Rover," etc.

WORDS AND THEIR MEANINGS AS USED BY US

I have listed some of the most-used words by us. Some are common words used by people elsewhere, but they still seem to be a great part of our language. Some are unique; some mispronounced by us; all are interesting.

— Slap dab - exactly
— Persacitly - exact
— Purt nite (also, purt near) - almost
— Tatters - potatoes
— Matters, matoes, tom-a-toes - tomatoes
— Pie plant - rhubarb
— Artie-choke - to us, the roots of a tall plant with daisy-like flowers. Sometimes called Jerusalem artichoke, a type of sunflower.
— Plum-granny (pomegranate) - to us, a small melon, nice smell, edible but not tasty.
— S'urp - syrup
— Cu'ron - carrion; flesh of dead animals. Also used to describe anything dirty.
— Off younder - outside the mountains
— A fer piece - a distance of many miles
— Hunk - slang for Hungarian
— Tallie - Italian
— Itlie - Italy

—Salet - greens
—Diddie - diaper
—Diddlies (also biddies) - baby chickens
—Agin dark - nightfall
—Smart - wise; also, industrious
—Honest - when referring to a woman or young girl, it meant she had high moral standards.
—Ready roll - cigarette
—Chaw - chew; also a portion of chewing tobacco, like to take a "chaw"
—Whoppin' - whipping
—Sang - ginseng
—Might - maybe; "I don't know if I might go."
—High falutin - self-esteem
—Raise cane - start a fight or trouble
—Halve a calf - get drunk
—Skunt - skinned; to remove the hide or skin from an animal
—Punkin - pumpkin
—Pasnet - parsnip
—Pack - to carry
—Tote - to carry
—Brought-on - came from another state. Also, something bought, not homemade. Anyone born outside the hills was a "brought-on" person.
—Homemade - made by hand
—Nubben - a small ear of corn
—Boster - a long pillow, as long as the bed was wide
—Piller - pillow
—Winder - window
—Kivers - Covers for the bed, quilts and blankets
—Headin' - anything used as a pillow
—Sumpin' - something
—Scace (also scurce) - not plentiful
—Whelps - ridges or raised places on the body, caused by a

slight blow; as, "Where he whipped him, it raised big whelps."

— Bumps - small raised places on the skin, often on the face

— Kur'er - cure; to dry meat. Also, to help a sickness

— Retch, reatch - pass something

— Fetch (also fotch) - to bring

— The big waters - the ocean

— Warsh out - tide waters. When heavy rains caused the creeks to overflow

— Warshed off - something carried away by the flood waters; "He got warshed off" meant his house was carried away by the creek or river.

— Potash - lye

— Milk gap - the place in the pasture where the cows were brought to be milked and fed each night and morning

— Hant - ain't; also, the word for "ghost"

— Kampee - camp

— Kampee boss - mining superintendent

— Hoss - horse

— A pot-licker - hound dog

— Agerfreet - to irritate someone

— Wool a baby - to fondle gently, caress

— Coffee sack - a burlap bag

— Backer - tobacco

— Hath - hearth; a stone before the fireplace in the chimney

— Waze - was

— Seed - saw, or have seen

— Thang - thing

— Kang - king

— Rang - ring

— Sprang - spring

— Brang - bring

— Ailin' - being sick

— Ailment - sickness or disease

— Blossom - flowers

— Missery - painful
— Scuffle - to wrestle
— Pal - pile
  chal - child
  whal - while
  fail - file
— Chim'nie - chimney
— Atter - after
— Caze - cause
— Youngen - child
— Littlest un - the baby
— Tal-a-ble - feeling well (In answer to the question, "How are you?")
— Tip - touch
— Frash meat - uncured meat (just slaughtered)
— Comers and goers - visitors
— Dander - dandruff
— Drawers - underwear
— Tooth drawers - a tool used to pull teeth. It looked like pliers, and was made of iron in the blacksmith shop.
— Laggions - leggings. Made of leather; a covering for the legs from the ankles to the knees.
— Messie gom - very dirty
— Pitiful looking - in the need of pity
— Themil - thimble
— Batch - amount
— Passel - a large amount
— Fust - first
— Cautched - caught
— Foutched on - brought from out of state
— Hurt feelin's - insulted
— Smearing cancel - giving advice
— Picking grass - animals grazing, eating weeds and grass
— Picking salet - gathering wild greens

—Angern - onion

—A poke bonnet - an old-fashioned bonnet, called a "poke" because it was used to carry things in like a poke (sack).

—Poke - a paper bag

—Tote - to carry

—Pime plank - true or exactly; "That's just pime plank how it looked."

—Sartin - certain

—Summerset - somersault

—Mail pockets - mail bags

—Mail boy - mail carrier

—Mail root - Mail route

—"Tweedle" someone - talk them into believing something

—Draw water - bring water up from the well or spring

—Contakerious - mean, hateful

—afeared - afraid

—Aidge - edge

—Allus - always

—Sunball - sun

—Moonball - moon

—Eyeball - eye. To eyeball someone: look them in the eye

—Warshboard or rub board - a washboard to wash clothes on

— Warsh - wash

— Born days - all your life

— Burin' ground - graveyard, cemetery

— Recollect - remember

— Good eatin' - good food

— Galluses - suspenders; maybe from the word gallows

— Bee gum - a bee hive; a place for bees, sometimes made from a hollow log.

— Holler - hollow; the space between two hills. Also, could mean the small stream. Also used to describe a log that the inside had been removed from, like a "holler log."

— Hunkers - haunches

— Hunkered - squatted. To sit down on your heels; "They hunkered down behind a log."

— Hog meat - pork

— Cow meat - beef

— Shelved - pushed

— Ketched - caught

— Leampe orel - lamp oil (kerosene)

— Trapisen - traveling

— Privy bush - a hedge bush

— Na'ar - narrow

— Pint plank - positively

— Dreck'ley - after a while; soon, but not just now

— Onerry - mean

— Pen - prison

— The silent - insane asylum

— A play party - a party or dance; any get-together that's just for fun.

— A play purty - toy

— A candy pullin' - a get-together of young folks to make and eat candy.

— Spruce up - get dressed up

— Quil - coil (a snake "quilled" before it bit)
— Raised - reared
— Renched - rinse
— A right smart - a large quantity
— Sass - all the food put away for winter, except meat and corn. "Sass" also meant to answer back in anger; to "sass back."
— Scringe - cringe; to shrink from fear
— Sidelin' - slanting; "Sidelin' ground" - steep; at an angle
— Tackey - ugly or cheap-looking
— Clever - hospitable
— Yarbs - herbs
— Disfurnish - to sell or give away so much of what you have that you are in need yourself
— Rue'in back - backing out of a trade; not accepting an agreement already made
— Yur - ear
— Sut - soot
— "Prank" with someone - bother or tease
— Scrouge - to place too close
— Tee-tote-ly - exactly
— Hist - lift or pull up
— Back set - relapse of a sickness
— Drank - drink
— Woe'ter - water
— Purt - active
— Staires - stars
— Gum boots - rubber boots
— Learned - teach
— Chicken crow - early morning; daylight
— Weren't - was not
— Worser - worse
— Auer - air
— Pichure - pitcher

—Pitcher - picture

—Cawcumber - cucumber

—Hunard - hundred

—Drowed up - to shrink; a cloth "drawed up" when you washed it

—A caution - a great wonder or great sight; (a "caution" to see)

—A "pone" of bread - a pan of bread (a whole pone; all of something). A pone could also mean a large, swollen place on the body.

—Crap - crop; the amount of corn one would plant

—Brash - brush; also pronounced "bressh"

—Safftee - soft

—Banger - bango

—Little bitty - very small

—Dane'ce - dance

—Biler - boiler

—Sank - sink

—Sank hole - a dent place in the field, or a mud-hole in the road

—Clur - clear

—Poyour - pure

—Dry up - hush; quit talking

—Shet - shut (close)

—Teggious - small; a "teggious" job; something hard to do, because it's small

—Techious - a touchy subject; sensitive

—A techious person - easily aroused to anger

—Learn by heart - memorize

—Growed-up - a grown person; also, a field that has been allowed to grow back to the weeds and trees

—Banter - dare; also, ask for a trade or barter ("I bantered him to jump from the barn roof," or "I bantered him to a horse trade."

—Flour bread - biscuits

— Hoe cake - bread; baked in under the grate

— Brand new - never been used; also, "spanking brand new"

— House plunder - furniture

— Layway (also waylay) - ambush; also could be to mean just to watch for someone to pass

— Bushwhack - to ambush someone to kill them; also means to cut the trees down and leave them lay, like for a pasture

— Sittin' alone - the ability of a baby to sit without help

— Catter cornered - at an angle

— Sulled up - won't talk or smile (sulled like a possum)

— Cravin - having a desire. Pregnant women were supposed to crave certain foods.

— A plenty - enough; never said just "plenty," but always with the "a"

— Branch water - pure, clear water

— Cuss - curse or swear

— Tightwad - stingy; (wod - the small bit of cotton used to load a gun)

— Dadburn it - slang; used in anger

— Jim dandy - extra good

— Limber jim - a small switch used to whip children

— Pully bone - wish bone

— Tittie - a woman's breast

— Tittie milk - breast milk from a woman

— Saplin - a young tree

— Slam bang - slang for loud noise

— Hollerin' distance - close enough to be heard

— Dry-land fish - edible mushrooms

— Mad'durs - mattress

— Gimmiee - give me

— Wuden - was not

— Samen'igues - salmon

— Gappe - yawn

— Wearin' things - clothes
— Bed clothes - blankets, sheets, quilts
— "Blinky" milk - milk just started to sour, still edible
— Funkey - spoiled; bad odor
— Pot licker
— Hoss - horse
— Dough beater - wife or cook
— Jab (or, job) - push
— Breakus - breakfast
— Spoom - spoon
— Tetch - touch
— Each - itch
— Squessee - squeeze
— Scutch - move over
— To "billie fie" - slander
— Eatin' hearty - a good appetite
— Yeller - yellow
— Feller - fellow
— Me'ler - mellow (an apple was "me'ler" when it was ripe)
— Pissen - poison
— Eatin' table - dining room table
— Side table - an extra table in the kitchen used to set the pots and pans and a place to prepare the meals; a kind of work bench
— A water bench - a small table or bench to set a bucket of water
— A warsh (wash) bench - a table or bench sometimes in the kitchen and sometimes just outside the kitchen door; held the pan, water pitcher and wash bowl; a place to wash the hands and face.
— Ma'nur - manure
— Creek bed - the path the creek followed. Often the creek bed was the only road.
— Tarnation - slang; an expression of surprise; "What in tarnation is that?"

— Blab mouth - talkative person

—Druther - rather

—Life saver - slang for gravy. Gravy was eaten as a dish, not an additive.

—Souper six - nickname for pinto beans; also called miner's strawberries

—Poppie caps - popcorn; also called "cap corn"

—Corn capper - corn popper; a long-handled pan made of wire, with a removable lid, used to pop popcorn

—Riddie bob - see saw

—Spar' grass - asparagus

—Poor doe - slang for water gravy (gravy made from water in place of milk, when no milk is available)

—Slonch ways - at an angle

—Plagued - embarrassed

—Plunder - household goods; household furnishing

—To plunder - ramble or look through; "I plundered through that old trunk."

—Cox's army - slang for a large crowd

—Getting riled (or getting riled up) - becoming angry

—Brile - broil

—Anch - inch

—Saiese (or says) - said

—Coppers - pennies

—Soap gourd - a very large gourd; for containers

—Larpin - taste good

—E'drop - eavesdrop

—Leak of the house - under the edge of the roof of the house

—Brimstone - sulphur

—Spit'tum - humidor

—Brar - briar

—Ba'ar - bear

—Garr - jar; shake loose

—Shelve - push

—Flung - throw; "He flung it away."
—Sasser - saucer
—Biler - boiler, as a coffee boiler
—Scutch - move over
—Melt - the spleen; part of a hog - edible
—Work brittle - loved to work
—Brickle (or brickley) - crunchy
—Smart - industrious; also means intelligent
—Cover'let, coverled - a hand-woven bedspread
—Ye-born-days - lifetime
—Brash (or breesh) - brush
—Culled (or culled over) - selecting the best
—Like - lack, to need; "I like one having enough."
—A furner - a foreign person
—Airship (also airie plane) - airplane
—Allus - always
—All-fired - powerful
—Ank - ink
—Play acting - pretend
—Apt to - likely
—Arn - iron
—Farplace - grate
—Bad off - real sick
—Sick un to death - terminally ill
—Kantuck - Kentucky
—A'mercky - America
—Old Fer'ginie - Virginia
—Old Anglin - England
—Frankfret - Frankfort
—Louieville (also Lu'vel) - Louisville
—Bawl - cry
—Cow bawl - mooing
—Blackguard - use obscene language
—Black gold - nickname for coal

—Chop block - a block of wood, sometimes a piece of log. A place to chop wood for fuel or for the stove; also used to climb upon to mount a horse

—Chuffy - short and stocky; fat

—Heavy set - a large person

—Martifie - to decay. Used when describing human flesh or bodies of animals

—Here atter (after) - eternity

—Saft - soft

—Ferder - farther

—Fester - a small boil formed around a splinter or briar that's been jabbed into the skin, and pus gathered

—Vulgerie - vulgar talk; obscene language

—Helt - hold

—Nigh cut - a shorter distance; "Take the nigh cut around the hill."

—Plum - real; "plum full," "plum drunk," or "plum tired"

—Pime blank (also plime blank) - exact; "That is just plime blank how it was."

—Blue John milk - just started to clabber, or sour, but edible

—Clabber milk - started to ferment, a semi-solid form

—Whey - the watery substance left when the clabber has been removed from the milk

—Lite bread - loaf bread

—A bridle path - a narrow path suitable for riding a horse along

—A log road - a road left after timber has been cut and removed

—A wagon road - a road suitable for wagons to travel

—A cow path - a path left by the cattle, but used by people when the hill was too steep for a road

—Sech - such

—Cap - a low place where two hills join

—Clift - cliff

—Nue - new

—Shore - sure

—Tight - stingy

—Snot - mucus

—Take care - watch out (get out of the way)

—Woneste - once

—Crane your neck - turn your head

—Foot log - a log laid across the creek to walk across on

—Out-a-whack - out of order

—A spring freash - flood waters

—Back then - in the past

—Dans'ee - dance

—Cuttin' a shine - mischievous

—Fanning the breeze - running fast

—Humdinger - large (a humdinger of a fight)

—A "shirt tail fight" - a fight between a man and his wife

—A knock-down-and-drag-out-fight - a big fight, usually among a lot of people

—Mock - imitate

—Get foundered - eat too much

—Screamers - nickname for the grains of popcorn that do not pop

—Tu'mar - tomorrow

—To ma'rr up - to sink; "You might ma'rr up in a mud hole."

—Rip-to-my-roys - slang for corduroy pants

—Hog wash - slang, meaning not true

—Youngens - children

—Yep - yes

—Nop - no

—Yeers - years

—Womern - woman

—Wish book (Also wish and want book) - catalog

—Widder - widow; both men and women were called "widders"

—A while back - some time ago

—Aggue - egg

—Hen berries (also cackle berries) - eggs

—Seeing as how - because of that

—Laige - leg

—Lasses - molasses

—Bee line - direct route

—Batch - amount; a "batch" of gingerbread

—Bone dry (also dried up) - completely dry, as, "the creek was bone dry"

—Dead eye - an expert sharpshooter

—Flaieries - flowers

—Deef - deaf

—A deef and dumb person - a deaf mute

—Coon - raccoon

—Corn shuck - corn husk

—Cow juice - slang for milk

—A little dab - a small amount

—Jest - just

—Dodger - a pancake of cornbread baked by placing it directly on the top of the stove

—Dope - soda pop

—Drug - dragged

—Duck - to dodge

—Drempted - dreamed

—'Capted - escaped

—Clever - generous

—Waill - wild

—Fanger - finger

—Stretching leather - rubber

—Ruck - rake

—Tuck - took; "I tuck and did that."

—Tick-tack night - Halloween

—Drug - drag

— Nueground - new ground; a ground just been cleared of trees
— Haare - hair
— Fiesty - sexy
— Murrey - marry
— Dry up - hush
— Barefooted - barefoot
— Whiddle - whittle
— Campe'fer - camphor
— Smart - to burn; the pain of a whipping
— Bolted meal - meal bought from the store, not home-ground
— Ponch - hog's stomach
— To "nuss" a baby - to hold it on your lap
— Rinds - groins
— Stri'ped - stripe
— Sir'up - syrup
— No faritey - not fair to someone
— Aim to - going to; "I aim to go to church."

DESCRIPTIVE PHRASES

All of our old folks were wonderful story-tellers. Their descriptive phrases added humor and interest, giving character to the tale. Many of the ones I have listed were of their own invention, some are used by people elsewhere, but I have included them because our folks used them too.

—Naked as a jay bird
—Sleeping like a log
—Smart as a whip (smart, meaning "wise")
—Working like a house on fire
—Working all power
—Looking like something on a stick
—Kicking up his heels and showing his oats
—Crooked as a black snake
—Crooked as a rail fence
—So stiff that a cat could not scratch it
—Like pull a eye tooth
—Mad as a wet hen
—As useless as a last year's bird's nest
—His ears are so thin you could sun bees through them
—Small as a squirrel
—Froze stiff as a poker
—As pretty as a peach with one side bit off
—As frisky as a young colt just let out to pasture

—Gone, world without end
—To fit to a tee-wonk-tum (exactly)
—Fair to meedlin (almost)
—Cool as a cucumber
—Long in the tooth
—Sulk like a possum
—Enough grub to feed a working
—Like trying to feed Cox's army
—Black as the ace of spades
—Until he turns blue on the face
—Looking wild as a deer
—Skinny as a rail fence
—Ready for the bone yard
—I would not give you air if I had you in a jug
—Sleeping spoon fashion
—As snug as a bear in a hole
—Digging your own grave
—Don't hold your breath until I do
—I would rather have a bear by the tail
—Half drunk or a little haffer
—I half raised you
—We were brung up together
—Riding shanks mare (walking)
—Sleeping with the dogs
—Yoked with the wrong woman
—Slow as an ox
—Stubborn as a mule
—Clumsy as a cow
—Her tongue tied in the middle and loose at both ends
—Head as big as a soap gourd
—Down in the mouth
—Running off at the mouth
—Running around like a chicken with its head cut off
—Sweating like a nigger at an election

How We Talked

—Just a spit and a holler away
—Out of hearing, out of mind
—Taste right where you hold it
—A cow so poor you could hang your hat on her hips
—As ill as a hornet
—As busy as a bee
—A face you could whip a din of wildcats with; or, I could take your face and whip a din of wildcats
—You are like a cow's tail, always behind
—If Kentucky was a cow, Knott County would be the tail
—She is about frying size
—As ugly as a mud fence
—As ugly as homemede sin
—As ugly as gouge
—Just a slip of a girl
—He looks like a Philadelphia lawyer
—So cross-eyed he can see the back of his head
—In answer to how old you are:

a) old enough to sleep by myself
b) as old as the hills and not half so pretty
c) old enough to have had the seven year itch three times
d) old enough not to die young

—You look as if you were born on Wednesday and looking both ways for Sunday
—So cross-eyed he can see both ways at once
—You look as if you were born in the middle of the week and can't find Sunday
—He don't know his head from a hole in the ground
—A house not big enough to whip a cat in
—A house with cracks you could throw a dog through
—A quilt with stitches long enough you could hook your toenails in

— Toenail climbing

— He wasn't born, a buzzard laid an egg on a rock and the sun hatched it

— You look like the little boy the gander kicked through the fence

— Knee high to a duck

— As bald as a buzzard

— As scared as a rabbit

— You may be a chip off the old block, but you look like a shavin' to me

— A nigger in the wood pile

— You look as if the chickens have been roosting in your ears

— So poor he would have to stand twice in the same place to make a shadow

— Ears big enough to hold a peck of seed corn

— One of Pharaoh's plagues and came too late

— Your head looks like a stumpful of grand-daddies

— You look as if you had been sucking the old sow

— Pretty as a speckle pup

— His head looks like a burnt maul

— It will be a cold day in hell before I do that

— Like a bat out of hell

— Like a snowball in hell

— I've got you in my sight and the lock pulled down

— When you get a good thing, remember where you got it at

— That's what I feed my tongue for, to talk

— He is not worth the powder and lead it would take to blow his brains out

— So poor the wind whistles through its bones

— If he was going off to starve, he would take something to eat with him

— As big as all outdoors

— A bloomin' idiot

— Alive and kicking
— He kicked the bucket (died)
— As mean as all get out
— Chief cook and bottle washer
— Don't clamp at the bits
— Whore hopper and bottle stopper
— Fly off the handle
— Frog in his throat
— Going from piller to post
— She gave him down the road (berated)
— To work like a dog; also, to work like a mule
— High as a Georgia pine (drunk)
— Hog wild and pig crazy
— Hows does that grab you?
— That takes the pumpkin
— I guess I nipped that in the bud
— Not worth a hill of beans
— You ain't got brain one
— You ain't got a lick of sense
— A pack of lies
— She is beginning to pouch out (look pregnant)
— It's a downright shame and scandal

How We Talked

— Ever since old Heck was a pup
— Like a snake in the grass
— It don't make a speck of difference
— Dressed in your Sunday-go-to-meeting clothes
— All dressed up and no wheres to go
— An accident going somewhere's to happen
— A story that won't hold water
— She took up with some old man (living with him)
— As tough as cow hide
— Looks weasley and puny
— With rhyme or reason
— Knee high to a grasshopper
— Sing like a bird
— The shank of the evening
— A young whipper-snapper
— Barefoot weather
— Riding bare back
— Well bless my time of day
— Could not hit the barn door
— The kit and caboodle
— Don' got his dander up
— Wearing a Mother Hubbard dress (maternity clothes)
— You are as slow as the seven-year itch
— You need not fear the rain, you are neither sugar nor salt, you won't melt
— Fit to be hog-tied
— No more sense than God gave a goose
— Like a stuck pig
— White as a ghost
— Acting like they had a worm in their tail

SOME NONSENSE PHRASES:
— Whose wagon chain got frowned
— The little boy the gander kicked through the fence

64

—Clean your nose on that are dish rag. If they's anything in this world I can't abide, it's pure nastiness

—She eats like a bird, a peck at a time

—Ma said to Paw: reatch around there and scratch my back, right there between my thighs

—I wintered him one summer, and summered him one winter

—I would like to swop you to a "yeller dog" and then kill the dog

—If I was you and you were me and you had been someone else, who would I be?

—If me and my folks liked you and your folks like you and your folks like me and my folks, there were never folks liked folks since folks liked folks

—Wear a tie to keep your feet warm

—A young boy was told to smear cream on his face and let the cat lick his beard off, for his first shave

—Tear down the house and put it up in the loft

—Somewhere in the second flat above the top of the hill

—I took a cold last night from sleeping out in the yard and forgot to shut the gate

—If you could iron out all the hills in Knott County, it would be bigger than Texas.

—I have over one-hundred things for dinner, all soup beans

—We got plenty to eat, pret nigh all tatters

—I was going along, slow like, woulden' even thinking about a snake, and wham! up jumped a frog

—We haven't had biscuits in so long the children would think they were turtles, have them in the floor, putting fire on their backs, trying to get them to crawl

—Come on and eat. I know you are welcome and I hope it's clean

—I wish I might be ground up into sausage meat and cast into the bottom of the sea if I am not telling you the truth

— My feet's running and my nose is a smelling. My nose is a running and my feet's smelling

— We have chicken and gravy ever' day, the chickens are in the yard and the gravy is on the table.

SOME NEWER PHRASES:

— When canned milk was first introduced into Appalachia, it was described as, "No manure to haul, no hay to pitch. You just job a hole in the son-of-a-b - - - -."

— "Buy an ice box and starve the pigs to death." Said of the first refrigerators, as up until then the leftovers had been fed to the pigs.

— When my kids were growing up, they had all kinds of pets, except pigeons. Ever so often one son would decide maybe he could change my mind. For days, it would be a battle of wills. He would talk nothing but pigeons. No matter what we said, he would turn it to something about pigeons. Now, when someone has a one-track mind, "He is wanting to buy pigeons."

— A "chickenhouse divorce." Sometimes a man and a woman will get divorced from each other just so she can get government aid through the child welfare program (aid for dependent children). The husband would stay close by in a small house, pretending to no longer live with the wife. Sometimes this outhouse where he lived had been a chicken house, so, the phrase "chickenhouse divorce."

— A "happy pappy" or "mushrat" were men working on a government program for unemployed fathers.

— "Instead-of-coffee" - instant coffee

— "Aught-to-be-a-mule" - automobile

— "Round meat" - bologna

NAMES OF PEOPLE, PLACES, AND THINGS

I have just included a few names of animals, insects, plants, and birds that we pronounce the names differently, have our own name for them, or have some superstition about them.

The "grave robber" was an animal that was feared because it was supposed to have dug into newly-dug graves and eat the bodies. I have not been able to prove nor disprove if there was such an animal. It was described to be the size of a fox, only larger around, black or dark brown, short legs, long pointed nose, long sharp teeth (could have been a wolverine). Our folks built small houses over their graves to protect them from these "grave robbers." They believed in them, feared, and hated them even if they were true or mythical.

We used some animals for food, some we used the skins (the groundhog and deer), some were useful for their feathers (ducks, geese, and turkeys).

— "Crawdad" (also called the "crow dabber") - crawfish

— "Mud dobber" - a member of the wasp family that does not sting and builds a nest of mud, in which it places dead spiders for the young to eat when the eggs hatch. For this reason it was believed that the mud dobber turned into a spider, so many were killed because the spider was not liked, as it was thought to be poison.

— "Mussrat" - muskrat. Killed for its fur, also to get rid of it because it ate young ducks, their eggs, and garden plants planted close to the creek.

— "Coon" (also called a "ringtail") - raccoon. Killed for its hide and some people ate them. The raccoon destroyed the corn.

— "Possom" - o'possum. Killed for its hide and some folks ate them, but they were not counted as being good for food. A "blue belly possom" (summer young) was used as an expression of contempt, as "You are not worth as much as a blue belly possom."

— "Pack saddler" - a worm that was found on the blades of corn. We were always afraid of them when we were pulling the fodder. It stung by projecting spines from its back. It had a ring of these hair-like spines along its back that resembled a saddle.

— "Antie'mar" - ants

— "Grub worm" - Larva stage of a black beetle. It ate the roots of plants and was very destructive to cabbage. We got rid of them by putting cinders and ashes around the young cabbage plants.

— "June bug" - a bright-green beetle which also ate cabbage. Children caught them, tied a twine to one leg, and played with them, because they made a pretty, buzzing sound.

— "Garree" fly - jarfly. We loved to hear them "sing" and wondered at their ability to know when you touched the tree on which they were, for they would stop suddenly.

— "Lighten' bug" - firefly. We loved to catch them and play with them. Sometimes we would rub the bugs on our fingernails to make them glow in the dark.

— "Chinch bug" - a very awful, bad-scented bug that was found on plants, sometimes on berries. The chinch was a bed bug that got in the beds. We got rid of them by spraying the beds with kerosene oil, and "scalding" the beds with hot water.

— "Jack snapper"- a long, black beetle that made a loud snapping sound when it snapped its head. We children loved to play with them and make them snap their heads.

— "Doddle bug" - built its nest in sandy, dry places, usually under a cliff. Children loved to make them come out of their homes by circling their finger around the top and saying, "Doddle bug, doddle bug, fly away home, your house is on fire, your children will burn."

—"Grand-daddy" - a grand-daddy-long-legs. They were supposed to point one of their legs in the direction when asked where your cow was in the pasture.

—"Wooley worm" - A hairy worm believed to tell weather signs. A lot of dark-colored ones seen meant a cold winter; soft colors meant a warm winter. If there were a lot that were of many colors, then the winter would have different kinds of weather.

—"A thousand-legged worm" - a centipede.

—"Bessie bug" - a very active and excitable bug. We said of someone that had lost their mind as being as "crazy as a bessie bug."

—"Sow bugs" - a small bug usually found under old, decaying logs. Used to cure diseases by tying them in a rag and wearing them around the neck.

—"Stink bug" - a pretty, bright-green beetle with a yellow head, which gave off an awful odor.

—"Polecat" - skunk

—"Groundhog" (also called a "whistle pig") - woodchuck. The most useful small, wild animal. The body was used for food, the fat was "rendered out" and used as medicine (earache), the skin cured and used for thread, shoelaces, banjo heads, etc.

—"Ground squirrel" - chipmunk. Some folks ate them. Mostly killed to get rid of them; they were a great nuisance, as they dug up the seed corn.

—Birds:

Yeller hammer - wood hen
Whipperwill - whippoorwill
Pecker wood - woodpecker. Sometimes called the "red-head pecker wood."
Joe reed - I don't know the real name for this bird, but it made a sound as if it was saying, "Joe Read."

Spar - sparrow

Howke - hawk. These killed a lot of our chickens. A glass jar
on a tall pole was supposed to keep them away.

Scritch owl - screech owl. If one of these called close to the
house, it was the sign of death.

Snow birds - chickadee. Were supposed to flock together just
before it was going to snow.

Hummin' bird - hummingbird.

—Animals, known as "critters" or "varmits":

Cow brute - cow
Hoss - horse
Pot licker - hound dog
Wile cat - bobcat

—Insects

Yeller jacket - yellowjacket
Wasper - wasp
Cow fly - a small fly that bothered cows, very bad in the summer. One of the children would have to hold the cow's tail
while someone was milking so as to keep the cow from
switching her tail as she tried to rid herself of these flies.
Horse fly - a very large fly that bothered horses and cows.
They laid their eggs in under the skin of cows, rabbits, and
kittens, on their backs. When the eggs hatched the larva
made a sore in the animal, which was very painful, often
killing the rabbit or cat. The cow was able to stand it better.
We kept the fly from laying its eggs on the cow by putting
salt on their backs. As they licked the salt off, it got rid of
the eggs. The salt also killed the young flies.

—Names of some of our weeds and plants: again, I have only
listed the ones that have an interesting name or a unique name,
or one that was used for some purpose.

A. Greens - ones used for greens that were cooked.

   a. poke salet - the leaves, and also the stalks were eaten. They must be cooked in a lot of pork lard as they are poisonous. The stalks were rolled in meal and fried in grease.

   b. Groundhog's ear - so named because its leaves resembled the ear of the groundhog.

   c. Sheep's sour

   d. Sour vine - resembles the poison vine, except it has five leaves in a cluster; the poison variety has only three. We were told to remember the difference by the idea that the five were the fingers of our hand, therefore a sign of friendship.

   e. Wild mustard

   f. Plantain' - plantain, the most used. A plant that somewhat has the taste of cabbage. We still use this, sometimes putting it in our freezers, or canning it for winter use. Eaten with vinegar poured over it.

   g. Speckled dock

   h. Lambs quarter

   i. Yeller dock

   j. Blue sissel - thistle

B. These plants were eaten for salet (greens), but not cooked: they were salted and "killed" (pouring hot grease on them).

71

a. Winter lettuce
b. Crows foot - three leaves close together like a crow's foot. One variety of this plant is poison.
c. Chicken salet
d. Bird's leg
e. Shoe string
f. Ragged gut
g. Creasses
h. Shonnie
i. Sheeps tongue
j. Tangle gut

—Other plants and flowers:

Easter flowers - Jonquil
Fall roses - Zinnia
Dallie - Dahlia
Murrygoes - Marigold
Furne - Fern
Sissel - Thistle
Dog fennel- used to get rid of bugs
Chinch weed - so named because of its awful odor
Smart grass - used to get rid of fleas, also put in a hole of water to make the fish come to the top of the water and could then be caught.
Sang - ginseng. Used for medicine, mostly dug to sell.
Yeller root
Snake root
Pu'coon or Blood root
May apple - dug for the root. Some ate the fruit, but was poison.
Pop paws - eaten for the fruit
Simmons - Persimmons
Horse weeds - grew very tall; were used mostly to feed cows, horses, and chickens.

How We Talked

Hen gollop

Burrs - Spanish neddles; Sheeps burrs; Snach burrs; Cuckle burrs.

Jempson weed

Red root

Mullen

Rattle weed

Spegnet

Ground ivy

Penni'rile - Pennyroyal

Horehound

Balm

Branch mint (also called "creek mint")

Farewell Summer weed - bloomed just six weeks before frost

Dollar leaf plant

Pretty My Nights - 4 o'Clocks

Dog ticks - Castor beans

Ladies wash bowl - Tiger lily

Rose moss - Primrose

Easter bush - Formostha

— Plants and roots used for beverages:

Sassafack - sassafras

Spice wood - also a few small twigs cooked with a groundhog to rid it of the woodsy or earthy taste

Birch tree bark or twigs

Sweet anis roots

Mountain tea

— The most used plants, barks, and roots used for medicine:

Wild cherry bark

Peach tree bark

Blackberry roots

Slippery elm

Red stem ivy
Wild cane
Black gum bark
Cucumber tree (Wahoo)
White oak bark
Spruce pine
Privy bush
Sourwood
Chestnut tree leaves
Branch willow
Pussy willow
Buckeye - carried in pocket to cure rheumatism
Nightshed - Very poison. Used mixed with milk on sores.
Garlic - for colds and high blood
Ratsvien - kidney trouble and liver
Water weed (also called "Jewelweed")
Spicewood
Birch tree bark
Peppermint
Calamus
Fever weed
Wild rose petals (also called "May Rose")

The way we pronounce some of the well-known proper names: All names ending in "a" are pronounced as ending in "ie" or "y". So:

Marthie - Martha
Rosie - Rosa
Verney - Verna
Berthie - Bertha
Evey - Eva
Jeemes - James
Murry - Mary
E'lick - Alec

Vi'lorie - Valeria
Bar'brey - Barbara
Lee'an'er - Lenora
Ca'ther'rine - Catherine
Josie'fine - Josephine
Heel'un - Helen
Lue'eyes - Louise
Harm - Hairm
Eva'line - Evelyn
Fran'sis - Francis
More'ell - Morrell
Run'nells - Reynolds
Guer'hart - Gayheart
Tut - Tuttle
Macken'tush - McIntash
Rossie'felt - Roosevelt
Burgie - Amburgy
Sa'yeries - Sawyers
Lizzie'beth - Elizabeth
Kay'rue - Carew
Bishe - Abisha
Isom - Isham
Lean'urd - Lenard
Pur'us - Pierce
Glade'us - Gladys
Santie - Santa
Ce'lie - Celia
Vergie - Virginia
Gar'ie - Gary
Sa'ley - Sally
Napper - Napier
Be'at'trice - Beatrice

CHIMNEY CORNER LAWS: CUSTOMS OF THE HILLS

Hill people had a lot of old customs of their own, a way of life, of doing things, that were called "chimney corner laws." These were more strictly kept and observed than the real laws handed out by the government. In fact, one of the chimney corner laws, "never turn in one of your kinfolks to the law," meant protect him in any way you can. This was one time it was permissible to lie. The law and its enforcers were the enemies and all was fair in trying to outwit them. These chimney corner laws were taught to children at as early an age as they could recall being taught. It was just something you grew up knowing. If asked why they did something such and such a way, the answer would be, "I don't know, we just allus done it that way, and why quit now?"

There are too many of these chimney corner laws to list them all. I will just put down a few, so as to give an idea of what they are.

—Never go into another man's house if he is not at home, if it's just his wife and children there, unless one of the children is grown up and a male, or some other male relative is at home. Ask at the gate if "the old man's at home."

—Always ask anyone you meet to go home with you. If someone is passing your home, ask them to come in. They, in turn, must ask you to go home with them. If they are leaving your house, you must ask them to come back soon. This goes for everyone, not just your friends and acquaintances.

— You always invite anyone to "stay and have a bite" if it's close to mealtime, even if they are just passing the house, and surely if they are in your home. Also, to "stop and set a spell."

— Never talk loud or laugh while you are passing someone's house. This was very insulting.

— If you found someone's stock (cows, sheep, horses) had "jumped the fence" and strayed from home, return them or let him know. If someone's milk cow was near your house near milk time and she needed to be milked, you must milk her, and if he did not ask for the milk, you were to keep it as your own.

— If you found a bee tree (a tree in which bees had made a hive and made honey), even if it was not on your land, chop a cross mark in the bark. No one else could cut the tree except you. The owner of the land could demand part of the honey, or keep the bees, which ever you both agreed on, but not both.

— Each man had a mark for his pigs; by making a split or notch in their ears (maybe both a clip and a notch), a notch and undercut for the left ear, a notch and an overcut for the right ear, or whatever combination he preferred. No one had the same. These were, at times, recorded on the court records. The hogs were allowed to run "wild," turned loose in the woods, and feed themselves on "mass" (nuts and roots). If a mother pig birthed a "gang" of pigs and the owner did not catch them and put his mark on them, when they were "weened" and quit running with the mother pig, they were counted as wild pigs and belonged to whoever caught them and put his brand on them. Chickens were marked by cutting off the end of one or more toes when they were little. Each person had his own mark depending on which toe, how many, and which foot, right or left.

— If it became known that a family was "in a hard place" (needed help) or got behind with their work in making a corn crop or garden, building a house or fence, or maybe had just gotten married, all the neighbors got together and had a "working." The women cooked and served a "good dinner," the men did the work. Sometimes there was a free supper. Also, sometimes the working was followed with a dance, depending upon the religious beliefs of the family. Our people were sturdy, hard-working people. They never grew tired - they could work all day and dance and "frolic" all night.

— If a pregnant woman "craved" for a certain food, if you had any, you must see that she got all she wanted to eat.

— If a pregnant woman asked a man to go to get a doctor or "granny woman" for her, he must never refuse to go, no matter what he was busy at.

— A man could refuse to let his wife be baptized into the church and his wish must be respected. This is no longer true.

— If you set a price on something and someone offered to buy at that price, you must accept the trade, never "rie back."

— When a man was shaking hands with a woman, he would sometimes scratch in her hand with one finger. This meant he was asking her for a sexual favor. In return he might get his face slapped, depending on the kind of woman it was. Or, she might answer, "Why don't you ask for it like a man, not beg for it like a dog."

— If one man's dog "treed" or "holed" an animal (ran an animal into a tree or hole in the ground), which was usually caught for food or fur, no other man dared kill the animal. It belonged to the owner of the dog.

— You must never speak evil about anyone dead. Once, a man died. He had been so mean all his life that all his neighbors hated him. At his burial someone asked, "Is there anyone here that can say anything good about him?" and one old man spoke up and said, "Well, he was a good whistler."

— You must never hit or slap a woman when she was pregnant. Some women took advantage of this.

— A man must watch two women fight without trying to stop them.

— You must never hit anyone wearing glasses.

— Never call a man a liar; you are saying "fightin' words." A man might kill you if you told him he was lying, because our folks did not lie.

— If you called a man a "S.O.B." you were insulting his mother. It was thought a disgrace to not fight if you were called this.

— No man would allow his women folks to go any distance from home without some male relative with them. This was out of love and respect, and his desire to protect her, not that he did not trust her.

— Never use obscene language in the hearing of a woman, or allow anyone else to, or while passing anyone's house.

— It was counted an insult to ask anyone for a debt.

— A handshake and a promise was all the agreement made between two mountain people, no matter how much money was involved. No man would ever break a promise after he had "shuck hands on it."

FOOD — GRUB
OR VITTLES

It would be impossible to write a cookbook of recipes in modern terminology describing dishes prepared by our Appalachian cooks in time past. They had no written forms of how to prepare a dish. They cooked on stoves heated with coal or wood; there was no way to regulate the heat. There were no measurements such as modern cooks use. A dab, a pinch, a handful, and a smear were some of the terms they used. Most girls learned by watching their mothers, and taught their daughters the same way. There is no assurance that the following directions will come out perfect every time, but they are recorded as near as possible to the way our folks "fixed them."

And, as for allowing so much for so many servings as modern recipes do, just so you had "a plenty and some to spare" was all that mattered to our people. Any self-respecting housewife in Appalachia would "druther been found dead in the middle of the road" than be caught at mealtime without enough for the family and more. They would have felt disgraced to have had all the bowls and platters empty and no more in the pots on the stove to refill them. The custom was (and still is) to cook more than enough for the family and if no one came in near mealtime to eat it, you gave it to the animals. It made its way back to the table through them. What did it matter? You raised all the food yourself, and always had much more than you could use. It was an insult to

80

not ask any visitor, or just even a passerby (someone passing the house) near mealtime to stop "and have a bite." It was counted good manners to belittle what you had to offer a guest to eat, no matter how plentiful. "You can make out for a little while, what we make out on all the time," or, "Why don't you stay for a week or until you get weak, whichever comes first." Or, you might be told, "Stay all night, I will set up with you all night before I would let you go to bed hungry." They always had enough for themselves and "the commers and the goers" (visitors).

To prepare a meal was to "fix a mess." The word for food was "grub" or "vittles." All food put away for winter use, except meat, milk, and bread, was "sass" - all dried, canned, and holed-away fruits, vegetables, berries, and salt-pickled foods (kraut, corn, beans, and cucumbers).

Their dishes were simple and easy to prepare. They grew everything themselves, even the spices (sage, dill, mints). The only shortening they used was pork grease. Anything else would have been "a make-do." Even when they used butter, it was not counted as good as pork grease. Their skillets and pots were iron, which makes a big difference when cooking from our utensils of today. So, with these warnings, here are the recipes in the language of our people.

—Red-eyed gravy (also called bay sop) - Processed meat cannot be used for this. It must be fresh meat - ham, pork chop, sweet meat, or lean bacon. After the meat has been fried, remove it from skillet, pour off into a bowl most of the grease, leaving about one-half cup. Place the skillet back on the stove, pour in about one-half pint of water. The water will begin to boil and loosen the residue left from the meat. Let boil until most of the water has boiled away. Pour into bowl and serve. Good over flour gravy, meat, fried and mashed potatoes.

—Flour or brown gravy - In an iron skillet put about four tablespoons of melted meat grease (if you use cold lard, a lump about the size of a large egg). Place on heat, stir in a small handful of flour. Keep stirring until the flour has turned brown. Pour in a pint and a half of milk. Stir constantly until thickened. Use more or less milk to assure the preferred thickness. Salt and pepper to taste. Serve with meat, fried apples, fried potatoes, or on hot biscuits. In Appalachia gravy was used as a dish, not just an additive. Most often it was for breakfast. Two-thirds meal and one-third flour can be used and make cornmeal gravy. Buttermilk can be substituted for the sweet milk, making sourmilk gravy. Water gravy was only used when there was no milk available. But, as it was thought that every meal must have gravy, sometimes water gravy was made, and nicknamed "poor do."

— Fried potatoes - Peel and slice a large bowl of potatoes, wash and drain off the excess water. Put about one-half pint of lard into an iron skillet. Again, bacon drippings are best. When grease becomes real hot, pour in the potatoes. Sprinkle with salt, cover with lid (a plate is better to use as it keeps in more heat). Let fry a few moments, remove lid. Stir with a knife or egg turner. (Never use a spoon.) Keep turning over and over from the bottom until they are brown. Potatoes can be cut into cubes or long, strips, if desired. Also, real small potatoes can be fried whole. (You only have these small ones if you raise them yourself.) Also good to add a diced onion to the potatoes and fry together. Serve with butter or gravy.

— Fried sweet potatoes - Sweet potatoes can be fried the same as Irish potatoes, only they are very easy to burn. Peel and slice the sweet potatoes. Wash and drain off the excess water. Pour into an iron skillet in which a small amount of lard has been allowed to melt. Sprinkle on top of the potatoes a small handful of sugar, a large pinch of salt. Cover with plate. (Brown sugar is best.) Let cook for a little while, until the moisture from washing the potatoes has caused the sugar to melt and become syrup. Stir often. These are very easy to burn. Serve topped with butter or gravy.

— Fried tomatoes - Slice six or seven large, full-grown green tomatoes. Remove "bud spot," don't peel. Slice two or three large, green sweet peppers and one very small red or hot pepper. Mix all together, sprinkle with just a little buttermilk (just enough to make them damp). Stir in a small handful of cornmeal and about half as much flour. Salt and pepper to taste. Pour into an iron skillet that has a small amount of lard pre-melted. Place on heat and let fry. Stir often. Let cook until meal becomes brown. Some folks like them sweetened with sugar. Also good to fry in large slices, one layer at a time, in deep fat, turning each over like pancakes. Served with soup beans, shucky beans, or as a side dish for any kind of meat.

— Fried summer squash - Prepare and fry as same as sweet potatoes, except you do not peel. Remove the seeds if they are not real young. If the seeds are not soft, remove them.

— Fried cabbage - Chop cabbage very fine. Add salt and pepper to taste. Pour into preheated iron skillet into which a small amount of lard has melted. (About two tablespoons of lard.) Do not cover. Stir constantly. Let cook for about five minutes, or until the cabbage lose their crispness.

— Fried apples - Peel, core, and slice length-wise a bowl of sour apples. Wash and drain off excess water. Pour into preheated iron skillet in which a small amount of lard has melted. Sprinkle with a large handful of sugar (brown sugar is best) and a small pinch of salt. Cover with a plate. The sugar will melt and draw out the juice from the apples. Stir often, as they are very easy to burn. Serve with biscuits and butter, flour gravy, sausages or bacon. A breakfast dish.

— Homemade syrup - Fill a skillet or saucepan with about one pint of water. Pour in three times as much sugar (brown sugar is best). Stir until all the sugar is melted. Let cook until desired thickness. (Remember, it will be thicker when it has cooled.) Remove quickly from heat. Do not let it overcook. Served over pancakes or with hot biscuits and butter.

— Every family had their own way to make hot biscuits and had them every morning for breakfast. To have biscuits was a status symbol. Sift a large pan of flour almost full. (We used only plain flour.) Make a hole in the middle, about one-third of the depth, with your hand. Put in this hole one tablespoon baking powder, one large pinch of soda, a small amount of salt, a big chunk of butter (about a fist size). Using the fingers, work the butter and dry ingredients into a small amount of the flour. Slowly pour in about one pint of milk. (If you use buttermilk you must use more soda.) Mix the milk with the flour. By gently tapping the sides of the pan, you can keep adding more flour as you need it to make a thick dough. Knead the dough, pinch off small amounts (size of biscuits preferred) by using the sides of both hands. Form into biscuits. Place on greased pan and bake until done, a light brown. You can roll dough out and cut with biscuit cutter, but why bother?

—Cornbread - When using our own home-ground meal, use about two quarts of sifted meal. Add a teaspoon baking soda, another of salt, one small cup of buttermilk. Add enough water to make a soft dough. Stir and mix well. Pour into a preheated, slightly greased pan. Bake until top is brown. In our stoves the side nearest to the fire got brown first, so the pan had to be turned around after one side got brown so the other then could brown.

To use "bolted meal" or store-bought meal, you must use one part flour to three parts meal. Some folks like to add an egg to the mixture.

The brand sifted from our home-ground meal was fed to the chickens or cooked for the pigs. After sifting the brand a second time a small, fine-cracked grain was obtained. This was cooked in water, making a thick paste. Sugar was added and eaten as a cereal, like grits.

By using hot water to make cornbread we made what we called "scalded bread." It was very good to eat with milk. We sometimes added molasses to make molasses bread. Cooked cushaw or pumpkin was added also. Cracklin' bread was made by adding the cracklins (left over meat scraps from making [rendering] lard).

If the fire wasn't hot enough to make the bread bake fast enough, it was said to be "sun baked." If the bread was not brown someone was sure to say, "You must have scared this bread to death, it looks so pale."

If a woman let her bread burn, then her husband was angry at her. (Superstition)

—Stiff Jacks, or molasses candy - Pour into a large skillet or iron cooker about one quart of molasses. Add about one small teacup of water and a small pinch of soda. Bring to a boil. Let boil until it will "spin a thread" when allowed to drip from a spoon. Pour into a large greased pan or platter. Allow to cool. Break into pieces, do not cut. Nuts can be added if preferred. Serve as a snack.

—Popcorn balls - Pop corn. Do not add salt or butter. Prepare molasses the same as for candy. Pour over popcorn while hot. Stir until all corn is covered. Smear hands with butter or wet hands with water. Form popcorn into balls, pressing gently to make them stick together. Place on large platter, not touching each other. Eat as a snack. Nuts can be added to the popcorn, if desired.

—Parched corn - Shell a few ears of the regular white corn,

normally used for feed or meal. Pour into an iron skillet. Add a small amount of grease and a large pinch of salt. Place on heat. Stir constantly, until brown. Serve as a snack. Becomes very "brickley" (crunchy).

— We roasted eggs, potatoes, sweet potatoes, apples, onions, and chestnuts under the grate in the hot ashes. Chestnuts are easy to burst. The eggs must have a hole (very small) made in them and a straw pushed into the hole to keep them from bursting when they get hot.

— Mush - In a large pot of boiling water (salted to taste) slowly pour with one hand, while stirring with a long-handled spoon in the other hand, enough meal to thicken to desired thickness. Allow to cool for a few seconds. Stir constantly. Serve by "dunking" spoonfuls into a bowl of milk. Eaten warm. Also good if allowed to become cold, sliced and fried like pancakes and eaten with syrup and butter, or molasses.

— Guy-my-grallin' - A kind of stew. In a large pot of water, preferably water in which meat has been cooked or preboiled, cook any vegetables in large chunks or whole. Just peel and wash the potatoes, onions, carrots. Quarter the cabbage. Cut the corn from the cob, string the green beans. Add salt and pepper to taste. Cook for one hour on the back of the stove (low heat) then add several large, sliced tomatoes and cook for another hour, or until tender. Keep adding water if any boils away. Serve with cornbread and milk. Nice to cook when you are going away from home or are going to be very busy. We always had Gut-my-grallin' on wash day.

— Shucky beans - To dry them, pick while still green, almost full grown. Remove the strings. Dry them by placing them in the sun, or stringing them on twine like beads, using a darning needle, and hanging them on a nail. Do not hang close together as they need to dry fast in the air, or they will mildew. To prepare them to eat, remove from string, soak in water for from one to two hours or more, wash through several waters, put into a large pot, cover with water. Add a big chunk of hog's jowl or salt pork. Allow to cook slowly for three to four hours. Keep covered with water by adding more as the water boils away. Add salt to taste. Let cook until almost all the water has boiled away. Some folks like to remove them from the water and fry in pork grease. Serve with pickled beets or sauerkraut and cornbread.

— Dried apples - To dry, our old folks had a "kiln" and dried bushels of dried apples each year. But, to just dry a few, you can dry them in the oven of the stove. Peel, quarter and remove the seeds and core, place on a cookie sheet or bread pan, one layer thick at a time. Place in the oven under very low heat. Stir often, as they will burn easily. They are cooked in a large amount of water with sugar added and eaten as a desert. Or, allow the water to all cook away (cooked down dry) and fry in a small amount of grease, sugar, and a little salt. But they were used most for to make fried apple pies, also called "moon pies," "moccasin pies" or "flip overs."

— Fried pies - Make a dough as for biscuits, roll and cut into squares about three or four inch size. Place a spoonful of apple butter (cooked apples can be used, also cooked dried apples) in one corner of the square of dough, turn other corner over to cover the apples. Pinch the dough together tight, fry in deep fat or bake in well-greased pan. "Smear" the top with more lard. Remove from pan and sprinkle with brown sugar and powdered cinnamon while hot. Serve warm.

— Old-fashioned gingerbread - Again, every family had a different recipe for gingerbread, but this is the one used by my family for generations:

10 lb. plain flour
2 pints sugar, one brown, the other white
½ lb. butter and ½ lb. lard
1 cup molasses
1 heaping Tablespoon ginger (more if desired real strong)
1 level teaspoon cinnamon, and half as much nutmeg

1 teaspoon soda
4 eggs
8 teaspoons baking powder
1 quart buttermilk

Sift all the flour into a large pan. Make a large round hollow in the middle of the flour one third deep. Put into this space all the dry ingredients. Mix with small amount of flour. Add eggs, soft lard, butter, and molasses. Mix well, using your hand. Add milk a little at a time. By tapping the sides of the pan, cause a little of the flour to fall into the mixture. Keep mixing with hand. Keep adding flour this way until you have a stiff dough. Knead until very stiff, or until all the flour is used. Pinch off a small piece and shape into long cakes. Place in preheated, greased pan. Pat smooth to about one-half inch thickness. (If you want, you can roll and cut with biscuit cutter or into squares, but our folks did not.) Smear the top of cakes with the white of egg, using a cloth tied to a fork. This gives them a shiny, glossy look. Put into oven and bake until brown. Good served with butter, milk, coffee, or alone. Good eaten warm, but will keep for weeks.

—Stack cake - Sometimes called old-fashioned fruit cake. Make the dough the same as for gingerbread, but bake in a skillet or cake pan, each cake as large as the pan, and about one inch thick. "Smear" a plate with apple butter. Place one cake on the apple butter, put more apple butter on it, another cake, more apple butter, and so on. Make stack as high as you want, at least four or five. Cooked apples, applesauce, crushed peaches, and berries of any kind can be used in place of the apple butter. Cooked fried apples were also used.

—Apple butter - Cook apples until tender or soft. (Some remove the core, skin, and seeds before cooking; some preferred the taste the peeling gave the apples.) Allow the apples to cool and push them through a sifter (we now use a food mill) by using the hands. This way you remove all the seeds, skins, and cores and make the apples smooth. Add sugar (about one part sugar to three parts apples). Add cinnamon and spice to taste. Cook until very stiff, stirring often with long-handled spoon or paddle. Apple butter is easy to burn. Put into jars and seal. Our folks used to put into crocks and churns and cover with beeswax, as they had no glass jars. Sometimes they used molasses in place of the sugar. With molasses the apple butter will keep for weeks without spoiling.

— Old fashioned chicken and dumplin's - Put a cut-up chicken in a pot of water. Add salt and cook until tender. Add more water if needed. (Our folks used a full-grown hen complete with the head, neck, feet, liver, gizzard, egg bag, little eggs, and all the fat . . . the more fat the better. That's what gave them the good flavor.) Remove the chicken from the pot. You should have at least a half pot of "gruel" left in the pot. If not, add more water. Bring to a rolling boil and drop in fist size "globs" of biscuit dough, as many as the gruel will cover. Allow to cook about twenty minutes. Take from heat, cover pot, and allow to "steam" for another ten minutes. Nowdays folks roll the dough and cut into strips; it's not the same and by no way as good.

Our folks made dumplings in the stock where fresh meat had been cooked. We also used apples, berries, rhubarb, even vinegar, to make dumplings, with sugar added. Spice was also added to the vinegar water. A "barefoot dumplin'" was made from water, grease, and salt.

— Chicken gravy - Cook the chicken in a large amount of water. Remove from pot. Fill a small bowl about two-thirds full with milk. Beat in a few spoons of flour, pour into the boiling "gruel," and let cook until smooth. More or less flour can be added to get the desired thickness. Salt and pepper to taste.

— Squirrel gravy - Same as chicken gravy, except you use a squirrel in place of the chicken. Always served with young sweet potatoes.

—Fried chicken (southern style) - Roll cut-up pieces of young chicken in a mixture of two parts meal and one part flour. Salt and pepper to taste, place in preheated iron skillet of real hot lard (have at least one inch of lard). As soon as bottom side gets brown, turn each piece over. Place on lower heat, cover with plate, and cook or fry until tender. It took longer to fry our home-raised chickens because they "run loose" and grew slower, but had a much better flavor.

—Homemade hominy - Must use iron or enamel pot. Fill pot with water; add lye (about one heapin' spoonful to each gallon of shelled corn). The regular white corn used for feed or bread is best. Pour in corn and cook until husk can be easily removed. (Test by rubbing a few grains with fingers.) Remove from heat and wash through several waters, rubbing with hands until all husks are gone and the taste of lye is gone. Put into a pot of clear water and cook until tender. You will need a much larger pot for this second cooking, as the corn will "swell," but it does not have to be an iron pot this time. Homemade hominy is good to just sprinkle with salt and eat as a snack; also good fried in lard and served as a vegetable dish. We used to make gallons at a time in a "mink kittle" outside. It was a tradition to always make hominy when we had our first snow.

—Homemade jelly - Apples, peaches, pears, all berries, rhubarb, elderberries, wild grapes, and cherries were used. As apple juice was the easier to get to "jell," it was often mixed with the other juices. Cook the berries or fruit in a lot of water, until tender. Strain out all the fruit to get the water. Add three parts sugar to one part juice. Cook, stirring often. Test by letting a small amount drop from spoon. When two or more drops cling together the jelly is ready to be removed from the heat. Pour into jars and seal. We used melted paraffin to seal the jars. Blackberries can be used without cooking them. It takes more berries, but the taste is better. Crush the berries and run through a sifter or food mill to get the juice. Boil with sugar and make as other jelly. The remaining parts of the berries can be mixed with sugar—the same amount of sugar and berries—and boiled to make jam.

—Beverages:

Sassafrack (*Sassafras*) *tea* - Dig the sassafras roots. Wash and peel the outside rough bark. Cut off the remaining center bark of the roots into small pieces and boil in water. Strain and add sugar and drink while hot. Remember, it's very strong. A very small piece will flavor a big pot of tea.

Spicewood tea - Use the small limbs or twigs. Break into small lengths. Boil in water, add sugar, and drink hot. A few twigs of spicewood was added to the water when cooking a groundhog. It was supposed to remove the "woodsy" and "earthy" taste.

Birch tea - Scrape the bark from the small limbs or twigs of the birch tree. Strain, add sugar, and drink hot. Also good cold.

Ginger tea - Boil a few "races" (the unground roots of the ginger plant) in water. Strain, add sugar, and drink hot. Some folks added whiskey to ginger tea.

Mountain tea - Boil the leaves of the mountain tea plant. Strain, add sugar, drink hot or let get cold. Has a wintergreen flavor.

Creek mint tea - Gather only the leaves and top stems of the creek mint plant. Slightly crush. Put into cold water and let "steep" for a few hours. Strain; add sugar (just a little). Serve cold.

Beer - From beer seeds, a fungus plant that looked like bread crumbs. They reproduced by dividing and grew in water sweetened with molasses and kept in a warm, dry, dark place. Ever few days the water could be poured off and used. This made a nice, refreshing drink, non-intoxicating. The jar was refilled and more molasses added, and more beer in a few days. When the beer seeds got too many for the jar, some could be removed for another start in another jar. Even if allowed to dry, they would live for many days.

Coffee - When coffee was first introduced into Appalachia, it came to us green, in one-hundred pound sacks. It had to be roasted or "browned" in the oven in a bread pan, then ground by hand in a coffee grinder, boiled in a coffee "biler," and served hot and black. No one ever used sugar or cream.

—Homemade butter - Strain fresh milk, just milked from the cow, into a sterilized churn, using a thin cloth or "store bought" strainer. Everything about milk must be sterilized. We did it with boiling water. Milk will "pick up" any odor it comes in contact with, and spoil the flavor of the milk and butter. The churn was covered with a cloth and set before the grate where it would keep warm but not get hot. Let set for about six or eight hours, until the milk "turns." The milk will become clabbored. Test by tilting the churn to one side. If the milk drops loose from the side, then it's ready to be churned. Using a churn dasher (two pieces of wood about two inches wide and one-half inch thick and five inches long, nailed in a cross to the end of a long stick) with an up and down motion, you mix the milk. The churn lid had a hole in the middle that let the dasher fit through and kept the milk from splashing out as you churned the milk. It will take about fifteen minutes of this churning before the butter will begin to form in small "gobblets" on top of the milk. If the butter is beginning to form into small balls about the size of peas and will not stick together, then the milk is too cold. Add some hot water to the churn. If the butter is thin and looks melted, it's too hot, so add some cold water. "Gather" the butter by swishing the milk around with the dasher just below the top of the milk. Remove the butter from the top of the milk with a spoon or tea cup. Put into a bowl. Beat the remaining milk out by using a fork like whipping cream. Wash out the extra milk by adding water. Keep on doing this until all milk is removed. Salt to taste. Milk can also be churned in a jar. You just have to shake the jar until the butter gathers ("comes").

—Killed salet - Some of the greens we used were not cooked, but eaten raw. They were "looked" (checked for bugs and rotting spots), washed, sprinkled with salt, and wilted or "killed" by pouring real hot pork grease over them.

—Cooked greens - They were cleaned and washed and pre-boiled in a lot of water. They were then taken out and reheated in pork grease and salt.

—Walnut candy - To three parts sugar (brown sugar is best) and one part cream or milk, add as many walnut kernels as you want (other nuts can be used). Cook in an iron skillet or iron pot until the mixture "spins a thread" when allowed to drip from a spoon. Take from the heat and beat until it begins to thicken. Pour into a greased platter. Allow to partly cool. Cut into squares and serve. Good warm or cold. If you make candy without the nuts then you must add butter, one tablespoon to each cup of sugar used.

—Potatoes cooked with their jackets on - Wash potatoes, put into pot. Cover with water, boil until tender. Serve with salt and butter, or sour cream. Children would often take an empty lard bucket to school with them and cook potatoes this way on the "pot bellied stove" used to heat the schoolroom, and eat them for their dinner. The teacher did not mind, she usually joined them.

—Roasting corn - Use young corn, when the grains will still run "milk" when jabbed with the fingernail. Turn back the shuck to expose the ear of corn, but do not break the shuck loose from the ear. Inspect for worms, bugs, and rotting spots, clean away all silks. Turn the shuck back over the ear of corn and fasten the end by tying some of the shucks together. Dip into water, to wet shuck so it will not burn. Place on hot coals of fire (a large fire built outside and allowed to turn to hot coals) turning once or twice. Let remain until tender. Serve with salt and butter. We had a corn roast like the modern wiener roast.

—To fry corn, select three or four large ears of corn. Test to see if it's ready for use by pinching the grains to see if they will "run milk." Remove silks and any bad spots after shucking. Using a very sharp knife, slice off the very tip of the grains all way around the ear. With the back of the knife, scrape over the grains, removing the creamy inside of the grain. Only the husk will be left.

Mix with a small amount of water, a large sprinkle of flour, salt to taste. If you use the regular white corn, you must also add a little sugar; if you use the sugar or sweet corn, then no sugar is needed. Pour mixture into a preheated skillet in which a few teaspoons of lard has melted. Stir constantly until the color changes from white (or yellow) to a clear color. Serve as a vegetable dish.

— Whole grain corn - Cut corn from the cob in layers, by cutting the grains in half, then the other half; or, cut in whole grains. Put in preheated skillet in which about two tablespoons of lard has melted and fry to cook in a small amount of water in a pot. Salt to taste. Cook until almost dry. Serve.

— Fresh meat - The bones of the hogs were cooked and eaten as soon as they could be after the hog was slaughtered, because we had no way to keep them. We cooked them in water and salt. If we cooked all the water out we called it "cooking them down to the dry grease." Sometimes we left a lot of water and made dumplings. Sometimes we cooked vegetables with the meat, usually potatoes. Some of the names we gave the different parts of the hog were:

a. the fan or blade bone - shoulder bone
b. chine bone - large bone in the fore (front) leg
c. ma'ar (marrow) bone - the large bone in the back leg; ham
d. hock bone - the bone near foot
e. knuckle bone - top of foot
f. sweetmeat - the muscle near the back bone
g. melt - spleen
h. lights - lungs
i. sweetbread - the muscle holding the internal organs together
j. ponch - stomach

— Hogs headcheese - Save the liquid in which the hog's head has been cooked. Bring it to boil. Slowly, add enough meal to make a mushy thickness, stirring all the while you are pouring the meal. Let cook for a few minutes. Be careful to not let it lump. Allow to cool. Eat as is or slice and fry.

— Souse meat - Sauce meat. Remove the bones from a cooked hog's head and feet. Cook the ears, liver, kidneys, and melt. Mix with the head and feet and chop real fine. Add a large cup of vinegar, sage, salt, and red and black pepper. Put into a churn or large crock. Press all the excess liquid fat out by placing large stones wrapped in cloths on top and let remain overnight. Can be eaten as is, or sliced and fried.

— Pepper sauce - Pepper and dry sage were sprinkled into hot grease, salted, and used as a gravy over meat, beans, and vegetables. Also, small red peppers covered with vinegar were kept in a bottle and used as a sauce to pour over meat, vegetables, meats, and greens.

— Slaw or salad dressing - Add a few tablespoons of sour cream to a small cup of vinegar. Add sugar, salt, and black pepper to taste. Use over slaw or salad.

— Deviled eggs - Boil, peel, and cut in halves as many as you want to use. Remove the "yeller" (yolk). Mash and mix with a small amount of vinegar, butter, sugar and salt. Fill the white halves with this mixture, serve cold.

— Pickled eggs - Boil and peel the desired number of eggs. Remove the pickled beets from the water and vinegar in which they were pickled. Add a little more vinegar, put eggs in this liquid. Let remain overnight. They will stay fresh for days. A traditional dish for Easter.

— Some people would make blood puddin'. I am glad to say I never ate any. They would catch the blood from a hog when it was killed, and use as a flavoring to make pudding. Just follow any recipe for pudding.

— White cake or plain cake - Use three large cups flour, one cup sugar, three egg yolks, one heaping teaspoon baking powder, one cup melted butter. Mix, stir. Enough to make three layers. Bake in round cake pan or iron skillet. Bake until slightly brown or until a broom straw stuck into the cake comes out clean. When cool, stack on plate and cover with "frasting." Decorate with cinnamon berries (hot shot candy). Frosting is made by adding sugar to the egg whites and beating them until they are stiff enough to "stand up in a mound." The "eye" of the egg must be removed before using them for the frosting. (The eye is the fertilization of the egg, not found in commercial eggs, as hens are kept from the roosters.)

—Sweet milk pie - When we had "left over" biscuits, we used them in a sweet milk pie, also called a "poor man's pie." A sauce was made from sweet milk and sugar, thickened with flour and boiled. It was then spread over the split biscuits, alternating the sauce and biscuits. We also used fruit and berries in place of the sauce. Sometimes we flavored the sauce with vinegar and sugar and spice.

—Sweet milk dip - Sugar and cream, maybe a little spice added (or cinnamon) made a good dip to use poured over gingerbread, sweet bread, or cake that was about to get too old and dry.

—Sweet bread was made just like gingerbread except you did not use any spice or cinnamon, but a little more sugar, no molasses, and some more butter.

—Dried punkins (pumpkins), cushaw, or squash - To dry them, cut into one inch rings, peel and remove seeds, string on a green stick hung close to the fire. As they become dry, remove and string on a cloth string and hang from the rafter or in the barn loft. Cook the same as shucky beans, only it doesn't take so long. Some like to add sugar or molasses, and not the meat.

—Cushaw - A long-necked squash, very large, sometimes weighing as much as fifteen pounds or more. We dried the soft shell or cooked them stewed down, also by adding sugar and spices. We made cushaw butter just like apple butter. The hard shell ones we cut into chunks (sometimes using an axe to cut them, they were so hard), "smeared" the tops with brown sugar, lard, or butter, and baked in the oven. They tasted like sweet potatoes. We also stewed the pumpkins for pies and made "pun-kin butter."

—Homemade sausage - All the scraps ("scrapy") pieces of meat left over when "cutting up a hog" were ground by using a hand-turned sausage mill. Salt and sage were added (we grew our own sage in the garden). There was no certain amount of salt or sage, as each family had their own way of making sausage. Some was dried for future use by stuffing it into sections of the pre-emptied and cleaned "guts" (intestines) of the hog. Another way, and the one used by our family, was to put it inside corn shucks. To prepare the shucks, remove the ear of corn, letting the shuck still stay attached to the shank (the part that holds it to the stalk). Stuff the sausage inside. Tie the end of the shuck together at the end by using a piece of the shuck and hang from the ceiling of the barn or "smoke house," making sure the air can circulate around all sides. It would keep this way for weeks, and be delicious. To prepare, just shape into patties and fry like meat. Served with flour gravy, hot biscuits, or fried apples.

—Sulfured or smoked apples - To smoke, peel the apples, slice them, and put them into a barrel, one layer at a time. A small amount of sulfur was burned on top of each "batch," and a hole was made in the bottom of the barrel to let out the juice. A quilt over the top of the barrel was used to keep in the smoke. They would keep all winter. The sulfur was burned by putting a little in a bowl and a hot piece of iron placed in it (usually an old file was used for the piece of iron). To prepare smoked apples, they must be soaked for a few hours in cold water and then washed to remove the sulfur taste. Then, use as any other apple. I like them served with blackberry jelly. They were supposed to be good for your health.

—Dryland fish - Edible mushrooms. The morel variety, found wild in the woods in early spring, under old trees in the rotting leaves. To prepare, wash in cold water, split open, roll in meal and flour, add salt and fry like chicken. Serve as a meat dish.

—To cook wild greens, clean and wash, cook in a large pot of water. Add a piece of salt bacon, salt, and cook until tender, letting almost all the water boil away. Or, don't add the meat and take from the water when tender and fry in grease. Some wild greens are poison if a lot of grease is not used, but we used pork grease for almost everything.

—Poke salet (greens) must be preboiled as it can be poison. Cook in a large pot of water for awhile. Take out, wash, and cook again until tender, in a different water. Add a lot of grease. The lard will "kill" the poison. The young stalks of the poke salad can be fried; peel, slice, roll in meal and flour, and deep fry.

—Homemade lye soap - To every four pounds of lard (or the equivalent of meat scraps, cracklin's, bones, and hog's guts) add one can of lye (long ago it came in balls) and four to five gallons of water. Boil in an iron kettle or enamel kettle only. It is best to have it outside. (We placed the kettle on a furnace made of rocks stacked in two piles with an opening between for the fire.) Stir with a long-handled paddle or "soap stick." Add a little water, if needed, to keep from boiling over. Some folks said to make soap at the old moon, while others said the new moon to keep it from boiling over. To test, when finished, drop some into cold water. If it congeals and breaks apart when cut, it is "done." Another way to test it is to let some drip from the paddle. If two or more drops cling together, it is ready to be taken off the fire. Remove from the fire and add two more gallons of water. Stir well and allow to cool. Let set overnight, remove any excess grease that has formed on top. This can be saved and used in the next "batch" of soap. Cut into squares and place in a cool, dark place, making sure each piece does not touch the others, so it can dry quickly. It will be ready for use as soon as made, but is better if allowed to dry. Homemade soap was not only used for cleaning purposes, but to take off dandruff, freckles; kill chiggers; kill worms around fruit trees; kill worms in hogs; and mixed with sugar, to make a salve for boils, stone bruises, and burns.

—Cold water soap - Put one can of lye (or one ball) into a little over a quart of cold water in an iron or enamel pot only. When the lye melts the water will become warm. Stir until all the lye is melted, using a long-handled wooden paddle. Allow to cool, add about six pounds of melted lard. Pour slowly and stir while pouring. Continue to stir for about fifteen or twenty minutes, or until it gets very hard to stir. As it begins to thicken, pour into molds or cut into squares. You must cut it before it gets real cold and hard. Allow to dry for a few days in a cool, dark place. Can be used at once.

—Lye was called potash, and for a long time we made our own. A small hole was made in the side of a barrel near the bottom. The barrel was filled with ashes from the fireplace. Water was added and caught as it dripped from the hole, into another barrel. It was then used to make soap and hominy.

—We grew a small variety of peaches that we called "cling stones" because they had to be cut from the stone. They were smaller than the size of an egg. We peeled these and canned them whole in sugar. Sometimes we pickled them. Cooked in water and sugar and vinegar and canned, they were real good.

As I said before, this was not intended to be a cookbook, but to tell the way we cooked, and mostly how we talked, how we taught our young folks to cook. You would have to already know how to cook before you could use this. Yet, I hope it will be of some use to you and bring back memories to those that lived and cooked as I did. And, to prove to the others that we were not a "poor starving people." Our meals were plain, but good, nourishing, and free from chemicals. Maybe we knew nothing about vitamins and a balanced diet, but we had a "square meal three times a day" that was raised, prepared, and eaten each and every day. We were willing to share with those that did not have. The world would be a better place to live if there were still folks like our old folks, living by themselves, for themselves, and undisturbed by the "do-gooders."

WHISKEY — LIKKER, MOUNTAIN DEW, MOONSHINE, WHITE LIGHTNIN'

Making whiskey was not thought of by hill people as being immoral. It was just another way of making a living, and as for the government, it had just better leave us alone. A "revenuer" (officer) was hated by both young and old. We no longer have many men that make moonshine whiskey, and those that do don't make the real corn whiskey like our old-timers did. The stuff they make now is more harmful. The real "corn likker" was made from corn, no sugar added. It would not hurt you, nor make you crazy drunk. It was used for medicine as well as just to drink. Even the preachers drank it. I have listed the names of the parts of the "still" and the terms as they said them.

—Still - from the word "distill." It could mean the whole set-up, everything needed to make whiskey, or just the large copper drum used to cook or heat the mash. Sometimes an old oil drum was used; also, two washtubs could be used by welding them together at the tops, with the bottom of one removed for an opening.

—Mash - the ground corn or meal (now used, but not by the old-timers) mixed with sugar. Fifty pounds of sugar were used to each sixty gallon barrel of mash and water.

—Malt corn - The corn was shelled, put in a sack, buried under the ground, and let remain until it sprouted, then ground into meal.

Sometimes a sausage mill was used. If the corn was used without being dried before being ground, it was called "green malt"; if dried, (it was better to let it dry) it was called "dry malt."

— The worm condenser - a long, coiled, copper pipe.

— A flake stand - a small barrel to hold the worm, filled with water. The water coiled the worm, causing the hot steam coming through to condense and become a liquid.

— Slop - the remaining residue left after the whiskey was made. Some was used to put back into the barrels of mash for the next "run" to help it to ferment quicker.

— The cap - the lid or top, which was used to seal the top of the copper drum in which the mash was cooked. It was sealed on with paste made from water and flour.

— Workin' off - the process of the fermenting of the mixture of sugar, water, and mash. This liquid was called beer before it was distilled. The first stage was called "sweet beer." It was nice to drink, had a nice taste, but was not intoxicating.

— Furnace - a place built of rocks and mud, for the fire to cook the mash in the copper drum. Sometimes the drum was put about half-way deep into the hole in the ground and the fire built around it. A "groundhog" furnace was best; a tunnel was dug with an opening at each end. The drum sat over one opening, the fire was built at the other. It was very important that the fire was kept at a low degree, just hot enough to keep the mixture cooking, yet it must not be allowed to burn.

— Backin's - the first liquid to be produced was alcohol with a very high percentage. The next was not quite so high, the last was very low and was called "backin's" because it was sometimes put back into the "first run" to "temper" it (make it weaker).

— Doublin's - run through the still twice

— Singletin's - run through only once

— A run off - the whole process of cooking the mash and collecting the finished product, the whiskey.

—Setting up a still - Building the still completely; the barrels to hold the mash for it to ferment, the furnace, the drum to boil it in and the worm.

—A thumping keg - as the hot steam went through the "worm" and condensed into a liquid, it made a thumping sound; this was called the "thumping keg."

—Getting turned in - being reported to the law enforcement officials. Very few people would "turn in a neighbor" for making whiskey. It would almost always be for spite to someone they hated for some other reason.

—Getting cut up - the law enforcement officials always destroyed a still, when they found one, by cutting up the barrels, worm, and drum, and pouring out the mash.

—Sour mash - the mixture of malt corn and sugar and water after it was "worked off" and became sour and ready to be cooked.

—Tempering whiskey - adding water to the strongest alcohol to make it weak enough to be used as whiskey. To test the amount of alcohol, a little was put in a small, clean bottle, shaken, and watched for "beads" (bubbles) to form on top. When the bubbles were evenly formed, half under the water line and half out, and would break on this line, it was one hundred proof. If the beads went away too fast, the alcohol content was too high. If they stayed too long, it was too low. The right amount was reached by adding more or less water or "backin's" to the stronger liquid.

—Home brew - a kind of intoxicating drink made by using red malt.

—Whoe shot - slang for an alcoholic drink for home use in small quantities

—Bootlegger - selling whiskey without a government permit

—A rat house - a small house with a little window that had a small wooden shutter with a hole through it, through which the transaction of selling whiskey was done without the buyer seeing

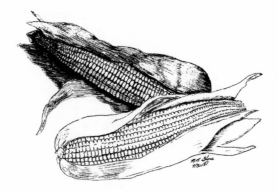

or hearing anyone. Sometimes a hollow tree was used for the same purpose. You left your money in the tree, went around the bend in the road, waited for a little while, came back, and looked in the hole in the tree. Your money was gone and your whiskey was there. What kept them from just keeping your money? Mountain honesty.

— Running off a batch or making a run off - the process of making whiskey.

— Whiskey was used for medicine for toothache (drink or hold it on the tooth to kill the pain), headache, stomach ache, rheumatism, snake bite (to drink or pour on wound), as a disinfectant for cuts and bruises, for broken bones, and to bring stains from clothes (it took the clothes from a man's back).

— Whiskey was also added to the herbal teas to help preserve them and to make them more enticing to drink.

— Whiskey was added to vinegar and camphor. A cloth wet in the mixture was placed on the face and hands of the dead, to keep them from turning black before burial.

— A non-intoxicating drink was made from blackberries. Cook the berries, add sugar (about one pint of sugar to the gallon of berries), set them in a dark, cool place and let them "work off" (ferment), then strain off the liquid and drink. About one gallon of berries to two gallons of water.

—A stew or hot toddie - a mixture of whiskey, water, sugar and ginger, heated and drank hot to help cure a cold or cough, and to make measles, chicken pox, or hives "break out." Drink just before going to bed to sleep; it will cause you to sweat, thus getting rid of the fever. Also used for rheumatism.

—Alkeyhol - alcohol

—Sometimes, if the fire got too hot under the still, it caused the mash to get mixed with the whiskey, ruining it. Then it was said that the still had "puked."

RELIGION

Of all the changes that progress has brought to Appalachia, our church has suffered the least. It's almost the same as it was two hundred years ago when our folks came here. Except for better houses with modern plumbing, there is little or no change. There are several denominations, but Baptist is predominant, and they are subdivided into United, Freewill, Missionary, and ours, Old Regular Baptist. In Knott County at least ninety percent of the people are of the Baptist belief. Not all are affiliated with any church, but they will tell you that that's the church they "believe in." Like people everywhere, we are very defensive and protective of our way of worship. We will welcome outsiders into our home, and invite them to visit our church, but in no way can they bring changes to our religion. The government tried that and failed. It's one part of our culture that has not been exploited by writers or television. As we say, it's a very "tetchie" subject. I have no intention of offending anyone by listing some of the words and phrases used by our church members, past and present. I am one of them. I love, honor, understand, and respect them all. I only want to help preserve something that's beautiful for the future generation to remember and enjoy, and to share with others our way of life.

About every four or five miles up and down each and every hollow you will find one of our church buildings. Long ago, when most of them were built, folks had no way to travel except by

foot or on horseback, so the churches were built close. Each
little church had its own name. Many are worth listing. Some
are biblical, some not; some are named for someone (like the
"Little Sarah," named for my mother); some are only of the place
where they are located. All are beautiful and interesting. I have
only listed a few.

Mount Olive	Samaria
Hollybush	New Home
Ivy Point	Little Zion
Pilgrim's Home	Defeated Creek
Little Dove	Rose of Sharon
Reynolds Fork	Mothers Home
Cedar Grove	Old Beaver
Happy Home	Providence

There are many more too numerous to mention. Each has a
moderator, assistant moderator, clerk, treasurer, several deacons,
and a number of preachers. There is no limit to how many preachers
there can be; anyone that feels he has been called by God, and has
met the standards of the church, can preach. All work without pay.

— A meetin' - the church service, made up of singing, praying,
and preaching. Each church meets once a month, two days — on a
Saturday and the following Sunday. Neighboring churches have
different weekends to meet. Like, one has the first Saturday and
Sunday of the month, another the second, etc. Then, some have an
extra gatherin' on the odd weekend that comes in some months.

— To "jine" (join) the church - to become a member by telling
the church you think God has forgiven you your sins, and you
want to be baptized.

— Given' your hand - asking for membership.

— To be borned agin' - to be forgiven of your sins by Jesus
Christ and given a new life through Him. A free gift from God.

— Bible read - used to describe one that has read and studied
the Bible. We do not believe that a person has to study to be-

come a preacher; his sermons are given to him from God. And sermons do not have to be prepared before being delivered. But, we believe that everyone should read and study the Bible, to show themselves worthy.

— Laid to my account - the sins that we have been charged with and found guilty of.

— It must have so ordered - the belief that something happened because it was pre-planned by a Higher Power to happen just when and where it did, and that man had no power over the process or results.

— The Good Man - Our people thought of God as being too sacred to mention His name, calling Him, "The Good Man." The Bible was called the "Good Book." Satan was the "Bad Man."

— To "church" someone - have him or her dismissed from church, to no longer belong as a member, because they had done something unbecoming to the rules of the church.

a. to be "thrown out of church" means the same as "church" them.
b. to "take their name off the Book" could mean the same, yet it could mean they requested to have their name just removed for a little while and could come back whenever they wanted to.
c. to be "set aside" - not dismissed from membership, just to have their name put away for awhile, until something is settled about their guilt or non-guilt about something.

— Called to preach - by a revelation from God, made known by Him that He requires one that receives the revelation to become a preacher.

— Trying to do right - realizing that you are a lost sinner and want to do something about it by beginning to change your sinful ways. Trying to do right by serving the Lord, and no longer the devil. Yet we know that we cannot save ourselves, no matter what we do. It's only through the saving grace of our Lord Jesus and His mercy that we are saved.

—Give out the next meeting - announce the place and time of the next service. Many are "given out" at the close of each "gatherin'" for a different time and place. Lots of times folks have "church in their home," another carry-over from when we had few or no church-houses. Everyone is "cordially" invited to come. If in the home, all are served something to eat after the service.

—Winding up the meeting - also said "for meeting to break," meaning to come to a close.

—Having a travel - the journey from nature to Grace. The time between when you realize you are a lost sinner and when God forgives you of your sins and you become a Christian. Some believe it takes days, weeks, even years. Some believe it is instant.

—Giving out a song - In some places it's called "lining a song." Long ago few people could read, few had song books, no one could read music. So, one person would read the song, two lines at a time. The congregation would sing those two lines and the one "giving out the song" would then read two more lines (in today's modern terminology of harmony, everyone sang lead) and so on until the song was finished. Some people can give out a song in such a way with such a beautiful rhythmical chant that it is more wonderful than the song itself. Many of the songs were composed by our church members.

Although our Christians would be angry if someone outside said anything they took to be disrespectful about their church, they often joke among themselves. Here is a joke about a man giving out a song:

An old man stood on the platform in front of the church, opened his songbook and said, "I am getting old, I can not see. I did not bring my specks with me." As what he had said rhymed, the people thought it part of his song, so they sang it.

I said, "I'm getting old, my eyes are dim, and I can scarcely

see to read this hymn." They sang that. Again, the old man tried to explain. "I did not give that out to sing. I only said my eyes are dim." They again sang that.

"I did not give that out at all. I believe the devil is in you all," he shouted. And they sang again.

"I see you won't let me alone. You can sing yourself. I am going home." And they did, and he did.

— To sing someone down - If one of the preachers got "carried away" (became so involved in what he was preaching that he forgot the time) someone would start a song, reminding him to finish.

— To take a part - One preacher "opens" (stands up and begins the service); one holds prayer; then, two or more (as many as wants to if they have time) preach. After this, one calls dismissal. What each does is called "taking a part."

— Open the church door - not just open the church house door, but to ask "If there is anyone that feels that God has passed by and pardoned their sins and they want to join the church, do so." They usually say this just as they are "winding up church," as they sing the last song.

— Getting your letter - If someone, for some reason, wants to change their membership from one church to another (of the same faith and order) they are given a letter to take to the other church. It must be given to the second church before ninety days.

— To answer in full love and fellowship - to ask the church at the beginning of the Saturday meeting (when all the business of the church is done) if there is any disturbance or disorder among the church members. If they can answer in full love and fellowship, they do it by remaining silent.

— Agin' bobbed hair - A woman must wear her hair long. In the past, if a woman had short hair she was not allowed to join the church. Now she must promise to not cut it any more. Men must keep their hair cut short.

— Agin' music and dancing - No music is allowed in church. No member is allowed to play any musical instrument at any time. At first when they "come out" radios and televisions were not accepted in their homes, but now they are. In the past many of our young people would build a small house close by where they would keep their radio, television, and music. At one time wearing a tie was counted a sin, as there was no useful need for a tie, it was worn "fer looks" (pride).

— Double marriage - A person having been divorced or married to someone that had been married before, as long as their former partners were living, are said to be "double married." Some churches will not accept them. Others will accept them, but will not let them preach. Churches that do let them cannot preach with those that do not. Perplexing? I don't understand it either.

— The innocent party - The partner in a divorce that is innocent of having asked, or given cause, for the divorce. The innocent party is allowed to join the church. Some places he is allowed to preach. Some say if God has forgiven you, then you are all innocent.

— To silent someone - to not allow them to preach. Many were silenced if they were "double married."

— Dinner on the ground - Many of the churches serve a free

dinner just after the religious service. This began long ago when people came for miles on horseback, on foot, or in wagons. They needed to eat before returning home. Now, with fast cars and restaurants, they no longer need to eat at church. It's just carried on for fun and enjoyment. Many times in the past the meeting was on the graveyard (held in a covered platform with open sides). Seats were made of logs or planks. The food was brought from home and was eaten and shared while they sat on the ground. Now, it's served inside the church house. Some have kitchens in the basements, some have makeshift tables, plywood lain on the backs of benches.

A little girl that had grown up in the north was visiting her aunt for the first time, and was looking forward to having dinner on the ground. She was very disappointed. She said, "I thought I was going to get to see all those old people eat their dinner off the ground, like the chickens do."

—Mo'ral - memorial. In remembrance of all the dead on the graveyard. When our folks first settled here in the hills of Appalachia, they had very little connection with a church, except through the circuit rider preacher, who traveled in a circuit, visiting only once a year. When their loved ones died they were buried without any religious service, except singing by the neighbors and friends. Maybe someone would read something from the Bible, if they had one. The preacher, on his next visit to the community, would conduct the belated funeral, for all the folks in each graveyard, at different dates for neighboring graveyards. For a long time after we began to have plenty of preachers, we still called this yearly service a "funeral meeting." Sometime in the twenties the name was changed to a "Memorial meeting." But none of the customs or traditions have changed. There are two days of preaching, singing, and praying on the graveyard. A stand and seats are built, the graveyard cleaned of all briars and weeds. The graves are decorated with flowers (now store bought; in the past they were grown at home or made from crepe paper).

White embroidered sheets are placed over the graves. Dinner on the ground is cooked and served by the families of the dear departed ones gone on.

— Preparing for burial - Before the body became stiff it was placed on the bed (after the feather bed had been removed) or planks lying across two chairs in a horizontal position, face upwards. Arms were crossed on the chest, feet tied together, and coins laid on the eye lids. The mouth was tied shut by tying a cloth coming under the chin, up over the top of the head. A cloth wet in camphor and whiskey was placed over the hands and face to keep them from turning black.

— Having a clur (clear) mind - being well satisfied, untroubled, with no doubts. The church service was always closed with these words, "If all minds feel clear and satisfied, we will look to the Lord for a blessing and be dismissed in order."

— Belongin' to the church - being a member of the church.

— Back sliding - being a member of the church and then going back into sin. Old Regular's believed a Christian could not backslide. Some believe they can. Some say if you backslide you are lost, and can never get forgiven.

— Being deceived - to honestly think you are a Christian, when you have not been born again. Some have been deceived and some have been deceivers, pretending to be Christians when they know they are not.

— A hippercrit (hypocrite) - a person pretending to be a Christian when he is not.

— Being right or gettin' right - becoming a born-again Christian.

— Brought up in the right belief - being taught the right rules, customs, and beliefs of a certain church.

— To cotee (quote) - to repeat a phrase from the Bible, giving chapter and verse, from memory. Many of our old folks could "cotee" large portions of the Bible correctly.

— Being showed something - having a revelation from God. Lots of people were shown things, both past and present, and things going to come to pass in the future. Many knew when they were going to die.

—Faith doctoring - Of all the many things misrepresented and misunderstood about Appalachia, this is first. It's thought by many outsiders to be something compared with witch doctoring, and a hocus-pocus chant. It's the true faith that Christians have in the promise made by Jesus, in the words of the Bible, and their belief in Him, that He does hear and answer prayer. All credit is given to Him for the healing, not to the faith doctor (healer). Some people are believed to have the "gift of healing" given to them by God, but they do not want any credit given to them for what they do. It's all done in faith. The person receiving the healing must also have faith. I guess some doctors would say it was a case of your mind over body.

—The laying on of hands - The deacons and ordained ministers lay (place) their hands on a sick person and pray for them to get well, always saying, "Your will be done Lord, and not ours."

—Sick-un-to-death - terminally ill.

—Having a gift, a talent - Christians believed that God gave everyone of us some gift—to sing, to preach, to pray, understanding, healing, and many others. All should be used to, and for, the Glory of God.

—A song ballet - song ballad. The written form of a song, usually handwritten. From the word ballad. Our folks learned to sing by ear and from memory. They did not sing "love songs." That was what they called all the old ballads that were sung by the folks that were not church members.

—Burin' ground - cemetery, or graveyard. Each family had their own "plot." They "reverined" their dead to almost a worship.

—A burin' - funeral.

—A dry-land Baptist - nickname for someone that has all the appearances and actions of a Christian, believing in the Baptist church, yet has never been baptized.

—The here atter (after) - life after death.

—To be baptized - done in running water (flowing water of a river or creek), standing with the back toward the way the water is flowing, immersion back foremost until completely under. Done by two church members (one must be an ordained minister) with these words, "I baptize you my sister or brother (name) in the name of the Father, the Son, and the Holy Ghost."

—Leaving good hopes (or, "talking pretty" before one dies) - a person saying, just before he dies, that he is going to heaven after death.

—The Lord's supper (also called "sacrament" or "communion") - Held once each year. Each eats one bite of unleaven bread (baked without anything added to the flour), one sip of wine, and wash each other's feet. In remembrance of Jesus and His last supper.

—Sound doctoring (doctrine) - the preaching and teaching of the religious beliefs of a church, based on their interpretations of the Bible. Unsound doctrine is anything preached or taught that they did not approve of.

—Women are not allowed to take any part in preaching or teaching in the Old Regular Baptist Church. They can help sing, but not give out a song. They cannot lead prayer. They must remain silent.

—All the church members sit on a raised platform in the back of the church, men on one side, women on the other. This is not a rule, just the custom. All the visitors sit in the front facing the platform, or stand, as it is called. Again, the men on one side, women on the other.

—Old Regulars do not ask for a collection, but do ask for anyone that wants to to give a donation of money for the upkeep of the church house, and for someone in need. The preachers do not receive any salary.

—Giving your experience - telling the church when and how you were saved, and that you believe you have been saved.

—Going behind your experience - to bring up something in

the church that draws attention to some wrong-doing you did while you were yet a sinner, before you were born again.

— At one time the Old Regulars believed that they were the one and only church that would enter heaven. They still will not have anything to do with any other churches, not even other Baptists.

There is a story told of a man who died and went to Heaven. Saint Peter was showing the new arrival over Heaven. "Here is where the Catholic lives, in the cathedral. The Jews are in this synagogue," and so on. The newcomer said, "But who lives away over there across the creek all by themselves in those little log cabins?" "Hush," said Saint Peter. "That's the Old Regular Baptists. They think they are the only ones up here. If they found out different, they would leave."

— Knowing doctrine - the belief that a Christian did or did not know if they were going to Heaven when they died, a question that causes a lot of controversy among Christians.

— Old Regulars do not have Sunday school nor Bible study. Children are allowed and encouraged to attend church, but are not allowed to join.

— Some other words and rules of the Old Regular Baptist:

1. The Old Regular Baptists always kneel when praying in public. Only the men hold or lead prayer.
2. They are always baptized in flowing water, the creek or the river. Many times it will be in the winter. I have seen them cut the ice for a baptizing.
3. If one of their members has done something against the rules of the church, then two other members of the same sex will visit them in private and discuss the matter with them before it is brought up in church. If the accused one denies the charge, then they must have "gospel proof" (two other members have to have seen or heard enough to prove

evidence). If they cannot give gospel proof, the accused one is declared innocent. This is called "dealing with someone."

4. Using tobacco is not looked upon as a sin by the Old Regular Baptists. In fact, most of the members either smoke or chew tobacco, even in the church house. Now some churches have put up "No Smoking" signs, not because they think it's a sin to use tobacco, but just for the satisfaction of the non-smokers.

5. In the far past, our church members also used whiskey. It was not counted a sin to drink, even the preachers did, just so they did not drink enough to make them drunk. Now if anyone drank whiskey, he or she would be "thrown out of the church."

6. They believed that God spoke to them through dreams. They "took stock in dreams" (meaning that they believed that what they dreamed was a revelation sent from God).

SCHOOL

Our one-room schools are another source of misunderstanding that have been distorted and misrepresented by writers and journalists. Until the mid-sixties we had small schools. True, they only taught the eight grades, but the closeness, friendship, and sharing between the teachers and students was a great loss when these schools were discontinued. The school was so much in harmony with the family life, there was no shock to the young child beginning school. The few times that a teacher was whipped or run off have been exaggerated and blown all out of proportion. Most always the teacher was a relative of most of his students, and "kin." They really loved each other, and he was a neighbor and friend to all the rest. There were only five months and a half of school each year, and the salary for teachers in 1905 was $57.42 a month. In the early sixties, for nine months the teacher got almost two hundred a month.

Words and their meanings as we used them:

—Grammer school - grade school

—Gittin' a larnin' (or, book larnin') - education

—A good scribe - good penmanship. Each summer there would be a few weeks of school just to teach anyone that wanted to, to learn to write. It was called "writing school."

—Figgerin' - doing arithmetic

—Scribblin' - writing

117

— Well read - well-educated

— Learning by heart - memorizing something

— Saying a piece - repeating a poem. It was required as a part of our education to memorize a lot of the well-known poems and repeat them on Friday afternoon.

— Take up books - begin classes

— Let out school - dismiss school

— First recess - a fifteen minute break in the morning, when the students were allowed to use the outhouse or get a drink of water.

— Long recess - A one hour break at noon. Some children brought their dinner (the word "lunch" was not used). Some went home, if they lived close enough.

— Laying the book in the door - When someone wanted to visit the little outhouse, he would hold up his hand and on receiving a nod from the teacher, he would take his book and place it in the door. The book would remain there, telling everyone that someone was out. On his return, he would get his book and someone else was then free to go out. If some student remained out too long, the teacher might send someone after him, or go to the door and yell at him to return.

— Ciphern - writing and counting numbers

— Box supper (sometimes called a "pie supper") - held when they needed to raise money for something extra for the school or Christmas presents for the students. Each woman or young girl that wanted to took part. She prepared a box of food, two of each thing, and took it to the school on a previously selected night. The teacher auctioned off these boxes to the men-folks. The man that bought the box got to eat with the woman that had brought it. It was supposed to have been a secret what box belonged to who, yet each woman managed to let the one she wanted to buy it know which one was hers. There would be a lot more entertainment the same night.

— A spelling bee (also called a "spelling match") - Almost every

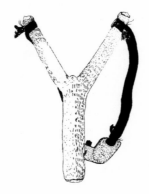

Friday afternoon all the students were lined up and given words to spell, one each. When a word was misspelled, that person sat down and was out of the match. The one left standing longest was the winner. Sometimes they would choose sides, one against the other, or the girls against the boys.

—Keepin' school - teaching school

—Staying in after school - kept after school for punishment. This was not done very often, because the teacher needed to get home to do the work he needed to do, raising his food, and the students were needed at home by their parents. So, the punishments were most often a whipping with a hickory limb.

—Times'ies - multiplication table

—Take a wayes - subtraction

—Countin' - addition

—Measuring a sled - All teachers were expected to "figger out" how many bushels a sled would hold. As people used no standard measurement when they built their sleds, this was a new problem each and every time. This was very difficult; a teacher would have lost respect and maybe his job if he had not done this favor for his neighbors.

—Singin' school - Sometimes, in some places, when "real school" was not going on, a teacher would meet each evening at

119

the schoolhouse to teach folks how to sing. Not to read music, just songs, and how to sing them, mostly just from ear.

—Writing school - Sometimes the teacher would meet with people of the community, in the schoolhouse when it was not being used to conduct regular classes, to teach penmanship.

—Moonlight school - Sometime just after the turn of the century the government promoted a system where a teacher came to the homes and taught the old and the handicapped people to read and write. It did not last long.

—A good scribe - one that can write well

—Scribblin' - writing

—Ink was made from pokeberry juice, pens were made from goose feathers. (The long ones from the wings.)

In these old-fashioned schools, each morning they gave the flag salute before coming in. There was always a flag hanging from a tall pole, by the side of the door. One of the student's job was to see that it was put up each morning and taken down every evening and if and when it rained. When they came they always sang, "America," or some other patriotic song. Then, the teacher read one or more verses from the Bible and they all repeated the Lord's Prayer before beginning classes. We did not begin having so much trouble in the school until we took the Bible out. Where Christ is not taught, the devil will be. Also, when they had to consolidate the small schools the children lost so much. Now more time and effort is placed on how good you can play ball than on how good you can read. We are growing bigger but dumber folks.

CHILDREN'S RHYMES

Some are funny, some teach a lesson, some are sung when doing a job of work; all are part of our mountain heritage, taught to one generation by the older one, passed on and on by word of mouth. Some may have been brought to the mountains from Europe. Some may have been learned from the Indians.

(To count toes)
Here's Will Willson.
Here's Tom Dunkins
Here's Long Rach
And here's Betty Bobkins.
And here's poor little shoe whackey, shoe whackey, shoe.

This little pig says, "I want some wheat."
This little pig says, "Where are you going to get it at?"
This little pig says, "Out of Mossie's barn."
This little pig says, "I will run and tell."
This little pig says, "Whee, whee, whee, I can't get over the
    door sill with this big bag of wheat."

Shoe the old horse, he has to go to mill.
Shoe the little colt, its feet are tender.
Shoe the old horse, he carries the load.

How We Talked

Shoe the little colt, he walks the fastest.
Shoe them both, shoe them both, shoe them both.
(Said as you pat the bottom of baby's feet, first one, then
    the other.)

"Let's go to bed," said sleepy head.
"Let's wait awhile," said slow.
"Hang on the pot" said greedy gut.
"Let's eat before we go."

Uncle Bish, jumped the jist (joist).
Tore his shirt once or twice.

Hickory stirrups and a white oak saddle.
A boy and a girl a riding a straddle.

A whistlin' woman and a crowing hen always come to some
    bad end.

New moon, true moon, let me see my love soon.
If I marry before I die
Let me hear a bird sing.
If I die before I marry
Let me hear my coffin ring.

Monday's child is fair of face.
Tuesday's child is full of grace.
Wednesday's child has far to go.
Thursday's child is full of woe.
Friday's child is lovin' and givin'.
Saturday's child works hard for a livin'.
But the child that is born on the Sabbath day
Is fair and wise and good and gay.

Marry in white, prove to be right.
Marry in blue, always be true.
Marry in brown, live in town.
Marry in black, wish yourself back.
Marry in green, ashamed to be seen.
Marry in yellow, ashamed of your fellow.
Marry in gray, you will rue the day.
Marry in red, you will wish yourself dead.
Marry in pink, you won't know what you think.
Marry in rose, money goes.
Marry in purple, rhyme it yourself.

William my trimney toe, he is a good man.
Catches hens, puts them in pens.
Some lay eggs, some none.
Wire briar, limber lock, five geese in a flock.
Some flew east, some flew west, some flew over the
     cuckoo's nest.
Enty menty, carry corn, apple seed and briar thorn.
You may sneak out with the old rotten dish clout.

Big head, little wit; little head, 'nary bit.

From the saddle to the ground, mercy sought and mercy
     found.

Needles, pins, triplet, twins.
What goes up the chimney? Smoke.
Hope this wish will not be broke.
Fingers, toes, this is the way our wishes goes.
Tip, touch, blue come true, tip glass, come to pass.

Sneeze on Monday, sneeze for health.
Sneeze on Tuesday, sneeze for wealth.

How We Talked

Sneeze on Wednesday, sneeze for a letter.
Sneeze on Thursday, something better.
Sneeze on Friday, sneeze for sorrow.
Sneeze on Saturday, see your sweetheart tomorrow.
And if you sneeze on the Sabbath day,
The news of a death is on the way.

Morning red and evening gray, set the traveler on his way.
Morning gray and evening red, pour the rain down on his
    head.

Churn butter churn, churn butter churn.
Come butter come, come butter come.
Peter is waiting at the gate, waiting for his butter cake.
(Sung while churning)

See saw, pull and draw. Margie will have a new master.
She won't get but a penny a day, if she don't see saw faster.
(Sung while sawing wood)

Snake baked a hoe cake, put a frog to mind it. Frog went to
    sleep and a lizzard came and stold it. Bring back my hoe
    cake, you long-tail Nanny-Oh.

Chickey, my chickey, my commie coe.
I went to the well to wash my toe.
When I got back my chimney was gone.
Cluck, old witch, what time is it?

Place my shoes in the form of a T, and dream of the boy
    whose bride I will be.
The color of his eyes, the color of his hair, the color of his
    suit and his everyday wear.

How We Talked

Backer Joe cut off his toe, and hung it up to dry.
Said, "Ezzie Belle, will I get well, or will I have to die?"
Backer Joe cut off his toe and hung it up to dry.
Said, "Ezzie Belle, will I get well, or will I die and go
   to — —?"

Me and my gal went a huckleberry huntin'.
She fell down and I saw sumpen'.

My gal Sal went up the hill.
I went along behind her.
She stooped over to tie her shoe
And I saw her coffee grinder.

Howdy do, how are you? Got any backer? Give me a chew.
I hain't got none but a few old crumbs.
Get away from here you lazy old bum.

The one before pegs the door.
The one in the middle plays the fiddle.
The one behind drinks the wine.
(Said when you sleep three in a bed, which often happened
   when folks stayed overnight.)

How We Talked

If I had some milk I would make some mush if I had some
meal.

Bessie bug, Bessie bug, fly away home.
Your house is on fire and your children will burn.
All but one and her name's Ann, she crawled under the
puddin' pan.

Lost one calf, one hind foot white, other same alike. Anyone
find calf, pay everybody five dollars.

I want to be buried in a hickory coffin.
So I can go through hell just a cracklin' and a poppin'.

Granddaddy nettie nottie, all legs and no body.
Which way did my cow go?

Bob Bob White, is your apples ripe? No, not quite. Will
your dog bite? Yes, after night.

Good night, sleep tight.
Don't let the bed bugs bite.
Wake up bright in the morning bright.
To do your best with all your might.

The animals had a fair, the birds and beasts were there.
The old baboon, by the light of the moon, was combing the
elephant's hair.
The monkey, he got drunk, and fell against the elephant's
trunk.
The elephant sneezed, and fell to his knees, and what
became of the poor little monkey, too mankey, too munk.

How We Talked

Tobacco is an evil weed.
We'll have no saving of its seed.
It spoils your breath
and burns your clothes.
And makes a chimney of your nose.
Little birds don't smoke nor chew it.
And little boys should never do it.

Cut your nails on Monday, cut for health.
Cut them on Tuesday, cut for wealth.
Cut them on Wednesday, cut for news.
Cut them on Thursday, cut for a new pair of shoes.
Cut them on Friday, cut them for sorrow.
Cut them on Saturday, see your sweetheart tomorrow.
And a man had better never been born
That cuts his nails on Sunday morn.

Apples, apples, my nose itches, yonder comes a man with a
   hole in his britches.

Find a pin and pick it up
And all that day you will have good luck.
Find a pin and let it lay
You will have bad luck all that day.

If anybody will bring me a steer bull heifer calf, the first
day of last week, he shall be well rewarded a pint of pigeon's milk, churned in a cat's horn. Likewise, the crutch
of a laying duck. Also, one peck of Irish potatoes dug out
of his own patch, providing he will pay the digger one
thousand, fast asleep, enough to make a dog laugh to see a
puddin' creep.

How We Talked

Yonder comes a high man, a lean man, a low man, a lumpkin.
Joe said the worm, "He eat a pot of dumplin's.
A cow and a half, an ox and a half.
A four-year-old bull.
And his belly wasn't full."

"Snow, snow," said the widder, as she gave her children the
last piece of bread and put on the last stick of wood. (Said
when it looked as if it were going to snow.)

Cussey, tossey, my bear skin,
It's going to be busted by this wind.
Some places bare, all of them thin.
Usey, tossey, my bear skin.

The north wind doth blow and we will have snow.
And what will poor robin do then, poor thing, poor thing.
He will set in the barn and keep himself warm.
And hide his head under his wing, poor thing, poor thing.

Star light, star bright, the brightest star that I have seen
tonight. I wish I may, I wish I might, have the wish I have
tonight.

Teacher, teacher, don't whip me, whip that boy behind that
tree. He stold the honey, I stold the money, teacher, teacher,
ain't that funny.

Possom in the papaw patch, picking up papaws, putting
them in his pocket to make him a papaw pie.

How much wood would a woodchuck chuck, if a woodchuck would chuck wood?

A man of words and not of deeds, is like a garden full of
    weeds.
And when the weeds begin to grow, it's like a garden full of
    snow.
And when the snow begins to melt, it's like a garden full of hemp.
And when the hemp begins to fly, it's like an eagle in the sky.
And when the sky begins to roar, it's like a lion at the door.
And when the door begins to crack, it's like a hickory at
    your back
And when your back begins to smart, it's like a spindle in
    your heart.
And when your heart begins to bleed, it's like a dead man
    indeed,
Phew! don't a dead man stink.

Heat a hammer with three nails.
Heat a cat with nine tails.
Whip Jack and spare Tom.
Blow the bellows, he is a good old man.
I had a little cuddy horse, his name was "Cuddy Gray."
He could fumble, he could trot, through the towns and over
    rocks.
Mary, Mary, are you home? Yes, Margrette, that I am.
I wish the home the gentle man got.
The old mare fell down and broke the mustard pot.
Pick it up and lose it not.

Jammie Martin kissed a nigger.
Run honey, the Dukes are a'coming.

Glad to see you, little bird. It was your little chirp I heard.
What did you intend to say? "Give something this cold day."
That I will, and plenty too, all these crumbs I saved for you.
Don't be frightened, here's a treat. I will stay and see you eat.

How We Talked

Shocking tales I have heard of you, chirp and tell me if they
    are true.
To steal from neighbors is a shame, leaving you with all the
    blame.
Thomas says you steal his wheat, John complains the plums
    you eat.
Choose the ripest for your share, never asking whose they
    are.
But I will not try to know what you did so long ago.
Here's your breakfast, eat away, and come again some other
    day.

The ground was all covered with snow one day,
And two little sisters were busy at play.
A snow bird was sitting close by on a tree.
So merrily singing his chicky-a-dee-dee.
He hadn't been singing his tune very long
Until little Emma heard him, so loud was his song.
Oh, sister, look out through the window and see
There's a dear little bird, singing "chicky-a-dee-dee."
Oh, mother, do get him some stockin's and shoes.
A nice little hat, and a frock if he choose.
I wish he would come in to the parlor and see
How warm we would keep him, poor chick-a-dee-dee.
The bird had flown down for a few crumbs of bread,
And heard every word that little Emma had said.
"I'm grateful," said he "for the wish you express,
But I have no occasion for such a fine dress.
I would remain with my little limbs free, than to hobble
    around singing chick-a-dee-dee.
For this is the way God meant birdies to be."
And he flew away, singing chick-a-dee-dee.

There was once a dear cricket who did nothing but sing
Through the warm summer months of summer and spring.
Surprised was the cricket when he turned to his home.
His cupboard was bare and winter had come.
Not a crumb could be found, on the snow-covered ground.
Not a flower could he see, not a leaf on a tree.
At last the poor cricket, with hunger made bold,
All dripping with wet, and trembling with cold
To the house of the ant, he went begging for food.
"Dear ant," he begins "will you not be so good.
To help a poor fellow who has not no food.
A coat for my back, and shoes for my feet.
A shelter from the rain, and a mouthful to eat.
I wish only to borrow, I will pay back tomorrow.
Without help I will die from hunger and sorrow."
Said the ant to the cricket, "Don't you know, my dear
     friend,
We ants never borrow, we ants never lend.
Is it true, my dear friend, you lay nothing by
When the weather was warm and the weather was dry?"
Said the cricket, "Not I, my heart was so delight, I sang by
     day and night.
All things looked then so gay, I sang summer away."
"You sang, so you say, now sing winter away."
Then, slamming the door in the poor cricket's face
He went and sat down in his warm, cozy place.
And said, "I am sure I too would be poor
If I idled away the warm summer day.
But I think this rule both right and good:
Who lives without work should live without food."

CHILDREN'S TOYS, SNACKS, AND GAMES

Snacks:

— Scraping the outer bark of the birch and beech tree to get the sap. Some mixed the sap with sugar and let it set overnight.

— The small sprouts of the beech nuts, when they just have the first two leaves.

— Mountain tea - found on the top of hills and along the ridges. We ate the berries and chewed the leaves, which have a wintergreen flavor.

— Sweet anis - Dig and chew the roots of this plant, which has a licorice flavor.

— Eat the flowers and buds of the redbud tree. Some children got sick after eating these. They must have gotten bugs or spiders, because the buds are not poison.

— The roots of the Artie-choke, a tall plant with yellow flowers like daisies and tuber roots like potatoes.

— Smoked and chewed the leaves of the "life ever-lasting" plant (also called "rabbit tobacco").

— Smoked cigarettes made from corn silks, rolled in pieces of poke paper (brown paper bags). We made pipes from corn cobs.

— Drank the liquid or sap water by tapping the "sugar tree" (maple); also boiled it to make syrup.

— Smoked pieces of the smoke vine for pretend cigarettes.

—Papaws - a fruit of the papaw bush.

—Some children ate May apples. They are supposed to be poisonous.

—We had a lot of blackberries, "raseberries" (raspberries), huckleberries, wild strawberries, and "hozzies" (haws).

—Warnets (walnuts), "hazenuts" (hazelnuts), hickory nuts, beechnuts, summer grapes, and possum grapes.

—Cushaw seeds were eaten raw and roasted. We grew a lot of sunflowers, but did not know you could eat the seeds.

—Snow cream - to a large pan or bowl of fresh snow, add enough milk or cream to make a smooth thickness. Sweeten and add a little vanilla or some other flavor.

—Parch corn - the regular white corn used for feed or bread. Brown in a hot skillet, to which has been added a little salt and grease. Stir until it becomes brown and "crunchie" or "bricklie." Eat as popcorn.

—"Crumble in" - Large pieces of cornbread and crust were soaked in milk. This is what most kids took to school for their lunch, in an empty lard bucket, a spoon to eat it with in their pocket.

Toys and Games for Children:

—Whizzor button - A twine was run through the two holes in a large button and tied in a loop. By holding one end of the loop with one hand and the other end with the other, the button in the middle, swing the button, twirling it around and around until the twine gets wrapped around itself and becomes tight. Then, by letting it first loose just a little, then pulling it tight, you will get a whizzing noise. Our older folks used the bones in a hog's foot, making holes by burning them in with a hot wire. They strung them on a string, in groups of two and three, and by pulling the string they could make music.

— When shucking (husking) corn, if just a few ears for seed or bread, or a whole crib full, the work was made more pleasant by a counting game. Finding a white ear did not count anything. A red ear was twenty points, a blue fifty, and a speckled one fifteen. A "sque-ball" (one of many colors) was one hundred points. Score was kept, and the one with the most points when the job was finished won. The first one to find a red ear got to kiss the girl of his choice. Sometimes boys would cheat by bringing a red ear from home. (Not to win the game, but to get to kiss the girl.)

— Hully Gully - a game for very small children, teaching them to count and do small sums. Fifty grains of corn were used. Each player took half. The one to begin the game took a few grains in his hand and said, "hully gully"; second player, "how many?"; first player, "nine or tennie" (meaning not over ten); "you guess." Then, the second player guessed how many grains the first one had in his hand. If he guessed right, the first one must give him all the corn he had in his hand. If he guessed over the amount, then he must give the other the number over. If under, then the one with the corn in his hand must give to the other the number of grains between what had been guessed and the actual number. The one having the most at the end of the game won, or when one won all the corn. Also played with nuts or buttons.

— Five Up (sometimes called seven up, depending on the number used) - played with a pinlet or a piece of charcoal from the fireplace. The small dent on one side of the grains of corn were darkened or "blackened." As many players as wanted to could play. Each player took turns shaking the corn in his hands and tossing them on the ground or table top. All grains with the black side turned up counted points. If all turned up were black, it counted double. If no black ones turned up, the player lost all his points and started back at zero. The first one to reach one hundred won.

— Fox and Geese - A pattern was drawn on a piece of cardboard (see drawing). Twenty-two grains of white corn were geese, two red grains were the foxes. The rules are somewhat like checkers. All the geese are placed on one side of the board on the spaces where the lines cross, the foxes on the other. The players choose wherever they think is best. Each player begins to advance toward the other, one move at a time from one cross to the next, taking turns. The geese can only move forward, the foxes can move either way, sideways, forward, or backward. If the fox finds himself next to a goose with an empty space on the other side, he can jump the goose and catch it and remove

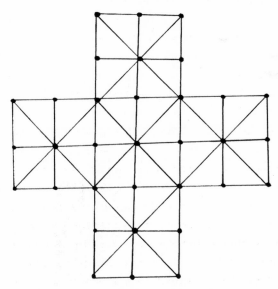

A Fox and Goose Board

it from the board. The object of the game is for the fox to catch all the geese, or for the geese to surround the fox and have him "cornered" until he can no longer make a move.

—A top or "dancer" was made from an empty thread spool. One spool makes two dancers. Whittle all around both sides (leaving the edge already on the spool) sloping toward the middle. Bring to a point and cut in two. Sharpen the end. Whittle a small peg, fit into the hole in the spool (must fit tight). Allow to protrude about one inch on smooth side. Sharpen other end to a sharp point. Place pointed end on any smooth surface. With finger and thumb, twirl the peg. Let loose quickly. The toy will spin for several seconds.

—Marvils (marbles) - a game played by both children and men. The marbles were made by taking a small chunk of a stone which we called "marvel rock" because it was the hardest stone we have (not real marble), as most of our stones are either slate or sandstone. After chipping a small hole in a large rock lying close to the creek, the small chunk was put in this hole. A small stream of the creek was then channeled and forced to flow over the hole containing the small chunk, thus causing it to turn around and around. In a few days it would be worn smooth and round. When it got to the right size, it was removed and another one put in. Sometimes it took weeks to make just one marble, but once made they last forever, handed down from one generation to another. Sometimes, if not carefully watched, the creek would rise after a rain and the marbles would be lost.

Some expressions used in the game of marbles:

a. To "fudge" - to place your hand over the line drawn as a starting place (counted cheating), going beyond span
b. Keepsies - a game where all the marbles were placed in a ring (a line drawn in a circle on the ground). Each player took turns trying to knock them out by hitting them with another marble flipped with the thumb lying against the

closed fist. Each player got to keep all the marbles he knocked outside the sides of the ring.

c. Holly Rolly - a game of marbles where the object was to get the marbles to roll into a hole by shooting it across the ground, by flipping another marble and hitting it. There were three holes in a row about a yard apart, then another hole at a much further distance. This last hole was called the bull hole. The winner must get his marble to hole in all the holes first. When one missed the hole, he lost his turn to the other player.

d. Tall - the marble used to "shoot" with (hit the other marbles)

e. A span - measured by placing the hand thumb down on the line, spreading the fingers, reaching as far as you can without moving the thumb and making a mark on the ground with the end of the forefinger to determine the spot to shoot from. People with long hands had an advantage.

f. Upsies - allowed to place one fist on the ground to rest the other one on when shooting the marbles

g. Anties - placing the marble on a small mound of dirt so as to be more able to hit it

h. Pea jibs - very small marbles, sometimes given away with gum or candy

i. Aggies - glass marbles

j. Saw logs - slang for large marbles

—Toys were made from cornstalks; little animals, cows, pigs, horses, chickens. The dry stalks were used. The inside "pith" (soft spongy part) was cut into short lengths for the bodies, heads, feet, and legs, fastened together by sticking small splints of the outside hard part of the cornstalk (use your own imagination) through the spongy parts. These could also be put together in a way to produce sound, by flopping the ends of the splints, thus a small, pretend organ or piano.

—A pop gun - made to shoot spitballs or paper wads. The barrel was a short length of a limb from the elder bush (which has a nice hollow inside). Remove the pith. Whittle a plunger from a piece of poplar wood, leaving a knob at one end, shaping the rest to fit tightly inside the hollow of the barrel, about three-fourths of an inch short of the end. To load, make a spit ball from paper, push into one end of barrel using plunger; "tamp" it in to fit very tight. Push another spit ball into other end, after blowing air into barrel and holding finger over opening so air cannot escape (to build up pressure). Now, another spitball on top of the first one. Place small end of plunger against last spit ball. Strike the other end with the palm of your hand. The force of the air will cause the first spit ball to come out with a loud popping sound, and force enough to "raise a blister." From then on you have to only use two spit balls each time you reload.

—Sling shot - We would find a forked limb shaped like a "Y," about the thickness of your finger. Cut the top prongs about two and a half inches long, the bottom about five inches, enough for a good hold. Cut two narrow strips of rubber (before rubber, deerskin was used) about eighteen inches long, shorter for a small child. Fasten by tying at the ends of the top prongs, along a small groove which you must first cut near the end, to hold the end of rubber. Tie real tight, using a twine or strong thread, wrapping the ends of rubber along the groove and catching it together to tie. Now, the other ends of the two pieces of rubber are connected together with a piece of leather about two inches by four, a small hole in each side. The ends of rubber are drawn through these holes and again tied with twine or strong thread. (The leather was usually cut from an old shoe.) Small creek gravels made fine ammunition. To use, place rock in pad, hold long end of prong in left hand; with right hand, pull hard on rubber bands to stretch for tension. Release. The rock will shoot for a long way with a lot of force. In fact, our older people killed small animals with sling shots.

—Dolls were made from corn shucks. They were things of art, with no resemblance to the small ones now sold in handicraft shops. I wish I knew how to make them like the ones our grandmothers made, but I have not been able to find anyone that now knows how. There were also beautiful dolls whittled from wood with moveable arms, legs, and heads, dressed in clothes made from quilt scraps and yarn hair. Rag dolls were stuffed with yarn or home-raised cotton, with button eyes and mouth and nose stitched on from colored threads. Young girls were taught to sew by the age of eight or ten.

—It was the custom to give a child a whipping on its birthday, one stroke for each year and one to grow on. The friends tried to catch them and put them under the table or bed, all in fun. It was counted good luck to put butter on someone's nose on their birthday.

—A "riddie bob" - see-saw. A plank or pole was placed across a large log so as to balance each end. One or two children would sit on each end. With a slight push with their feet, they could make first one end go up and then the other. As one end went up, the other came down. They also made their own merry-go-rounds from logs.

—Balls were made from yarn or twine covered with groundhog hide or deer skin. A game we played which we called "round town" was very much like baseball, with a batter, pitcher, and first, second, and third base, homeplate, and striking out.

—A swing was made by hanging a rope from the branch of a tree. A small piece of wood was used for a seat. Sometimes we would find a stout grapevine growing in such a way as to be used for a swing. Some used an old tire hung from a tree.

—A small piece of grapevine was used for a jump rope. Some for just one child; often two would hold the ends, one at each end, while another jumped over while they threw the vine over and over.

—A rollie hoop - A small iron hoop, usually from a wagon

hub, was rolled along the road with a long, stiff wire (found in rolls of roofing, placed there to protect it while being shipped) with a hook bent in one end to fit over the edge of the wheel. It took a lot of practice to be able to balance them, but a lot of fun once you did.

—A playhouse - All little girls had a pretend home under the shade of a large tree or in one end of the barn loft. Flat rocks covered with slabs of moss for beds and chairs; scraps of broken dishes; empty tin cans and jar lids made wonderful dishes; acorns, with a very little amount of imagination, became cups and saucers; broken twigs became forks and knives, hollow ones for spoons; baking mud pies and cooking weeds for greens; taking care of their rag dolls, learning to be homemakers and mothers as they played. The children were often given a small plot of ground for themselves where they could grow real vegetables, again learning while they played.

—There were the usual games played at school: London Bridge, Ring around the Rosie, Hop Scotch, Go Sheepy Go, Fox and Dog (a game of tag), Antie Over (a game of ball where the ball is thrown over the house), Jackstones (small pieces of a broken churn or crock, or little rocks, for jacks), Froggie in the Meadow, Hide and Go Seek.

—Pitching horseshoes - Two short stakes were driven into the ground several yards apart. There were four players, two partners. One each stood at opposite stakes. Use four horseshoes. Each player tossed two, one at a time, at the stakes. The object was to try to get the horseshoe to fit around the stake. If the shoe circled the stake it was a "ringer," counting ten points. If it fell leaning against the stake, it was a "leaner," counting six points. If no ringer nor leaner was made, then the shoe falling closer to the stake counted one point. If a player tossed his shoe on top of another "ringer" already made, the first lost his points for the ringer and they went to the one whose shoe was on top. Also the same for a leaner. The one to reach a number previously agreed upon won.

— A candy pulling - a get-together for young people to make and eat candy. They also played kissing games: "Please and Displease" - one person passed a hat or basket and each player dropped into it some personal item as a forfeit (comb, knife, watch, ring, or hair ribbon). Another person sat in a chair while someone else held over his head one of the forfeits one at a time saying, "heavy, heavy, over your head." The one sitting in the chair asked, "Fine or superfine?" ("Fine" meant the object belonged to a boy, "superfine" meant it was a girl.) "Pleased or displeased?" he was asked. If he said "Pleased," he was asked what it would take to please him any better, and he would say the person to whom the forfeit belonged must do something. It could be anything he could think up — maybe kiss his best girl, stand on his head, bark like a dog, stick his head in a bucket of water, whatever it was, he must do it before he was given back his forfeit.

— Picking cherries - another kissing game. A boy and a girl caught hands and started climbing from opposite sides up the rungs of a chair. On each step up on one rung to another, they must kiss before going on to the next rung. As they came back down they would kiss again on each stop. This may sound easy, but it's very hard to balance and kiss. A lot of fun and kissing. If they fell off, they had to start all over again.

— Hanging the Doorknob - One person was asked to catch hold of the doorknob with his left hand, place his right hand over his left shoulder, then choose some girl. She would take his right hand in her left one and put her right one over her left shoulder and choose a boy, and so on, boy, girl, boy, girl, until everyone was called. Then, number one kissed number two, number two kissed number three, and on down the line. The last one turned and kissed the one next to him and on back to the beginning. When it got back to the first one, he must kiss the doorknob he has been holding onto. The point is to kiss without letting loose of the two others' hands you are holding on to. Very difficult, and a lot of laughs.

—Walking the Lonesome Mile - A boy and girl stood at opposite sides of the room and began walking toward each other. As they pass, the boy says, "I am walking the lonesome mile." She answers, "I have too." When they pass again on their return trip he says, "I love peaches." "I do too," she answers. "I love kisses." If she answers this time, "I do too," they kiss. If she says, "I don't" and runs, then he tries to catch her and get his kiss.

—What and How - All the players sat in a circle, except two. Of these two the first one goes to each player and whispers to him, "I give you (whatever he wants to say - car, ball, worm, toothpick, just whatever comes to his mind). The second one then goes to each one and tells each what to do with the gift the first one gave him without knowing what it was. Later, each player must tell the group what the first person gave him and what the second told him to do with it. The results were sometimes very amusing. There was another similar game, only this time there were three players. The first tells each where he was last night, the second who he was with, and the third what they were doing. The results were sometimes very funny. With a little imagination the whispers could come up with some wild combinations.

—We also played Thimble, Thimble, Who Has the Thimble (sometimes called, Button, Button, who has the Button) - It's played the same way.

—Club Fist - The first player puts his fist on his knee with the thumb sticking up, the next one catches hold of the first one's thumb with his fist and sticks his thumb up. The next one does the same, on and on, until all the players have a thumb in their hands. The first one says, "What you got there?" "Club fist," comes the answer. "Take it off or I'll knock it off." If the answer is "Knock it off," he knocks it off, and so on until there is only one left. Then he begins to ask the remaining player:

"What you got there?"

"Bread and cheese."

"Where is my share?"

"The cat's got it."

"Where's the cat?"

"In the woods."

"Where's the wood?"

"Fire burned it."

"Where is the fire?"

"Water squinced it."

"Where is the water?"

"The ox drank it."

"Where is the ox?"

"The butcher stabbed it."

"Where is the butcher?"

"Rope hung him."

"Where is the rope?"

"Knife cut it."

"Where is the knife?"

"Hammer broke it."

"Where's the hammer?"

"Dead and buried behind the old church door, and if anyone speaks, laughs, shows his teeth, he will get five boxes and ten nails." If anyone did any of these things, he got hit with a fist, which was the five boxes, and scratched with ten finger nails.

—At bean-stringings, corn-shuckings, apple-peelings, quiltings, corn-hoeings, and barn-raisings, lots of work that must be done in order to survive was turned into a social event, a get-together of neighbors, family, and friends. Work changed to play and was enjoyed by all. They played at work and worked at play, happy, carefree, enjoying life and each other.

WEATHER SIGNS
AND SEASONS

The weather meant a lot to our people. In a way, it controlled their lives. There was nothing they could do about it, but there was a lot they learned by watching and remembering. For a long time they did not have calendars, almanacs, watches, or clocks. They had their own devices to "keep track of time and space." Watching Mother Nature to know when it was going to rain, snow, or "be a long dry spell" was taken into consideration each and every day, so as to know when to plant and when to gather. When your very survival depends on growing food, then the way and the how was very important. Even when to do the laundry depended on the weather. Dry wood must be gathered, rain water caught in a barrel placed under the "leak of the house" (under the side of the roof) or dipped up from the creek, the sunshine to dry the clothes on the line. In winter, if they became frozen before they got dry, they could break and be ruined. Oh, how wonderful a feeling to wake up in the night and hear the soft gentle rain falling on a board roof, knowing you had just finished hoeing your garden, set tubs under the edge of the roof to catch water, brought in plenty of wood, and fastened up the little chickens.

—On New Year's day, before daylight, go outside with a lighted torch. If the smoke goes straight up, it will be a dry year. If it floats out, it will be a wet year.

—On the first new moon in December, count the numbers

of stars in the circle around the moon. That's the number of big snows you will have that winter.

—For every time it thunders in February, it will frost on the corresponding day in May.

—For every big fog in August, a big snow that winter; each little fog, a little snow. Some people kept a gourd hanging on the porch. For each fog they would put in a gravel. That winter, for each snow, as it happened, they would take out one of the gravels. It was more times accurate than not.

—If the corners of the new moon were turned up, the next few days would be dry; if turned down (letting the water out) it was going to be rainy.

—Blackberry winter - a few cold days in May when the blackberries bloom.

—Dogwood winter - a few cold days in April when the dogwoods bloom.

—Redwood winter - a few cold days in April when the redbuds bloom.

—Indian summer - a few warm days in October when there is a haze over the sky. Folks said it was the Indians burning off the prairies so new grass could grow for their buffalo herds.

—The depth of the snow was described as: a skiff of snow; ankle-deep; knee-deep; straddle-deep; over your head. The small, grainy snow was called "homney (hominy) snow." A windy snow was said to be snowing "cross-legged."

—Falling weather - a change in the weather for the worse.

—A very heavy, blinding snow was called "good weather to steal a sheep." Once, or so the story goes, a man made a bet with his neighbor that he could steal one of his sheep and tell him when he did, and yet get by without getting caught. The thief went to his neighbor's sheep shed during a big snow storm, killed one of the sheep, put it in a sack, took it on his back, went past the door of his neighbor's house and called him to the door. The snow was so thick he could just see. The man told him, "I have the weather (name of a she sheep) on my back and the wind in my face."

— The first three days of May were the "barren days." Nothing would bear any seeds if planted on these days. Corn would grow big and tall, but there would be little or no ears of corn.

— Some people were able to taste snow in the water the day before a big snow.

— Old folks' bones ached before a snow or rain.

— The first three days in a season determined the weather for the next three months.

— If it rains on Monday, it will rain three days that week.

— March borrowed twelve days from February and froze the old woman's cow to death.

— There were some days known as "emery days." On these days, if you chopped on a tree it would die. If a person got hurt on these days, the wound would be slow getting well.

— On New Year's eve, if your shadow could be seen with two prints, you would die that year.

— If the first person to visit you on New Year's day was a lazy person, you would not raise any chickens that year. If they were not lazy, you would have good luck with all your chickens.

— Whatever you worked at on New Year's day, you would do that all that year.

— If you sweep your house on New Year's day, you were sweeping one of your family out, you would lose one of them that year. They would die, leave home, or get married.

— If the bottom of the leaves turn up on a tree, it's going to rain.

— If the dew clung to the spider's web, it was going to rain.

— If the chickie-dee birds (snow birds) gather together under trees, it's going to snow that night.

— When you hear a cricket in the house during the winter, it's going to "freeze up."

— When you could hear the wind whistling in the chimney, it was a sign of snow.

— A heavy dew was a sign of a hot day.

— Mares' tails clouds meant rain soon.

— If the morning fog does not "hang on," it's going to rain.

— Ring around the moon, rain soon; ring around the sun, rain none.

— If it comes a sudden shower and the chickens run for shelter, the rain will not last long; but, if they remain out in the rain, then it's going to rain all day.

— "Begin before seven, then quit before eleven." Rain. Also true of snow.

— Rules when to plant or gather your crops:

a. Dig potatoes on the "light of the moon" in October.
b. Plant all vines on the 10th day of May. Watermelon, muskmelon, squash, cucumbers; also on "twin days" (Aquarius)
c. Plant Irish potatoes on St. Patrick's Day.
d. Plant peas, onions, and lettuce on Valentine's Day.
e. Plant turnips on July 25.
f. Everything should be gathered by Thanksgiving Day.
g. Make soap on the new moon and it won't boil over.
h. Kill hogs on "dark nights" and the meat will not curl up when fried.
i. Potatoes planted on the new of the moon will grow deeper

in the ground. If planted on the "dark nights" they will
grow near the top of the ground and be easy dug.

— If a black cat turns its tail toward the fire and sits that way,
it is going to snow soon.

— If flowers bloom out of season, it means weather without
reason.

— If the sky is red at sunrise, it means the sun has water in its
eye, so it will rain soon.

— When dew is on the grass, rain will come to pass.

— Three months after hearing the first katydid, there will be
the first frost.

— Wooly worms tell what kind of winter there will be: light
color - snow; dark color - wet; multi-colored - varied weather.

— If you see crows feeding on the ground in September, then
there will be a very cold, bad winter that year.

— If a hoot calls from the north side of the mountain, it means
bad weather; if from the south side, it's the sign of coming good
weather.

— Wind from the east, bad weather; wind from the west, good
weather.

MEDICAL TERMS: CURES AND SUPERSTITIONS

These are medical terms and remedies used by our folks. I will not attempt to say the cures used would work every time, and do not mean that anyone should use them, but I have tried some of them and found that they did help. I know that some of the herbs they used were good. All the terms and names are authentic.

—Creel - to turn or twist the ankle when walking; or, to "creel over dead." Could come from the word "reel" like to "reel and rock."

—A bile (also called a "risin'") - meaning a boil. An extra large boil was called a "carbuncle" because it resembled the red garnet stone. Boils were drawn to a head (to cause the pus to gather) by placing a thin slice of bacon or fat back over the infected place and let remain overnight. Some used turpentine mixed in brown sugar; also, lye soap and brown sugar or a wilted leaf from a beet plant. A wilted cabbage leaf was another cure, or the thin inner lining of an egg, egg white and alum. A poltice made from lard and cornmeal was thought by others to be the only cure for a boil. Superstition: a boil or blister must never be "picked" or lanced before sundown.

—A stone bruise - a kind of boil that came on the bottom of the foot, usually on the heel, caused by going barefoot and bruising the foot on the sharp stones. Cure: Stick the heel in a warm cow pile (fresh cow manure); a mixture of salt and meal scalded with hot water, or any other cure used for a boil. The skin of the foot was made more tough by going barefoot, causing the infection to be more difficult to get to break and drain. A stone bruise was very painful, and could cause one to have to stay in for a long time and not be able to walk for months.

—"Jobbing" a nail in the foot was another hazard from going barefoot; also stepping on broken glass. All were treated with turpentine, soaked in salt water and Epsom salts. Many got thorns stuck in the feet - the same treatment as boils.

—Toe each (itch) - The skin in the small wrinkles along the underside of the toes became broken. Dirt and sand irritated it more. Cures: a piece of yarn thread tied around the toe through the cut, and worn for days; the juice or sap from the milkweed plant put in the infected part (this hurt more than the disease); stick the toe into the stream of cow urine as it came from the cow.

—Fall or summer sores - Sores that came on children's legs and feet. Could have been caused by infection from mosquito bites and made worse by wading in the filthy waters of the creek. Thought to be contagious. Cure: lard and sulfur mixed to make a salve; rosin and sheep's tallow, mixed; also, a salve made from the nightshed plant (this plant was very poison and must be used with care) mixed with cream.

—Bad cold - common cold. Always said as one word, bad-cold. It was not thought to be contagious, but to be brought on by exposure to the night air. Cure: give a laxative always: Epsom salts, castor oil, Black Draught; rub chest and back with Vick's salve, onion poltice made from roasted onions; kerosene oil. Give to drink a stew made from whiskey, sugar, and water, heated and taken just before going to bed. (To make you sweat the cold out from your body.) Also, hot ginger tea. Another cure was catnip tea, all taken just before going to bed. Others used spicewood tea and some combined two or more of these.

—Summer complaint - an upset stomach, diarrhea, vomiting, in small children, most often in their second year. Caused by their

failure to be able to adjust to the food given them, as they were fed the same rough food that the rest of the family ate. Cure: blackberry juice, castor oil, and one drop of turpentine; given very little to eat, little or no water (which they needed so much); bore a hole in a silver dime, thread it on a string and let the child wear it around its neck; tie three "sow bugs" (found under old tubs, planks, or old clothes that have lain on the ground for some time) in a cloth and let the child wear them around its neck until the bugs dry away.

—Pneumonia (pronounced "nuemornie") - very dangerous, probably caused more deaths than any other cause in the hills. Cure: given spinit tea to bring down the fever; Farewell Summer weed tea, blackberry roots tea, bervine tea.

—Expression: "Some ailment is a going around." - When there was some disease or sickness that they knew no name for, they would just call it some unknown ailment.

—When children lost their baby teeth, they were told that if they did not put their tongue in the vacant spot, that a gold tooth would come back in the place of the one removed. If the tooth was thrown on the ground and a dog picked it up and ate it, then the tooth coming in would be a dog's tooth or a tush. If a chicken ate the tooth, it would never grow back.

—Running off (diarrhea) - also called the "back door trots"; cure: small dose of castor oil and turpentine; peach tree bark scraped upwards as the limbs grew on the tree, made into tea (you scraped the limbs downward if you wanted someone to quit vomiting); creek mint crushed and put in cold water to drink. A person was said to be "runnin' off at the mouth" if a very talkative person.

—Bound up - constipation. Cure: the root of the calmus boiled to make tea. Expression: "Someone bound up so tight you could not blow him loose with powder and fuse." Expression: If you were "bound up," you took something "to work you." A bowel movement was "having a passage."

—Gravel - cystetis, acute infection in the bladder or neck of the bladder. Cure: tea made from the "he plantain weed"; also, spignet plant, steeped (put in cup and covered with hot water). Pour off the water and drink. Superstition: If you crossed the water or creek going upstream, it would cause you to have trouble with your kidneys or bladder. Always cross the creek in the direction in which it was flowing.

—Piles - hemorrhoids. Cure: use the fuzzy leaves of the mullen plant as toilet paper; sit on a hot chip from the white oak tree; bathe in salt water, use butter for a salve.

—Rum'a'tis - rheumatism. Cure: a hot toddy made from whiskey and vinegar; rub arms and legs with turpentine, kerosene, linament; split poke root and put in whiskey and drink (poke root is poisonous). Superstition - Carry a buckeye in your pocket; carry a rock that was found in a bird's nest in your pocket; turn your shoes upside down under your bed each night as you sleep.

—Consumption - tuberculosis. Believed to "run in the families" (inherited). Cure: wild cherry bark, yellow root tea, sandbriar roots tea (to help the cough - they knew no cure).

—Giant fellum - meaning "joint fellum," an infection in the joints of the fingers. Cure: treat same as any other boil. Split finger with a sharp knife after heating the knife in the fire.

—Different expressions for being sick:

a. got the punnies - just not feeling well
b. right smart - doing just fine
c. good shape - just fine
d. bad off - real sick
e. on the mend - getting better
f. puning around - not real sick, yet not quite well
g. stirring around - well enough to get out of bed
h. down and out - past going
i. lay a' dying - not going to ever get well
j. hiphoed - thinking you are sick, but you really are not

—Sick at your stomach - nausea; wanting to vomit. Also means disgusting. "It makes me sick at my stomach the way some folks act." Cure: creek mint steeped in cold water; tea made from peach tree bark (scraped down toward the trunk of the tree); chew on a match stem.

—Fit'ie'tie - asafetida, an awful smelling product, bought in stores. Thought to help keep anyone wearing it on a string around the neck from catching a disease; you were shunned by everyone, as it made you smell so awful that no one got close enough to you for you to catch any sickness.

—Falling off - losing weight. The fatter one was, the better health he was thought to be in.

—Mending - gaining weight, growing like a pig.

—If a woman nursing a baby got her feet wet, it was thought to cause the baby to get sick.

—Weed in the breast - mastitis. Especially common after birth of a baby, but could be anytime a mother is breast-feeding a baby. Cure: catnip poltice; also, drink catnip tea. Superstition: caused by crossing over running water.

—Seven year etch (itch) - caused by a parasite being under the skin. Thought to last for seven years. Cure: rubbing on the body a mixture of sulfur and grease for nine nights without bathing. Then, bathe and burn or scald all clothes worn and bed linens used. Another cure is to bathe in water in which red stem ivy has been boiled. Some used poke root in place of the ivy. Expressions: if someone was asked how old he was, he might answer, "I guess I am twenty-one, for I have had the seven year itch three times." It was thought to be very disgraceful to have the itch.

—A retarded person was called "feeble minded."

—"Being out of your head" meant being delirious from fever.

—A crazy person was said "to be off."

—If a person fainted you "brought him back" by "working with him" and caused him to "come to."

—An after-effect of some sickness was said to "settle" in you somewhere or to "fall" in some part of your body. Measles might fall in your legs, fever in your eyes or legs. The mumps could fall in a woman's breast or in a man in his sex organs and cause him to be sterile.

—Little children were said to be "liver grown" if they were listless and not active. Cure: lay them on their stomach on your lap, bring their left foot up over their back and touch their right hand, then do the same with the right foot and left hand. If they meet, then everything is all right. It does not hurt the child. In fact, they seem to like it.

—Tooth pullers or tooth drawers - a kind of pliers made in the black-smith shop. Mountain people could endure a lot of pain, and had to. Each community had someone that owned a pair of tooth-pullers. I remember my father had some and kept them in the drawers of the sewing machine. Every few weeks someone would come with an aching tooth. Father would sit him down in a straight back chair, give him a good "swig" of whiskey, take one himself, and pull the tooth. The patient would wash out his mouth with another mouthful of moonshine, and they both went back to work.

—Toothache - This is where faith doctoring was used most. Faith doctoring is one thing least understood by outsiders. It's thought of as something like witch doctoring, a hocus pocus chant. Not so. It's the beautiful faith of Christians in the promise of God through the belief in His Son to answer prayer. Cure for toothache: hold whiskey on tooth; hold open mouth over hot water in a cup; any kind of hot poltice, especially catnip. Some used carbide in the cavity to kill the nerve. This sometimes caused the tooth to burst (very dangerous). To "jump a tooth out" put a nail against the tooth and strike the nail with a sharp blow, thus causing it to come out. Yes, people did this. Another expression: "The only cure for toothache is cold steel" (pull it). Another: "I never had my teeth pulled, I just let them rot out naturally." A woman was supposed to lose a tooth for each child she birthed, for the child absorbed the calcium needed for its growth.

— Broken bones - Once when my husband was plowing the field the plow kicked him (the plow caught behind a root and bounced back) and broke two of his ribs. He never stopped work. We had to live and there was only one time to grow the food that we had to have. In fact, he did not know that he had broken his ribs until a few years ago when he had X-rays made for something else. Sometimes a broken bone was set, but most always not. An empty, circular box, like an oat box, was used for a brace. Brown paper bags soaked in vinegar were used to reduce the swelling.

— Thrown out of place - dislocated. Treatment the same as for a broken bone.

— Proud flesh - an excessive development of infection around a wound or ulcer. Removed by burning it.

— Blood pisin (poison) - Wash in whiskey (very painful), vinegar, Epsom salts; take a laxative. Superstition: if the red streaks went toward the heart and met, you would die.

— Your blood turning to water - maybe meant to describe leukemia.

— Your blood turning to sugar - maybe diabetes.

— Shingles - a rash on the body. Cure: the warm blood of a black chicken. Also, sparks from a flint thrown against the body and burning the rash. Superstition: if the rash went around the body, you would die.

—A rash was called a "breaking out." Like, poison ivy caused you to "break out."

—Gapes - yawn.

—Belch - burp. Was not counted ill manners to belch. If you belched while you were eating, it meant you were half full.

—He cups - hiccups. Cure: nine "sups" of water from a teacup; if someone could get you to believe a lie; get scared; breathe into a paper bag; drink water while holding the head upside down.

—Dander - dandruff. Cure: wash hair in the juice caught from a cut grapevine; use homemade lye soap to wash hair; catch rain water to wash hair (also thought to make hair grow).

—Blackheads - pimples. Thought to be worms under the skin that eat your body after death. Also called "caggey bumps." They were thought to come on the face when a person got old enough to have sexual desires.

—A fester - infection caused by a splinter or briar getting stuck into the skin and pus gathering. Cure: same as a boil. It had to fester before it would "come to a head" and burst and come out.

—Cu'rup'shun - pus.

—Colic - Young babies were thought to have the ten-day colic. Cure: one person held a horse collar, two others passed the baby from one side to the other, through the opening in the collar nine times, always feet first; a teaspoon full of whiskey was burned, making a blue blaze, then was cooled and given to the baby. A grown person—drink hot water "just as hot as you could stand it"; also, tea made from Jones root, also red root tea. Cramp colic could have been gallstone attacks. Cure: same as for colic. There was also something called "bowel consumption"—could have been stomach cancer. It was always fatal.

—Thrash - a rash inside the baby's mouth, thought to sure

mean death if it went down the throat and on through the bowels. Cure: have someone who has never seen their daddy blow in the child's mouth; drink water from some man's shoe. (You must get him to let you have the shoe without telling him what you want with it, and he must be someone that is no kin to the baby.) To keep a baby from ever having thrash, have the father hold the baby in front of the window in such a way that the sun will shine into the mouth of the baby before it ever touches any other part of its body. Yellowroot tea was good to cure the thrash.

—Hives or bold hives - a rash some newborn babies have. Cure: catnip tea. If the baby did not break out with this rash after drinking the tea, the rash was said to have "gone back in" and the baby would die. Then, the baby must be "scarified." Someone would take a razor and cut the baby between the shoulders on the back. Then, using a thimble with a hole in the bottom, a few drops of blood were sucked out and put in a spoon and fed to the baby. An empty hornet's nest hung over the baby's bed will help to keep the baby well. Just a "tetch of whiskey" (what will stick to a broom straw when dipped into the whiskey) added to a spoonful of breast milk from the mother was good for almost anything that the baby had in the line of sickness. So the baby would have a clear and pretty skin, they took the wet diaper off the baby and washed it in its own urine.

—Chicken pox - Cure: sit under the chicken roost for a while every night. The chickens usually roosted in trees in the yard.

—Measles - Cure: drink "nannie tea," a tea made from sheep manure tied in a rag and boiled in water; a stew made from whiskey, sugar, and ginger. If the rash was allowed to "go back in" too soon, it would cause a "back set" (relapse) and "settle" in the ears, eyes, legs, or arms.

—Whooping cough - Cure: drink a white mare's milk; pour some kerosene into a spoon, light it, and quickly blow out the flame. Mix with honey or sugar; also, tea made from wild cherry bark, sweetened with honey; a red flannel cloth, wet with onion juice, placed on chest. Poltice made from roasted onions.

—Yur ake - earache. Groundhog grease poured into the ear; blow cigarette smoke into ear; machine oil poured in ear; warm urine, taken from who had the pain, and put into the ear.

—Hed'dake - headache. Said as one word. Some were called "a sun pain." Cure: stay out of the sun; go to the north side of a spring of water, pick up a gravel (small stone), throw it over your left shoulder with your right hand—do this for nine mornings straight; tea made from possum bush bark (pussy willow). "Sick" headaches were another kind. They lasted for days with nausea and vomiting. Probably migraine. Cure: no food or water; hot or cold poltice made from meal, salt, catnip, and many other things. Others used a hot tea made from black pepper. Taking a laxative was believed to help. Some folks took a coffee headache when they missed drinking their coffee. Cure: drink coffee, or smell the steam from it.

—Nose bleed - another time when faith doctoring was used. Some people were believed to have a "special gift" to "stop blood." Cure: hold a piece of silver money in the roof of the mouth; press the fingers against the temples. To stop wounds from bleeding, crush winter fern and place on open cut; soot from the fireplace (this often left an awful scar, as the blackness of the soot cured up in the skin).

—Sore neck - tonsillitis. The older generation thought that "the pallet of the mouth fell down" (a lowering of the roof of the mouth). They would pull the ears upward and pull the hair on the head, thinking this would bring it back in place. Another cure was to sleep with your sock tied around your neck. This had more sense, as the socks were made from yarn and gave some heat to the sore throat, but must have been very uncomfortable and scratchy. Another cure was tea from willow bark. Also, peach tree bark, sweetened with honey. I was told that once a group of children lined up on the Knott County courthouse steps and the doctor clipped their tonsils out, one by one, as the others stood and watched, and sent them home. Many had to walk for miles. Some parents refused to let their children have their tonsils removed, saying, "If God had not had a use for them, He would not have had them to grow in the first place."

—Hart burn - heartburn. Cure: eat burnt bread, raw potatoes; chew on a match stem. Superstition: if you had heartburn during pregnancy you would have a "dry birth" (little or no fluid during delivery).

—Pank eye - pink eye, a contagious inflammation of the eyes, causing them to have a red or pink color. Thought that you could catch it by just looking at a person that had it. Cure: wash the eyes with tea made from catnip, peach tree bark, Jempson weed (this will change the color of your eyes for a few hours); put castor oil in the eyes; milk "tittie milk" in the eyes (breast milk). Expression: "Anyone that would take the pink eye would take anything that they could get their hands on." Another cure was to chew on the bark of the "pivy" bush (an evergreen hedge).

—Burns - With an open fireplace, a lot of children got burned. Maybe one out of every twenty families had a child to get burned to death—"got burnt up." Almost all got a large burn. Cure for burns: scrape a raw potato; baking soda; melted butter; Vick's salve; juice from a house plant we called "mother-in-law's tongue" (because it was so long and slimy, with barbs). Some folks were believed to have the gift of being able to "draw out fire from a burn" by blowing so many cold then so many hot breaths, saying, "out fire, out devil, out fire, out devil." Superstition: never pick a blister before sundown. Another superstition was that if a baby's diaper got burned, then the baby to whom the diaper belonged would get burned. The diapers got burned a lot because they were dried on a string stretched across above the fireplace. Sometimes they were used over and over again before being washed. To prevent diaper rash, clay was taken from between the rock in the chimney, pounded to a powder, tied in a rag, and dusted on the baby.

—Heart sick and weak trembles - symptoms of going into shock; very weak, nervous, and nauseous. Brought on by over-work, running too fast, being frightened or upset. If you passed out, you were said to "just died away" and you must be "brought to" by being "worked with" (given camphor to smell, drink, rubbed on; cold water on face, a hot iron wrapped in a blanket and placed to the feet).

—Settin' up in bed - a unique way our folks had to help the sick to rest when in bed. A straight-back chair was turned upside down, the seat part on the bed, the back side at an angle. Pillows were on this, and you had a very nice resting place to recline or to eat while in bed.

—Sun struck - sunstroke. Lots of our people worked for long hours in the hot sun and became over-heated. Prevention: "lick salt" (put a small amount of salt in your hand and eat by licking it with your tongue). Sunstroke was thought to be brought on by drinking cold water when you were hot. Many of our people had sunstroke so bad that it resulted in destruction of the brain cells, causing them to "lose their mind."

—Struck by thunder - When a person got hit by lightning, it was believed that it was the thunder that did the damage. He was said to have been "thunder struck." An expression: "I wish thunder might strike me dead if it's not so."

—Childbed fever - an infection after childbirth. A lot of mothers died from this. Cure: same as any other fever—drink water in which the bark of the "slippery elmmin" has been soaked. Superstition: a new mother must not eat anything that grew on a vine - tomatoes, grapes, cucumbers, pumpkins, etc. Also, she must not eat anything that was pickled. She must not cross running water, or sit on the ground.

—Can't-help-its - woman's monthly period, menstruation. Also called "the curse." Superstition: a woman was thought to be unclean during this time. She must not walk through a cucumber patch. If she did, the vines would die. If she canned food, it would spoil. Bervine tea was taken to start the flow. If the flow was too much, she might say, "I am flooding to death."

— Puke, also "throw up" - Vomit. Cure: tea from the bark of the peach tree (be sure and scrape the bark from the limbs down towards the tree. By scraping the bark in this direction it prevented the contents of the stomach from coming up).

— A pregnant woman was said to:

a. buy a baby
b. ready to get down
c. in the family way
d. being big
e. a happy belly
f. the nine month fever

A miscarriage was called "happening with bad luck." To deliver a baby was to "catch it." The midwife was a "Granny woman." The incident was a "granny race." The father was expected to "run a granny race" when he went after the midwife. While he was waiting, he was said to be "sleeping with his shoes on."

Children were told that babies were brought by the hoot owl. When they heard the owl howling, "who, who" they thought it was asking, "who wants a baby?" They would all run out in the yard and shout, "We do, we do." No matter how large the family, or how small the house and income, a new baby was always welcome by everyone. Children were also told that the navel was the place where the wings had been attached and cut off—if they had not been removed, then the baby would have remained a hoot owl. When my third child was born my second one hunted in my feather bed for the wings. He wanted to send him back.

If a pregnant woman "craved" some special food, the father must get it for her or the baby would be "marked." It would stick out its tongue until it got to eat some of the food the mother had wanted. It was counted a sin for him to not get the food if he could. There was a beautiful story about some cherries that Mary (the mother of Christ) wanted. The limbs of the cherry tree were too high for her to reach. She asked Joseph to get them for her. In jealous anger he said, "Let the father of the child get them for you," and the tree bowed down of its own accord.

Expression: "If you want to keep your wife at home, keep her pregnant in the summer and barefoot in the winter." It was a shame for a pregnant woman to be seen in public. Breast feeding was called "giving the baby the 'tittie'" and no one was embarrassed by this.

—Kan'cer - cancer. A lot of our people died from what we called "bowel consumption"; could have been cancer of the stomach.

—Foundered - indigestion and diarrhea. When someone over-ate. We had no way to keep food fresh, especially meat. They would be so hungry for fresh meat when we killed our hogs that many would eat too much. Yet it was looked upon as being a very disgusting and shameful thing to get foundered. Cure: same as for diarrhea.

—The crazy bone, funny bone - the nerve in the elbow.

—Dew was thought to be poison to a wound or sore. If you walked in the dew you would catch dew poison. Night air was believed to be harmful. All old folks, sick people, and small children were not allowed to breathe the night air.

—Ringing noises heard in the ear were called "death bells," a warning that some of your friends or family were soon going to die. Left ear, a woman, right ear, a man.

—Whelps - when the skin "raised up" in spots or ridges, caused by insect bites, nettle weed, or a limb (whipping).

—Sty - an infection in the eye thought to be contagious; if you looked at someone that had one, you would get it. Cure: salt water; also, wash eye in catnip tea. Superstition: tie a gravel in a rag, drop it in the road where the road crossed, repeat "Sty, sty, leave my eye and catch the first person that passes by." It will then leave your eye and the next person coming along that road will soon have a sty. Another way was to steal someone's dishcloth and drop it in the road. The sty would then come on the eye of the person from whom you stole the dishcloth. Or, you could rub a black cat's tail through your eye. To squirt "tittie milk" in your eye was another cure.

—Wild hairs in your eyes - New eye lashes just beginning to grow in were very irritating to the eyes. Cure: have them pulled out, using tweezers. This was painful and irritating and just caused them to have to grow back again. Some folks learned that if you just let them be, that they got all right, but many folks just kept on pulling them out as they tried to grow back.

—The "bad ailment" - venereal disease. Also called "clap" or "pox" and believed that the more people one "gave it to," the lighter the disease would be to the one that had it to begin with. Cure: given a "kill or cure shot," an injection given by the doctor that was believed to either kill you or cure you.

—Rup'chur (rupture) - hernia. Cure: if a baby, fasten a silver dollar around the belly over the navel. Some made a "trust" (truss) from a heavy object sewn in a cloth.

—Flux or bloody flux - sometimes it was an ulcer of the stomach, thought to turn to cancer. Cure: eat squirrel gravy; eat mutton; ginseng tea with a little sugar added. Contagious. All water given to the patient must be boiled. Also, milk must be boiled.

—Insect bites - Wasps were called "waspers." "Chiggers" - a mite found on most weeds and grass and always on blackberry briars. Makes a large bump, itches; more likely to be lodged under the arms or groin. Can be picked out. Cure: salty grease; bath in homemade lye soap. Chiggers were called "the no see um, big feelum bug." Only found during the warm weather months. Wasps, hornets, bees and bumble stings were treated with wet clay, baking soda, or tobacco juice. A bee's stinger was removed.

The mud dobber is a wasp that does not sting. It builds a small mud house along logs or tree limbs, lays its eggs inside, kills spiders, and seals them up in with the eggs. When the eggs hatch the young wasps or mud dobbers eat the dead spiders. For this reason our old folks thought that one and the other were the same, that spiders were wasps.

There once was a resident of Caney that loved his land so much that he fought all progress. He would not allow anyone to travel over it. He did not like for planes to fly over. He had to be forced "by law" to let a road be built and for telephone poles, electric wire poles, etc. to be set on his property. Someone told that he tried to bring a law suit against a mud dobber because it was carrying mud from his land and building a nest on his neighbor's land. Now we describe anyone too protective of his property as "going to sue a mud dobber."

—Water dogs or thunder dogs - a small, worm-like animal that lives in the water. We were told that if one bites you, it would not let go until it thundered or a cow bawled. I don't think they bit at all.

—Corpins - a yellow-striped lizzard, thought to be poison, but were not.

—A poisonous snake - We pronounced the word "poison" as "pis'zin." We had three snakes that were poison: the rattler, copperhead, and the water snake (sometimes known as the water moccasin). As our people spent most of their awake hours in the field and woods, very few escaped being snake bit sometime during their lifetime. What with the hogs running loose (they ate the snakes) and the ever-occurring forest fires burning a lot more, there were still a lot of them around. Some people would go "snake hunting" "come a wet day or Sunday" when they could not work at their crops. They would all get together and take the dogs and go find the snake dens and burn them out by piling logs and setting them a fire. In getting ready for planting, the many small rocks were gathered into piles. This made a good place for snakes to hide. The cornstalks were placed on top of these rock piles and burned to kill the snakes, getting rid of the snakes and the trash at the same time. Cure for snake bite: snake weed. It was believed that man was as poison to the snake as the snake was to man. If, after biting a man, the snake did not get some of this snake weed to eat, it would die. So, it was best if you followed the snake and saw what weed it ate, and the same weed would help you. Other cures: kill a black chicken, place the still-warm "enterals" over the wound. The poison would be "drawn out" into the chicken. It would turn green from the poison. A bottle of turpentine would do the same. It must be a bottle that had never been opened before. Place the mouth of the bottle upside down over the wound. You could see the poison rise up in the bottle as it drew the poison out. Whiskey was used a lot, poured on the wound and given to the patient to drink. Also, to wash out the mouth of the one that had drawn out the poison by placing their mouth over the wound and sucking out the poison. Black snakes were feared because they were known to get into the house, find a baby, crawl into its mouth after the milk it smelled in the stomach, and choke the baby to death. We had to take our babies to work with us and leave them on a quilt under the shade of a tree while we worked close by. Again, snakes were a threat. Cats would also take a baby's breath, by sticking their heads into the baby's mouth.

—Brar - briar. Briars and thorns became embedded in the flesh. Cure: take out as soon as you can with a needle, pin, or sharp knife. A thorn that was not removed was said "to go to the bone." If they were too deep to get out, they were "drawn out" with a fat piece of meat or a mixture of soap and brown sugar. If just left alone they would "fester"—the pus gathered would push them out.

—Hip'hoed - meaning, "thinking you were sick when you weren't." Could have come from the word hypochondria.

—Tuck the big eye - Insomnia.

—Pack saddlers - a worm found on fodder, the blades of corn. It had a bunch of hairy spines on the back that stuck into your flesh when you touched them. Very painful. Cure: wet clay or tobacco juice.

—Swelled up - swollen. Cure: soak in hot salt water, Epsom salts, a poltice made from catnip, brown paper bag soaked in vinegar, also used camphor. An expression: "a swelled head" (inflated ego).

—A breaking out - any kind of rash caused by measles, poison ivy, chicken pox, heat, etc.

—Spring neddles - whelps and bumps that came in the spring. Probably from an allergy to weeds. Cure: make tea from the needle weed plant.

—Pision vine - poison ivy. An infection from touching the plant poison ivy. The acid from the plant burns the skin. Cure: juice from the Touch-Me-Not weed (these plants always grow together); lotion from boiling white oak chips; unsalted cream, skimmed from milk; calf slobber (spit from the calf mouth as it sucks the milk from the cow); slippery elm steeped in water (drink it and rub on skin).

—Chaffed skin - chapped skin. Cure: rub with sheep's tallow; make a lotion from unsalted butter.

—Kernels - lymph glands in the neck, arm pits, groin, when they become swollen from an infection in the body. Cure: make a cross with soot from the fireplace on the "kernel." If bruised, they would turn to a boil.

—A big pone swelled up - a phrase used to describe a large swollen place.

—If you had a fever blister on your lip - Superstition: you had told a lie. Admit to the lie and it would go away. Cure: rub the blister with some of the wax from your ear; chew the bark of the privy bush.

—Crampee - cramp in the legs. Cure: make a cross on the bottom of each foot with turpentine; sew a small amount of sulfur in a cloth and wear it in your shoe; eat a pinch of quince each day.

—Childbed fever - an infection resulting from childbirth, most always fatal. Cure: treat as any other fever — tea made from Farewell Summer weed or Pennyroyal weed. The fever was treated, not the infection.

— Milk leg - a blood clot, usually after the birth of a baby.

— Took down sick - became ill.

— To set up mortification - blood poison, or the dark color of the body of someone dead.

— Your "you know what" - unmentionables, private parts of your body.

— Die away - to faint. Cure: burn feathers under your nose. Also did this if one had trouble breathing.

— Tissic - asthma. Cure: measure the child's height on a sourwood stick, when he grew longer than the stick, he was cured of the tissic. Put a "lock of his hair" in an auger hole made in an oak tree.

— Upset stomach - Cure: tea made from wild cherry bark.

— Low blood - Cure: Yellow Dock; also, drink sassafras tea. (This was a good tasting tea and was often used just for the taste.)

— High blood - Cure: sassafras tea, pie plant (rhubarb).

I have only used the herbs, plants, roots, and barks used by my own family, the Owens and the Summer Slones. Different families used different cures for the same thing. Some combined superstition. Others did not. But all believed in faith doctoring, knowing that only through the power of God could anything help. I could in no way list all the cures and all the ways our people fought sickness. And I do not in any way intend this for to be used by anyone as a cure-all. I want more than anything to help preserve the way our mountain people talked, and thought. I do know that some of the plants, roots, and herbs they used were good, and many were better than the "stuff" the real doctors give you today, and some are the same thing in a different form. I believe that God guided them and taught them what to use because of foolish and superstitious ways. Many times they used the household things that they had because they had nothing else to use. Some of their remedies they brought with them when they came from Europe. Some they learned from the Indians and some they discovered by trial and error. They were passed on from one generation to another by word of mouth. Many are now forgotten. So many times when I would ask someone in my family did they remember this or that, they would first say "No," then in a day or two they would call me up and say, "Yes, now I remember. It's all come back to me." But, as I am trying more than anything to preserve the language of our people, I have first listed the word as we pronounced it, then the correct way to say it. But, as I am no expert, I can only try, but I do know how we talked better than someone who never lived here.

I have included many little short stories along with my list in the hope it will be more interesting. And, as I said, it's just about my own family. I am sure other folks have many family cures used only by them, and many stories. I can only say I wish I could include them all. But time and space do not permit.

A list of herbs and their uses:

— Horse radish - bladder trouble
— Rhubarb - high blood
— Yellow Dock - blood builder, rheumatism
— Wild cherry bark - upset stomach, cough, tuberculosis, whooping cough, tonsillitis
— Peach tree bark - cough, cold, tonsillitis, upset stomach, diarrhea, vomiting
— Catnip - cough, cold, measles, whooping cough, to make one sleep, to bring out the hives in a baby, as a poltice (toothache, earache, mastitis), reduce swelling
— Yellow root - mouth wash, mouth rash, strep throat, gum disease, stomach trouble
— Sassafras - blood stimulant, high blood, spring fever (just the "run down" feeling everyone has in the spring)
— Spicewood - kidney infection, bring down fever, to take the woodsy or earthy taste from a groundhog

— Redstem ivy - to get rid of the itch

— Ginseng - most dug to sell, cure ulcers

— Blackberry roots - pneumonia, diarrhea, upset stomach, summer complaint in the second summer of a child (sometimes called green diarrhea)

— Whiskey - cold, pneumonia, cough, rheumatism, colic, snake bite, fever, aching bones, toothache, flu

— Tobacco - snake bite, insect bite, tea from tobacco given to get a child rid of worms, in seed beans to repel insects, around trees and plants to kill worms

— Carbide - toothache, slack carbide in seed to repel insects ("slack carbide" means after it was used)

— Salt (mixed with water) - hemorrhoids, stys in eyes, sinus, insect stings, headache, toothache, to reduce swelling, dandruff

— Soap (homemade lye soap) - mixed with brown sugar for boils, stone bruises, embedded thorns, briars, splinters

— Turpentine - snake bite, insect stings, cuts and wounds, embedded nails, thorns, briars, splinters, stomach troubles (what would stick on a broom straw) colic, rheumatism, to reduce swelling, broken bones

— Castor oil - cough (burn in a spoon for a few seconds, blow out flame, then give to drink, very dangerous, could have been sucked into lungs), rheumatism, to repel insects, mixed with other things for cold, pneumonia, and flu

— Vinegar - reduce swelling, broken bones, upset stomach, heartburn

— Cream or butter - chapped hands or lips, burns, poison ivy, insect stings, toe itch, pink eye, sunburn

— Urine - cow urine used for toe itch, baby urine for clear complexion, earache

— Manure - sheep manure for measles, cow manure for stone bruises

— Cabbage leaves - wilted and used on boils

— Lard or grease - mixed with soap, turpentine, onions, rosin, brown sugar to make a salve to cure poison ivy, burns, colds, coughs, boils, poison

—Dry dirt or clay - on open wound to stop bleeding, burns, insect stings, pounded into a powder for diaper rash

—Soot - on open wound to stop bleeding

—Epsom salts - constipation, to reduce swelling, boils, broken bones

—Grapevine juice - make hair grow, dandruff, freckles, sunburn

—Milkweed - toe itch, pods used to stuff pillows

—Mulein - hemorrhoids

—Raw potatoes - burns, heartburn

—Jempson weed - pink eye

—Mutton - eat to cure flux, ulcers; mutton grease for burns, diaper rash, chapped hands and lips, used to soften leather, and as shoe polish

—Fat meat - to draw out a briar, thorn splinter, boil, or a stone bruise

—Slippery elm - a drink made by letting the bark steep in water to cure fever, poison ivy, burns, cuts, diaper rash, sunburn

—Plantain - bladder infection, menstruation trouble, also used as greens

—Poke root - itch, rheumatism, the berries were used to make ink, the leaves were used as greens, the stalks fried in lard and eaten

—Bervine - pneumonia, menstruation trouble

—Farewell Summer weed - pneumonia, bladder infection, kidney trouble

—Calmus- constipation

—Here are a lot more plants that I know they used, but I don't know just what for:

a. sage
b. basswood
c. mountain tea

d. sweet anis

e. buckeye (carried in pocket)

f. dandeline (dandelion) greens

g. dogwood

h. jewel weed

i. spinit

j. wintergreen

k. ratsvien

l. bloodroot (puccoon)

m. May apple

n. winter fern (used to stop bleeding)

o. thistle

p. dog fennil

q. chinch weed

r. smart grass

s. snake root

t. horse weed

u. hen gollop

v. neddle weed

w. tansy

x. rats vain

y. sumac

z. life-ever-lasting (also called rabbit tobacco)

A. chigger weed (also called stink weed)

B. rag weed

C. mortifie weed

D. pig weed

E. John's root

F. burrs

G. beggar lice

H. Spanish neddles

I. sheep burrs

J. snatch burrs

K. cucle burrs

Other uses for plants, barks, and roots:

—Roots were used to make dyes to color their yarn, cotton, and hemp thread

—Ink was made from the juice of the pokeberries

—Smart grass, also called smart weed, was boiled in water and the water used to kill insects, bugs, worms on vegetables, especially cabbage. By putting smart grass in a pond or creek, the fish would come to the top of the water and be easily caught.

—"Penee'rile" or Pennyroyal. Used green or dry, the leaves crumbled and sprinkled on the beds and floors to kill fleas and bed bugs. "Dog fennil weed" was also used for this.

—Ashes from the fireplace were used to kill bugs and worms on vegetables. Ashes were also used for fertilizer.

—Cinders from the fireplace put around young cabbage plants killed the grub worms.

—A cob soaked in kerosene placed in a cucumber hill or other vines got rid of the bugs that bothered them.

—To get rid of ants that were finding their way into the house, pour used coffee grounds along their road, or where they are entering the house. Used coffee grounds are good as a fertilizer, especially for house plants.

—Stems from the wild cane, a reed, were used to make walking canes, pipe stems, and fishing poles.

—Corncobs made pipes, jug stoppers, back scratchers, toilet paper, handles for tools (such as files, chisels)

—Turtle shells made soap dishes, also small scoops for corn or grain.

—The hides from animals were used for many things—shoes, moccasins, harnesses, bridles, belts, chair seats, bed springs, shoe laces, banjo heads

—Feathers were used to make pens to write with, as a swab to put medicine on sores or the inside of the throat, to oil a clock or gun. Feathers were also used to stuff pillows and beds.

—The seed pods of the milkweed plant were also used to stuff pillows.

—Gourds were used. The larger ones to hold lard, salt, sugar, soft soap. The smaller ones that had a very long handle to make dippers from which to drink water. A small, round variety (called hen foolers) were used for nest eggs. An egg must be left in the nest so the hen will return to lay more eggs. There was a pretty, bright-colored gourd we called a "dimercrat." It had no practical use, we just gave it to the children for a toy.

—Broom corn is a plant that belongs to the sugar cane family of plants. We grew it to make brooms and a "small sweep" to clean soot from the stove.

—Groundhog grease was used to put into the ears to cure the earache.

—Groundhog hide was used to make banjo heads. Small strips of the hide were treated with tallow and made pliable by pulling them over the back of a chair until they became soft, then used for shoe strings. Women also used these strings to tie their hair.

—Corn shucks were used to stuff mattresses, to make shaving brushes, also to make a brush to put the paste (made from flour) on the pages of newspapers and magazines that were then pasted upon the inside walls of the house. Homemade sausage was stuffed into corn shucks and hung from the ceiling to dry and keep for later use. Shucks were used in making the hot bed to sprout sweet potatoes.

—Broomsage was used to make small brooms, mostly to clean the soot from the coal-burning stove. It also made a brown or tan dye. Cloth "ticks" were stuffed with broomsage and used for mattresses. The green broomsage grass was used for pasture for the cattle and horses. Each spring the fields were burned off so as to let the new grass come back. The holes dug into the ground in which the potatoes, turnips, and apples were kept through the winter were lined with broomsage grass. Hens' nests were made from this dried grass.

—Sheep's tallow was used on shoes, saddles, bridles, harnesses, as a polish to make them more durable and water repellent. Used on the hands to cure chapped hands.

—Salt was used, mixed with soda, for toothpaste. Salt was used many ways as medicine. (See medical terms.)

—Vinegar had many uses, one was as a flavor substitute for fruit. (See food.) Also as medicine.

—Carbide was used in their carbide lamps. It was also used to kill the nerve in an aching tooth. This is very dangerous.

—Tobacco was used, also as medicine. It was also used to put in seed beans to keep the bugs out and dusted in the quilts to keep the moths away.

Some of the ailments for brutes or beasties; diseases in animals:

—Cows had the "murn" - Symptoms were like a cold; cough, runny nose, fever. Cure: poke root put inside an ear of corn. Take the "pith" (inside) out of the corn and put a small piece of poke root in it. The cow will eat it then. You can get her to eat it also if you put it in a shuck.

—Scours - diarrhea in cattle, young calves, when they first began to eat grass and weeds. Cure: boil blackberry roots, make a tea and mix it with meal so they will eat it.

—Holler horn - Something got wrong with cow's horns. Thought a worm got inside the horn. Cure: remove the horn by sawing it off.

—Holler tail - A worm of some kind got inside the tail of a cow, causing it to become limp. Cure: cut the tail off just above the limp place, close to the body.

—Hide bound - The hide or skin on the back of a cow "brute" became very tight, maybe from malnutrition, because it seems to happen to poor, unkept cattle. Cure: pull the hide loose, using your hands. Some used nails driven into a board and hit the cow on the back, piercing the hide with the nails.

—Wools in the back - the large "horse fly" laid its eggs under the skin on the back of the cows (also rabbits, kittens, squirrels).

When they hatched the larva were called "wools." Very painful. To prevent them, salt the cow by putting salt on her back. The cow will lick the salt off, thus getting rid of the eggs and killing the larva. If more than one cow was together, they would lick the salt off from each other's back.

—Distemper in dogs - symptoms like a cold. Cure: poke root in lard, gunpowder taken from a shotgun shell. Also sulfur and grease. Gunpowder was also given to a dog to make it mean, ready to bite, therefore a better watch dog.

—"Mange" in dogs - sores on the body. Cure: burn sulfur in the dog house. Burn dog bed (any straw or whatever it has been sleeping on). Make a mixture of sulfur and grease and rub on the dog's body. Mange is very contagious.

—"Quencie" in pigs - a cough. Cure: give lye soap cut up and put in dish water, and feed to them.

—"Heaves" in mules - hard to breathe.

—"Ham strung" in mules or horses - an injury to the shoulder.

—"Botts" in mules and horses - worms in the stomach. Give poke roots in corn.

—Colic in horses or mules - Cure: hold a saucerful of turpentine under the "nabble" (navel). The turpentine will be drawn up inside to the stomach.

—"Hip sweeney" - injury to the horse's or mule's hip.

—"Ring bone" - in horse's feet. Caused by standing in wet manure. Wash in salt water and grease.

—Foundered - when animals ate too much feed at one time. Cure: give linseed oil.

—"Stemming the fodder"- Sometimes when the horses or mules were too old to chew the fodder they would only eat the soft outside of the blades.

—When hogs were "trimmed," also called "changed" (castrated), crushed tomato leaves or elderberry tree leaves were used to keep flies away and to stop the bleeding. Some people ate this part that was cut from the hog. It was called "mountain oysters" or "hog's nuts."

— Children were told that cows "pawed up" the calves from out of the ground. The bull had to tell them where to paw to find them.

— Sometimes hens "got eggs broke in them" if they got a blow to the body, breaking the egg before it was laid. Always resulted in death. If found quickly enough, the hen was eaten by the family. Many times we lost hens by them hanging themselves, getting their heads caught between the two slats of the palling fence going around the yard. Again, if found while the body was warm, the hen was eaten. Often "accidently on purpose" by the man if he wanted chicken for dinner.

— The horse belonged to the man, the cow and the chickens were the woman's, the dog was the man's or the children's.

— Little chickens took something called the "gappes," always fatal. They also ate maggots (larva stage of the fly) and died from that. They got lice on their head. Cure: salty grease. Many got drowned in tubs of water left uncovered.

— Hogs also got lice. Cure: kerosene oil.

— Cows sometimes "sucked themselves" - took the milk from their own udder. We made a spindle of wood and ran it through the cow's nose to keep her from sucking herself.

— Sometimes a cow might want to kick while being milked. Then there was a "cow kicker" (made in the blacksmith shop). Two clamps fit over the cow's legs, just below the knees. They were connected with a short chain.

SUPERSTITIONS

— If you had hairy legs, you would be good at raising hogs.

— If you had big ears, you were clever (meaning generous or hospitable).

— If you had small ears you were stingy.

— If your nose itched, someone was coming for a visit. Left side meant a woman, right side meant a man.

— Don't sew anything for someone sick. If you do, they will never live to wear it.

— Don't sew anything while wearing it. If you do, you will get it torn off you.

— Don't begin any job of work on Saturday that you can't finish that day.

— If you start to say something and forget what it was, it was a lie.

— A baby that walks before it can crawl will have to crawl sometime during its lifetime.

— If the soft spot on a baby's head grows up before it's a year old, the baby will not live to get grown.

— It's bad luck for a hen to crow. If you kill the hen and eat her, the bad luck will be on the hen and you will have good luck.

— In the spring the first butterfly you see, you will soon get a new dress the same color as the butterfly.

— If a measuring worm is found on your clothes, he is measuring you for the new clothes you will soon get.

— If you dropped your dishrag (cloth) while you were washing the dishes, you were going to have a visitor soon. If you made a wish before picking it up, the first person you thought of would be the visitor.

— If when you were setting the table for a meal you accidently placed one too many forks or spoons at someone's plate, there was going to be a wedding in the family. If a knife, there was going to be a death.

— If it thunders real loud during the three weeks a hen is sitting on the eggs, waiting for them to hatch, the thunder will kill the chickens and they will die in the shell.

— A rabbit killed on a frosty morning was always fat. Rabbits were supposed to eat frost and get fat instantly.

— Don't eat beef and milk together. It's supposed to be "agin the Bible."

— Don't eat fish and milk together, they were supposed to be poison if eaten together.

— Don't break bread from a woman's hand. (The cornbread was baked in a large pone and placed on the table in one piece. Each one broke a large chunk from it.)

— If two people dried their hands on the same towel at the same time, they would marry in the same family.

— If a person's first toe on their foot (big toe) was bigger than the next one, they would be the boss in the family. If shorter than the second toe, then their spouse would be the boss.

— It's bad luck to cut (trim) your fingernails on Sunday. It will make you forgetful.

— If you comb or brush you hair after the sun goes down, it will make you forgetful.

— Don't patch old garments (articles of clothing) with a new piece of cloth.

— Good luck if it rains on a new grave.

— Bad luck if it rains on a new bride on her wedding day.

— The last person in a group of people leaving a graveyard will be the first one to die.

— Bad luck to step on a grave or over one.

— Bad luck for a bird to fly in at a window. If you catch it and carry it outside, it will change to good luck.

— The first red bird you see in the spring, make a wish before it flies. The wish will come true.

— If you and another person start to say the same thing at the same time, someone is coming to visit you. The visitor will be some-one that loves the person best that finished the sentence first.

— When you kill a snake, if you hang it up in a tree or on the fence, it will rain soon.

— If a boy wears beads, he will have to stay in jail as many days as there are number of beads.

— Laugh before breakfast, cry before supper.

— When working with someone, both using hoes, if you acci-dently hook the hoes together, the two people will work together next year.

— If it rains while the sun is shining, it will rain again at the same time next day.

— The first night you sleep under a new quilt that has not been used before, what you dream will come true.

— A quilt made from a star pattern or diamond-shaped pieces brings bad luck.

— You must make one mistake intentionally in the color scheme, the arrangement of the pattern, or the shape of the pieces when making a quilt, because only God makes anything perfect.

— Peelings from apples and counting the seeds; if you could peel an apple without getting a break in the peeling, throw the peeling over your right shoulder, letting it fall on the floor or ground. It will make the form of a letter. This letter will be the same as the first letter of your sweetheart's name. Count the seeds in an apple, letting each seed represent a letter of the alphabet like one is a, two is b, three is c ... the last one will be the initial of your future spouse.

— If the bottom of your right foot itches, you are going to walk on strange land (go somewhere that you have never been before). If it's the left foot, you will go somewhere where you are not welcome.

— If your left eye itches, you are going to be pleased about something. If it's your right eye that itches, then you are going to be made mad. You can cause it to happen to someone else by rubbing your eye and repeating their name.

— If your nose itches you will soon have a visitor or get a letter from someone. Right side a man, left side a woman. If you can keep from scratching your nose, the visitor will be a friend or the letter will bring good news.

— A dog that had long dew claws (the hind claws) will always make a good hunting dog.

— Remove a litter of puppies or kittens from the nest. The one that the mother takes back first will make the best dog or cat.

— It's bad luck to set out a pine tree or cedar tree. When it gets big enough to shade your grave, you will die.

— If you sweep around the chair in which someone is sitting, the person in the chair will not get married that year.

— Bad luck for a rocking chair to be allowed to rock by itself.

— Bad luck to open an umbrella in the house.

— Bad luck to bring a hoe into the house, unless you take it out walking backwards.

— Bad luck to come into a house by one door and go out by another.

— If you had white spots on your fingernails, each spot counted for a boy or girl friend. Some people said each spot meant a lie you had told.

— If you found an article of clothing in the road, if it was clean it was good luck. If it was dirty, bad luck. Never pick it up, unless you knew to whom it belonged.

— If you had started to go somewhere away from your house and had to return to the house for something you had forgotten, before continuing your trip, it was bad luck unless you made a cross in the road in the dirt with your foot, and spit in the cross.

— If you put a pully bone (wish bone) over the front door, the first person of the opposite sex that came through the door, if they were single (not married) and not a relative, they would be your future spouse.

— If children played with fire during the day, they would wet the bed that night.

— If children played with frogs they would have warts. To get rid of warts, tie as many gravels in a rag and drop it along the road at a place where the road crossed. If anyone picks up the rag, they will get the warts. There were many more cures for warts.

— If you burned a corncob, it would make your cow go dry (quit giving milk). If you boiled the milk, it would also make the cow go dry.

— When we asked where the smoke went, we were told that it went "off yander" where people made stretching leather (rubber) from it.

— When a new quilt was finished and removed from the frames where it had been quilted, all those that had helped with the quilting got hold of the corners and sides, stretched the quilt out, placed a cat in the middle, then shook the quilt. This scared the cat and it tried to get away. Whichever one it jumped out by would be the next one to get married.

— When a small baby began to talk, if the first word it said was "daddy," the next one to be born in that family would be a boy. If it said "mama" first, then the next one would be a girl.

— If you would keep some of the dirt from a person's footstep after they had left the house, then someday they would return.

— Never watch anyone going away from the house until they got out of sight. If you did, they would never return.

— If your right hand itched, you were going to shake hands with someone. If your left hand itched, you were going to get some unexpected money.

— If you thanked someone for a plant or a cutting from a plant that they gave you, it would not grow.

— If someone gave you an animal of any kind, it was bad luck. You must not accept it as a gift, but must give something in return. Often a person would bring an ear of corn from home and give it to the mother pig.

— It was bad luck to ask the name of a cow, horse, or dog, even if you were trading for them. It was all right to use the name, so as the new owner could hear it.

— It was bad luck to change a baby's name after you had once named it.

— Never burn anyone's hair after it was cut. It would cause them to have a headache. The "combings" (hair that got caught in the comb or brush when brushing the hair) must be kept in a dry place and not allowed to get wet. Often a hole was bored into the logs of the house and the hair pushed back into this hole. Another reason for not throwing the hair out into the yard on the ground was so the little young chickens would not get it tangled around their feet.

— If you tickled a baby (made it laugh by rubbing your fingers over its feet or ribs) it would cause it to stutter when it grew up.

— When it was snowing, we were told that old Mother Nature was shaking her feather bed.

— If you ironed a man's shirttail (the part that goes under the pants) it will make him feisty (sexy).

— If you have been offered the worth of something and do not sell it (a cow, horse, mule) it will soon die. It was a sin to sell a dog.

— When you sleep in a strange house, name the corners of the room the names of four of your friends. When you awake the next morning the corner toward which your face is turned will be the name of the one that loves you best.

— If a woman had good luck growing house plants, she was said to not love her husband. If she could not grow them, then she was said to love him.

— If a rooster stands in the door and crows looking inside, there will soon be a new addition to the family — a birth, a wedding, or someone come to live with the family to make it their home. If the rooster is looking outwards when it crows, then there will be a death or wedding, or one of the family will leave home soon.

— If a woman puts on a man's hat, it means that she wants to kiss him.

— Laughing is catching. If you laugh when you see someone fall, you will soon fall too.

— If you start to say something and forget what you were going to say, then it was a lie. If you start to say one person's name and say another, the person's name that you used is thinking of you.

— If your ear burns, someone is talking about you. Left ear, a woman, right ear, a man. Wet your finger with spit, make a cross on the ear that is burning, and say three times, "good, good, good, talk on; bad, bad, bad, hush."

— If you boil milk, the cow from which the milk came will go dry (quit giving any milk).

—Bad luck to build a house on the site where one has burned down.

—Bad luck to "set up a still" on the place where one has been cut up.

—Bad luck for a woman to go inside a coal mine. Some men would not work in a mine if they knew a woman had been inside.

—When you kill a chicken, if you lay it on its back, pull two feathers out of its wings and cross them on its breast, it will die quickly.

—Young girls were told that if they would put chicken manure on their breasts, it would make them grow.

—If you eat the gizzard and feet of a chicken, it will cause you to be pretty.

—If you changed a baby's clothes from the winter ones to the lighter ones that were for summer on the first day of May, it would keep the change from making the baby sick.

—If the hem of your dress turns up, kiss the hem and make a wish.

—If two people are walking together and one goes on one side of a tree and the other on the other side, they later have a fight. If one taps on the tree, it breaks the spell.

—If you want a dog to not leave home, bury some of its hair under the doorstep. Or, measure its tail on a stick and bury the stick.

—If you want a dog to hunt well, feed it the feet and "guts" of the animal you want it to hunt.

—Name a dog after a bad person and it will be a good dog.

—If a "water dog" bites you, it will hold on to you until it thunders or the cow bawls.

—Good luck for a cricket to live in your house.

—On old Christmas (January 6) the cows would "mue" at midnight and bees would buzz in their hive.

—Bees could not get honey from the honeysucker flower, a punishment put on them by God because they worked on Sunday.

—If a girl sat on the table, she would be an old maid.

—Bad luck to let a baby see itself in a "looking glass" before it's a year old.

—When building a fire, name it for someone. If it burns, they love you.

—If a woman lets her bread burn, it means her husband is mad at her.

—When a man was working in the coal mines, if his light began to flicker, his wife was seeing another man.

—Folks thought a child could be "marked" by something the mother saw or did while "carrying the baby." If she saw something that frightened her, she could determine where the mark would be by touching herself on the same spot on her own body.

—No one must be allowed to die while lying on a featherbed or feather pillow. Death would be harder for them.

—A woman pregnant with her first child could cut the split ends off someone's hair and the hair would grow back, no split ends, and the hair would be beautiful.

—A mole on the neck, money by the peck; a mole on the nose, money goes.

—An axe was placed under a woman's bed while she was giving birth to her child. The axe would cut the pains.

—Superstitions forewarning death:

a. If a bird flew in the house
b. A howling dog - if a dog howled in or near a graveyard the night after someone had been buried there, if his head was turned up the person had gone to Heaven; if down, they had gone to hell.
c. If a rooster crows at midnight
d. The last one to leave the graveyard will die soon.

185

e. If the wagon taking a body to the graveyard gets stuck in the mud, there will be another death in the same family.

f. If you use a razor that has been used to shave a dead person and cut yourself, you will soon die.

g. If a bird sits on a grave it means the person went to Heaven.

h. If it rains on a new-made grave, the person went to Heaven.

i. If you touch a dead person you can forget them quicker. It will also cure a wart if you rub it against a dead person. Also, birthmarks will go away after being touched to the face of someone dead.

— If you were eating something and dropped it, then someone else was craving whatever it was you were eating.

— If you dropped something you were eating, it was not nasty unless you dropped it for the third time.

— If two cats did not get along with each other and kept on fighting, you could tie their tails together and throw them across a clothesline, and they would never fight anymore after you took them down.

— Dreams - they believed that God sent dreams, but they also had a lot of superstitions about dreams:

a. To dream of a fish was the sign of a birth.

b. To dream of the dead was the sign of rain.

c. To dream of a naked woman was the sign of the death of a man; to dream of a naked man was the sign of the death of a woman.

d. To dream of a snake was the sign of the devil. If you killed the snake in your dream, it was a good sign. If you let it get away, it was the sign of trouble.

e. To dream of fire was the sign someone was going to make you angry.

f. To dream of lice, someone was going to tell a lie on you.

g. To dream out of season was trouble out of reason.

h. To dream of muddy water was the sign of trouble. If the water was clear, it was a good dream.

i. To dream of having a fight with someone was the sign of friendship. To dream of being kind to someone was the sign you would soon have trouble with that person.

j. To dream of a horse, if it was black, was a bad dream. If it was white, it was a good dream.

TERMS OF WORK AND
NAMES OF TOOLS

—Crap - Crop. Usually meant the amount of corn grown for each family.

—To tend a crop - The process of growing a crop of corn or other food. Also used the term "to tend the land."

—A truck patch - A garden.

—To clur (clear) a newground (always pronounced as one word) - To cut all the trees and remove them from a piece of ground. The trees were cut, the larger logs hauled away for firewood or buildings, the smaller trees and branches put into piles and burned. The stumps were pulled out with oxen, burned with fire, or blasted with dynamite.

—To burn brash (also pronounced "bresh") - Meaning brush, (the small limbs and twigs) left from clearing a new ground. Always done at night. All the neighbors came to help for fear the fire would get out of control and set the woods on fire.

—To grub - Cutting and digging out by the roots the sprouts, briars, and small bushes.

—Raking weeds or grubs - After the grubs were cut, they were let lay for a few days to dry, then they were "drug" by using hoes into piles and burned. The last year's cornstalks had to be done the same way.

—Shaving weeds - In a new ground or ground that was too steep to be plowed, the ground was prepared for planting by cutting the weeds and loosening the soil with a hoe by removing just a small layer of the topsoil and dragging it a few feet down the hill.

— A swith - The width you could reach with your hoe, as you shaved weeds.

— A threw - One row, from one end to the other of the field.

— A round - A row from one end to the other of the field and back again.

— A balk - The distance between two rows.

— "To yon enn an back" - To the other end and back.

— Digging in corn - When the ground could not be plowed, then the corn had to be planted with a hoe. A hole was dug about every three feet. Three to five grains of corn were dropped in and covered with dirt. A newground was more work, but grew better and bigger, and more, corn.

— "Drappin" beans, cushaws, punkins - All were planted in the corn. Two bean seeds in each hill of corn; cushaws and pumpkins, one every fourth hill, every fourth row.

— A corn planter - A tool used to plant corn in ground that had been plowed. A devise that makes a small hole in the ground and drops a few grains of corn and, on being released, covers them over as you bring the planter out. Some of our folks were so skilled with using the corn planter that they could plant corn just as fast as they could walk through the field.

— Plowing- Making the soil loose and killing the weeds.

a. Turning ground - plowing it so as to turn the weeds under, so they would decay and enrich the soil.

b. Breaking it for the first time - early in the spring, long before time to plant.

c. Breaking it the second time - a few weeks after the ground was plowed the first time it was plowed again, this time it was prepared ready for planting.

d. Laying off - making shallow trenches with the plow, for the rows of seeds.

e. A fer (furrow) - the trench in the ground made by the plow.

f. A short row - as our hills are so steep and sloping, many times a short row had to be added to bring the rows up even.

g. Double back - to finish first one row, and go back for another one.

—Scatterin' ma'nure - Manure from the barn shed, chicken house, and pig pen was used for fertilizer; also ashes and cinders from the fireplace.

—Pitching rocks - Each and every year the numerous small rocks had to be removed from the garden patch. Sometimes they were pitched onto an ever-growing pile. Sometimes the children hauled them off in a sled made from an old washtub with "runners."

—Trashing the under row - Our corn was planted in rows around the hill. It had to be hoed by beginning at the bottom and working upwards. Each row had to be finished ahead of the row above, as we raked the cut weeds from the top row onto the row below. If the weeds were raked onto the first row before it was hoed, it was being "trashed."

—Burning off a seed bed - Stalks, weeds, or brush were piled and burned on the spot planned to be used for a seed bed. The fire destroyed all the weed seed and insects. Also, it made a soft place for the small seeds, such as tobacco, pepper, cabbage, tomatoes; anything that must be transplanted later.

—Settin' out plants - Transplanting.

—Thinnin' and replantin' - If there were too many plants growing in a hill, some must be removed; if not enough, then more must be added. When hoeing corn for the first time (it was hoed twice) we had a pocketful of corn seed with us to replant the missing hills. Later, as this corn did not get grown as soon as the rest, we would go over the field and hunt for these ears for "roasting" ears for the table.

— Pulling fodder - The blades from corn were saved for feed for the horses and cows. It was stripped from the stalks just as soon as the ears of corn got full grown. If pulled too soon, it would damage the corn, causing it to not "fill out." If left too long, it would begin to dry and be no good for the animals. All the blades were stripped from the stalk except the one in back of the ear of corn. When you got a handful, you stuck it between two stalks of corn where it was gathered and tied into bundles by using one or two blades of the fodder to tie the rest with. This must be done early in the morning or late evening when there is some dampness in the air, as the fodder is very "brickley" when dry. The bundles were then stacked around a pole in a way so as only the top ones and the tips of the rest got wet when it rained. Some folks had a fodder house in the corn field in which they stored the fodder.

— Saving tops - After the blades of fodder were pulled, the tops of the corn stalks were cut just above the ear of corn, and tied into and put into shocks. To make a shock, put together four or five stalks of corn, yet standing close together, and tie them together at the top. Around these stack the other bundles, letting them stand up against the others. Tie them together at the top, using one of the extra tops.

Blade fodder was fed to the horses and tops given to the cows. The horses always seemed to belong to the father and the cow to the children and the mother. Cushaws and pumpkins were hid in the shocks of fodder to keep them safe from the frost, and brought in later.

—Ruffage - The name given to all fodder and hay given to stock for feed.

—Hoeing corn the first time - When the corn was about five inches high, it was hoed for the first time. If it were ground that could be plowed, the plow was run twice through between each row along each side of the corn, then with a hoe the weeds were cut between the hills and fresh soil "drug up" around the plants. If there were too many plants some were pulled, leaving only two to a hill. If any hills were missing then those hills were replanted.

—Laying by corn - The second time corn was hoed was when it was about knee high or about two weeks after the first time. You didn't have to be so careful this time, and you didn't bring so much soil up around the stalks. You didn't have to replant nor thin. We always had a celebration on the day we "layed by" our corn. We always were in competition with our neighbors in trying to beat and get ours done first.

—Out of the first weeds - Same thing as hoeing for the first time.

—Running away in the weeds - An expression used if our corn got weedy.

—Snaking the field or garden - An expression used to "poke fun" (laugh at) someone if they had let their corn or garden get a lot of weeds—saying that they would have to go through and run all the snakes out before they could hoe it.

—Gravling tatter (potatoes) - To get the young potatoes to eat, we would go along the row and look under the leaves. When we found a place where the soil "craced" we would dig in with a table fork and find a nice potato. It could be removed without damage to the rest of the plant.

—Picking beans - Gathering the beans from the vines.

—Saving seeds - Everyone must save the next year's seeds to plant again. They always saved more than they needed for themselves because nothing pleased them more than to have some to give to a neighbor. They wanted to save "a plenty."

—Bush whack - To cut small bushes or trees and leave them "lie" to keep land from "growing up" or to be used for a pasture.

—Deading a tree - Cutting a ring around a tree just through the bark, causing it to die but yet remain standing. This way it would dry out, decaying.

—Robbing bees - Taking the honey from bees. They would make a smoke from burning rags in under the beehive. This would tranquilize the bees, so they would not sting. Then, the honey bee could be removed from the hive without any trouble. When bees would swarm (the bees in the hive would divide and some would leave to form a new hive) we beat on a pan to make a noise and they would settle on a tree limb or something and we could get them into a new hive, a bee gum (the place to keep bees was made from a section of a hollow log.)

—Swopping work - Sometimes neighbors would swap work, by both families first doing the work that one needed done, then working for the other family. This helped out when one person's corn was not big enough to hoe and the other's was. And, it was a lot more fun for the children, especially if there were boys in one family and girls in the other.

—Working on the halves - When one person would furnish the materials and another would do the work, then both would take half as his share. I have often made quilts this way. We mountain folks had no money, but we knew how to manage without it and get along just as good.

—Hulling walnuts - Removing the outside hull from the walnuts. They were our largest and best nut, but getting that outside off was a messy and dirty job. The stain would remain for weeks on our hands, but they are not nearly as delicious if allowed to dry in the hulls. Some people made a hole in a piece of wood and hammered the walnut through. This got rid of the hull.

Some of the tools used:

— Hoes -

a. Shank hoe - a long-handled hoe with a long "shank" of iron connecting the hoe handle.
b. Grubbing hoe - had a shorter, thicker handle, the handle fitting into a hole in the blade of the hoe; used to "grub" or dig out the roots and sprouts.
c. Sang hoe - a very short-handled hoe with a narrow, sharp blade, used to dig ginseng and other roots that were to be sold or used for medicine and dyes.
d. Goose-necked hoe - A long handle fit into a crooked neck (the part next to the blade).
e. Laid hoe - When a hoe was used until the hoe part was almost worn away, a piece of an ole, worn-out saw or shovel was used to repair the hoe by being bolted on with bolts made in the blacksmith shop.

— Ma'tic - Mattock. A short-handled hoe with one side of the blade made like an axe, the other side like a narrow hoe, only thicker and with more strength. Used to loosen real hard soil or dig roots. Also used to dig out from their holes small animals such as groundhogs, rabbits, and snakes.

— Crowbar - An iron bar with a forked end, used to pull nails, or as a lever.

— Pick - Like a mattock, only with a pointed head. Used to pick out coal from a coal bank.

— A shevel - Shovel. We had cold-dirt, long handle fire-shovels we used for everything, but the most unique thing was what we children used the shovel for . . . sliding down the hill! By sitting on the broad bottom, letting the handle come up between our legs for a steering device, our feet on the handle, we did not need a sleigh.

—Plows - There were turning plows, hillside plows, turners, double shovel plows, and bottom plows, all homemade (made by hand). The iron part was made in the blacksmith shop (every community had one). They would hunt in the woods until they found a tree growing in just the right shape for handles, with a crook at the end. They also found "runners" for their sleds growing on the trees this way.

—Sleds - They made their different sleds for different jobs of work, each suitable to the work required.

a. Fodder sled - long, low, wide, light. Sometimes called a dryland sled.
b. Corn or coal sled - heavy, sturdy, high sides, not as wide as the fodder sled.
c. Rock sled - no sides.

When the "runners" wore out they were "half soled" by splicing a new piece along the bottom.

—Axes - There were many axes with different uses.

a. Double bet - cut on both sides of the blade.
b. Pole axe - cut only on one side; the other side was like a hammer or a maul.
c. Broad axe - blade only on one side; a real broad blade used to "hue" or make smooth logs and posts.

—Maul - Was made from a length of pole, whittled down to a "hand holt" size on one end; the other end left large, used as a hammer when making rails or driving posts into the ground.

—Fro - Made from iron, in the shape of an "L." The lower part was sharp; used to split wood when making rails, boards (shingles for the roofs).

—Cant hook - Swivel and "grabs" used in logging.

—Wagons - Were used for transportation; to haul groceries from the depot; to "peddle" fruit and vegetables to the mining camps. To "scotch" a wagon you placed a rock behind one wheel to make sure it stayed "parked."

—Buggy - Was a one-horse wagon.

—Hammers:

a. Claw hammer - used in carpenter work; had a "claw" with which to pull out nails.
b. Sledge hammer - a very large hammer, used to burst up rocks.
c. Bold pied hammer - with a round head, used to "brad" the harness and bridles, fasten them together, also to make them.
d. Horseshoe hammer - used when shoeing the horses. Very small.
e. Tack hammer - a very small hammer used to make or mend shoes.

—Splitting horn - A sharpened piece of a horn from a cow or deer, used to split large ears of corn so as to make them small enough for the calves or young cattle to eat.

—Hinges - For gates. Were made from worn-out horse shoes. The shoe was cut in two, the end of each turned back to form a loop and fitted together. The other end was nailed on each side of the gate. The bottom of the gate post was set in a hole in a rock to turn in. A weight on a chain stretching from each side caused the gate to swing shut by itself when opened.

—Hinges - For doors. Were made from the soles of old, worn-out shoes.

Our people knew many ways to make do with what they had, and I don't see how they did all the work that they did, yet they were happy and at peace with life. I know some of the things I have included in my writings are of no interest to anyone but me, but I do want it to be all recorded. That way, the old folks of the hills won't be forgotten.

COMMON FOLKS

To my five sons with love

FOREWORD

I first met Verna Mae Slone in 1982 at the Hindman Settlement School, Hindman, Kentucky, where I interviewed her for *Table Talk*, my second cookbook. We sat in chairs facing each other in a hallway. As we talked, the afternoon sun slanted through a high window and touched her silver-white hair, braided in two long plaits, which hung down on either side of her gentle, wrinkled face. Her eyes were a vibrant blue. Throughout the interview, she spoke with a soft mountain dialect, her words as clear and straightforward as her writing.

What My Heart Wants to Tell, the author's 1979 memoir about her father "Kitteneye" Slone, received much attention and over-shadowed her previous book, *Common Folks*, which was published in 1978. The print media frequently interviewed Slone and re-viewed her work. After the publication of *What My Heart Wants to Tell*, Verna Mae Slone, in her late seventies, joined the ranks of noted Appalachian writers such as Harriette Arnow, Wilma Dykeman, James Still, and Emma Bell Miles.

Slone shares her memories of attending Alice Lloyd College, getting married, and rearing five sons in *Common Folks*. I recall her telling me how she had prematurely named each son "Sarah Ellen" because her heart had always yearned for the daughter she never had. "I finally decided if I was to get a girl, I had to create one. So I wrote a book and named the little girl in it 'Sarah Ellen.'" Those with an appreciation of oral history or the folkways, folk medicine, and other aspects of life in Appalachia will find in *Common Folks* a rich first-person account that is difficult to put down. I believe this edition will be as welcome and valued as the 1975 reprint of *The Spirit of the Mountains* by Emma Bell Miles, which was originally published in 1905. Any reader would enjoy *Common Folks*, and it would be suitable material for use in an academic setting.

In *Common Folks* Slone describes areas of southeastern Kentucky that were irrevocably altered by industrial development, mining, and other intrusions from the modern world during her lifetime. She does not dwell overly long on the losses, but instead presents a clear, unadorned picture of her way of life and that of the people around her, revealing their natural paths as well as those dictated by society. Above all, Slone highlights the natural beauty of her surroundings as she tells the story of her life in Appalachia.

Sidney Saylor Farr

CHAPTER 1

As you can tell by the title I have used for my "scribblins," it is to be about common people. Folks who never did any great deeds, never became president, neither were involved in great scandals like Watergate, whose names were not known by newspaper reporters or television commentators, but were just common folks, loved by their families, and did the very best they could with what they had to do with. Folks who are worthy enough to be remembered, and not labeled as "hillbillies" because they were born in the hills. I want their grandchildren to know they had folks to be proud of, a way of life soon to be forgotten. Brave, sturdy, hard-working, God-fearing people, misunderstood by outsiders because their customs and speech belong only to them.

Well, if I am going to write my own autobiography, I guess the way to begin is with the information of where and when I was born. And I don't think I deserve a pat on the head nor a kick in the back for the accomplishment of either, for I had no control over the matter at all. In fact I was not even consulted. If I had been I might not have made a very wise decision, for I was not very wise at that stage of my existence. I thank an "all wise God" for making this all-important decision for me.

So with God holding the power over my life, He saw some

reason unknown to man for me to be born October the 9th, 1914, in a log house at the mouth of Trace on Caney Creek, in Knott County, Kentucky.

"Aut oh," I heard what you said when you read that. I heard you just as plain as daylight, you said, "Hillbilly!"

Hillbilly. A person as unreal as Frankenstein or the tooth fairy. But if you are born anywheres in Appalachia you are stuck with that label, glued on so tight, you will not become unstuck for all your born days, no matter what you do.

I was the twelfth child in the family of Isom and Sarah Slone. My mother lived only a few weeks after my birth. In those days a baby was never "put on a bottle," except in emergencies. During the three days of my mother's funeral, the neighbor women who had young babies divided their natural supply of milk with me. The quickest way to get a nipple was thirteen miles to Wayland over a wagon road or eight miles to Hindman on horseback. Folks did not buy bottles, they bought the nipples, "three for a dime," and used them over any empty medicine bottle they could find. Some folks would wrap cloth strings around a reed and place into the mouth of the bottle, to be used as a nipple.

Poor father, after making that long trip, coming home at nightfall, to find that his baby refused to take the bottle. For three days I just would not suck *that* milk from *that* bottle. My husband says I am still that stubborn when I set my head to either do something or not to do it.

My sisters would make me a "sugar tit," mixing sugar and butter together and tying it up in a clean rag. This I would eat. My father thought when I got hungry enough I would take the bottle, but he could see I was losing weight but not changing my mind.

My Aunt Cynthia Ann had been offering to take me. Her own baby, Lona, was over a year old; she could be weaned, and I could take her eating place. My father did not want any of his children to leave home, but at last in desperation he told my aunt she could take me, but with the understanding it was only until I was old enough to be fed, or learned to take milk from a glass. It was just a few weeks until I was back home enjoying my bottle. After they let up trying to make me, and gave me my own way, I agreed to give in.

And so it has been all my life. I will not say my way is best; you may not like what I do or say, you may agree or disagree. It does not make any difference with me. I will not change for anyone. You like me the way I am or go find someone you do like. I will respect you for what you are and will like what good I find in you. But you can't fool me, I can spot a phony a mile off. So with this warning, you can read the rest of this, at your own risk.

Now a history or true life story is very hard to write. If it was fiction you could let your imagination run wild. But to stick to fact, and make it interesting, is no "pie job." Also there are so many stories you would love to tell, but "as man is not an island unto himself," everything that has happened to one's ownself also concerns others, and just maybe they don't want it revealed. And many times they saw the same thing from a different angle.

If after reading this you think it is just a little too "goody goody," then please remember: we all have closet doors best left unopen, and do not want to "wash our dirty linen in public." It's not that I don't remember the ugly and bad, — pray God I wish I could forget some things — I just want to write in a way to hurt no one.

I am not ashamed of where I lived, of being poor, nothing that I think was God's will for me. I am ashamed of some of the things the devil got me into.

I don't think my life was interesting enough in itself to make anyone want to read about it, but I believe I lived in a place and time, a way of life, very unique and different, soon to be forgotten and lost. I wish to help preserve some of this.

I have very little education, I was a high school "drop-out." I believe God gave me a talent to put my thoughts on paper. If I had any training I honestly believe I could, so just try to wade through all the mistakes and get the thoughts anyway.

I do not intend to discuss sex, religion, or politics, farther than to say, I am a woman, a Baptist, and a Democrat. If you are different I do not think any less of you. If you are the same, you are no better in my sight. For these are just man-made words, and have nothing to do with the soul. If you are a Christian you belong to Christ. That's all that really counts. May God bless and keep you one and all.

CHAPTER 2

I will skip over the first three or four years of my life. I can remember my sisters taking me to school with them. I can "recollect" following my father everywhere he went, many hours playing in his "chair shop"; waiting on the outside of the coal bank, while he "picked out a coffee sackful" of coal. Riding the handles of his plow when he plowed the garden. Going with him to cut wood, pick berries, gather nuts. Riding the sled when he brought in the corn and fodder. I realize now I was just in his way, but he made me feel I was helping him, when all the time he was "takin' care of me."

One Saturday evening, when I was about five, Father told us we could go stay all night with our Uncle Will and Aunt Nance, as he was going to be gone for the night and did not like for us to be left at home by ourselves.

Boys, were we tickled! I can remember it all just like it was yesterday.

We all took a bath in the washtub in the kitchen behind the stove. I was the last one to get cleaned up, for fear I would get back dirty before we got started.

My Grandmother Owens had knit me a pair of long stockings made of bright red yarn. The weather was too warm for me to wear them, but I loved them and wanted to show them to my aunt and uncle.

My sister tried to tell me I should wear my new white cotton stockings. But when she saw that stubborn look on my face and remembering past experiences she said, "All right, I hope they burn you up." They were to get me in more trouble than to make my feet hot.

Father had caught Little Beck and saddled him for us. He was tied up in the shade of the "old weepin' willer" near the chop block. The cow was dry, so Vince had said he would feed and watch over everything for us. He lived up Trace just a little ways, in sight of our house.

My sisters were so slow getting ready! It seemed like hours before they got done primpin'. They put some corn for Little Beck in one side of the saddle bags, and some clean clothes for me in the other. I made like I did not see the new white cotton stockings going in with the other things.

Frances rode in the saddle. Edna, always the tomboy of the family, road a-straddle behind her. I sat on a "piller" in front. Renda and Vada walked. We were a little ways down the road when Renda noticed that O'Engle, our dog, was trying to "foller" us. She took him back and placed an old quilt on the porch floor near the door and told him to guard that old quilt. He would not leave there until she lectured and picked it back up. Not even my father could have touched it without getting dog bit.

I must have slept most of the way. I don't remember much of the ride. I know we went down the Caney road, up Aunt Lee Anner's holler, across Pigeon Roost and down Slone's Fork and up the holler where M. V. Slone now lives. Uncle Will and Aunt Nance lived there.

They had a very large family. Ida, their youngest, was the same age of Edna. There was no small ones my size, but that did not bother me none; I loved both my aunt and uncle, and enjoyed goin' to their house to stay all night.

Aunt Nance run down to the road to meet us. She took me down from the mule's back. The first thing I done was make her brag on my "purty red stockin's," which she wholeheartedly did. Uncle Will was "settin'" on the porch, leaning his homemade chair back against the wall. He told one of the boys to go put the mule up. Eva come out from the kitchen where she had been "gettin'" supper.

I was very interested in what we were having for supper. Aunt Nance told me, among other things, there was a large kettle of corn field peas now almost done, on the back of the stove. When I heard this I fairly jumped for joy and cried, "Oh, goody!"

Renda said, "Verna Mae, is there anything you like better than a plateful of corn field peas?"

And I said, "Yeah—two plates full." Uncle Will laughed and told Renda, "You can't get ahead of that one. She is just like her paw, allus full of devilment."

Soon we were at the table; I never ate anything except corn field peas and cornbread. Uncle Will tried to get me to have some of the other things, but I told him, why fill up space with something else when there were more corn field peas. He said he could not answer that.

Aunt Nance hated it when she heard her milk had turned, but I was tickled, I loved clabbered milk. I asked Aunt Nance to not stir mine up. When Renda heard me say that she said, "No, you are not eating it with your hands, like you do at home."

"Bet I do," I grinned at her. Uncle Will said, "I bet you do too."

Renda said, "She is spoiled rotten. Paw would kill us if we spanked her. She gets her way in everything. Why, the other night she woke up in the night, crying for water. She had us all out of bed before she decided which one could give her a drink. Then, when she picked Vada as being the lucky one of her choice, poor Vada had to guess if she would take the water from a glass, teacup, or the dipper. I guess it was an hour before we all got back to sleep."

After everyone quit laughing, Aunt Nance said, "Poor little thing, she hain't got any mommy."

When she said that I jumped down out of my chair, I stomped my foot and yelled, "I do too have a mommy. Renda is my mommy, I don't want you to say I don't have a mommy like other kids." I ran to Renda and climbed up in her lap and said, "Tell her, Renda, tell her you are my mommy."

Renda said, "If you say so, I guess I will have to agree."

Aunt Nance asked, "Why did you learn her to call you Mommy?"

"But I didn't, she just took it up herself. It plagues me sometimes when I am in a crowd and they don't know any better." She began rocking me and trying to get me to quit crying.

"Well, what's done is done, hush crying and I will take you with me to milk. My old cat has some little kittens under the barn. If you will get in a good humor with me, I'll show them to you."

Renda laughed. "It's just a homemade cry, see, there are no tears in her eyes."

"They do too, the tears are way back in my head, you just can't see 'um." I jumped down and ran to Aunt Nance, ready to go see the kittens.

They were back under the corn crib. I could not reach them. I was ready to try and drag one out with a long stick when Aunt Nance stopped me. When she finished milking the cow, she hung the bucket of warm foamy milk on a nail "drove" in the barn logs. She climbed up the ladder into the barn loft to look for eggs.

I started back to the house by myself. I was about halfway there when Aunt Nance screamed at me, "Run, honey, run to the house, that old gander sees your red stockin's and is takin' after you."

I looked behind me, and from the creek come a large gander with outspread wings and a long neck, calling insults and determining to devour me. Boy, but he sure was one big bird! I know naturalists and scientists say birds and animals cannot distinguish colors. But me and that old gander neither one nor the "tother" could read, so we did not know this. Proud as I was of my pretty red stockings, it was not them I was concerned with then; it was those little fat legs inside of those stockings I did not want that old gander to get a hold of. I started running with all power. But fast as I ran, that old gander was coming faster. He was so close behind me, that when I got inside the yard and shut the gate behind me, it smacked that old devil right in the face. It was a wonder it had not turned his bill back over his eyeballs. He did not give up that easy, but kept running up and down, jobbing his head through the fine cracks, squawking insults at me. Safe inside, I shook my fist at him and screamed back insult for insult.

All this racket and confusion brought everyone from the house. They all had a good laugh at my experience. Aunt Nance came from the barn with her bucket of milk. She untied her large white apron and shooed that old gander away from the yard fence. He went strutting back to his goose family.

She had a small basket of eggs, and right on top was a very large goose egg.

"I'll tell you, honey, how you can get even with that old gander fer scarin' the daylights out of you. I will fry you this goose egg for your breakfast."

I agreed with her real quick, for I was always interested in something good to eat, and I would doubly enjoy eating the offspring of that old gander.

Did you ever see what a plateful a large goose egg can make? It sure looks like a lot to place before a small five-year-old. I ate it all and enjoyed every bite, even sopping up the grease in which it had been fried, with one of Aunt Nance's big biscuits. I told Uncle Will they were almost as large as a turtle. He tried to get me to put one on the floor and place fire on its back and see if it was a turtle, but I knew he was just foolin'. I had other uses for that good flour bread.

That evening we had all set on the porch in the twilight. Uncle Will told us a lot of jokes and pranks that he and my father had gotten into.

"Well, you see, it was like this: Kitteneye was in jail fer something, I guess being in a fight with someone or other, or maybe fer being drunk. Anyway, he was the only one in jail at the time. Jailor Isom, that's our uncle, he was jailor then, and he had to go to Catlettsburg for some reason and he 'pointed me as deputy to take care of the jail and courthouse. Well, it was fodder pullin' time of year, and Kitteneye shore wuz worried, 'fraid Morrell and Vince and the other young'uns would not get the fodder saved in time. So I told him to go on home, and be back before Jailor Isom got back from Catlettsburg. Everything would have been fine, but you know what? The jailor came back one day before we was lookin' fer him. He come and got the keys that night. I wuz scared. I didn't know what to do, so I thought up this joke. Now Jim Smith, he had this old jenny, allus run loose all over town, and I took that jenny and put it in the cell where Kitteneye was supposed to be. I shore would have loved to have seed Uncle Isom's face when he started to give Kitteneye his breakfast next mornin'."

Aunt Nance said, "Yeah, and what about the time you all wuz up at Aunt Kate's, and you got to cuttin' up so much she told ye to take the door and leave, and you did. Took the door right off the pegs, and carried it on ye back, a way up the road. Good thing it was summertime, or poor Aunt Kate and her young'uns would have froze."

"Yeah," Uncle Will answered, "but we went back next day and hung her door back for her."

"And then I remember the time we got Matt to run through town without any clothes on. You see, me and Kitteneye made it up to do this. We had been walkin' all day and wuz real tarred, and just before we got into town, I said to Kitteneye, 'Let's all pull off and take a dip in the creek here, before we get in sight of folks' houses.' Matt agreed at once, and he did not notice that me and Kitteneye wuz a little slow in pullin' our things off. Soon as we seed that Matt wuz naked as a jay bird, Kitteneye throwed a rock in the bushes back of us and hollered, 'Look Will, there's a bear, run fer ye life!' Poor Matt, he did not take time to look, we all started out runnin', right through town we went. Matt wuz way ahead of us. Folks begin comin' to their doors to see what was goin' on. Everybody shouted, 'What's wrong, what's happenin'?'

"Kitteneye said, 'It's our brother, he has lost his mind, crazy as a bessie bug. Help us to catch him.' Soon, several men were runnin' after Matt and soon caught him. He kept trying to tell them the truth, but the more that he said, the more they thought he was crazy.

"Poor Matt, he wuz Maw's baby one. She never got over him gettin' killed like he did. Shot down, had his little girl by the hand, and he wuz buried off there amongst strangers. Maw asked fer his picture to be placed over her heart when she wuz buried." Uncle Will's voice trembled.

I did not like the way the talk had turned. I wanted to know all about my folks, but I liked the funny stories better.

Edna and Ida were catching some "lightnin' bugs" for me; I asked Uncle Will why the light was on the back end of the bug and he said, "Well, I guess they are like some folks, more interested in where they have been than where they are going."

I was sitting in Aunt Nance's lap. I knew to not try to set in Uncle Will's lap; I could ride on his back or walk holding his hand, but I could not crawl up in his lap, because he had a sore on his leg, a burn he had received when a baby. This sore never got well during his whole life.

Eva had made a "gnat smoke," by burning some old rags. Aunt Nance turned her apron up over my arms to protect them from the gnats.

I think if there was a Hall of Fame for articles of clothing, our mountain women's aprons would have to be placed in the most honored spot. Everyone wore aprons, dark ones on "weekie days," and white ones trimmed in lace or ruffles with "hamburg," all with two big pockets, tied in the back with a large bow made with the broad sash; these were the "Sunday go to meetin'" ones, but more useful than you could imagine. The pockets held their tobacco, or piece of gingerbread to be given to the children while they were at church. The pockets also came in handy to hold seeds to plant, when at work. By taking each corner of the bottom hem and tying them through the band at either side, they had a bag to use to carry anything—chips for a fire, eggs, little chickens, to pick beans, sallet (wild greens), apples. When a child was sitting in a lap, these aprons could be used as a blanket, to keep off gnats, the heat from the fire, or to hide an exposed breast when letting the child nurse.

Aunt Nance had used her apron to "flap" at that old gander, to scare him. She had used it to wipe away my tears. The apron could also be taken off and tied over the head when caught in a rain shower.

Yeah, these old-fashioned aprons sure had an important place in our lives.

Next morning when we started home, there was a disagreement on which way we would go back. We stopped at the mouth of the holler (which, by the way, is called Carter's Branch). Vada and Frances was for coming back the same way we had gone. Renda was for coming up Allum Cave because she wanted to stop at Aunt Nance Johnson's to see if she had any fall bean seed to spare. Edna wanted to come that way because they would also pass Sambo Johnson's house; Edna and Dorsie Johnson were good friends, and Edna wanted to see her.

"Well, that's two for one way and two for the other," Renda said. "Let's leave it up to Verna Mae. Just so we get home in time to do up our work agin' dark is all that really matters."

"Which is the longest way?" I asked. "Then I will get to ride more." And so it was decided that we come back home by the way of Allum Cave. It didn't seem very important at the time, but that small decision could have been a major turning point in my life. For on our way home I saw my future husband for the first time. If I had not met him then, would we have met at a later time in life? If we had not married, who would my children and grandchildren have been? I am not asking you for information. I know what I think. I just wanted to see what you believe about these things.

We stopped at Aunt Nance Johnson's and Renda got her bean seed. Aunt Nance Johnson was my father's oldest sister. The other Aunt Nance was my mother's sister. As it was close to dinner time, Aunt Nance would have us to stay and eat with her; when I learned she was having "home cured salt bacon" for dinner, they could not have dragged me away. Everyone had meat during the first of the winter, but this was a way up in the spring. Our meat had been used up for weeks.

We were soon on our way. As this was Sunday, no one was working. Every house we passed, the folks come out to the road and talked with us, asking us to come in, asking about our father, and saying, "Why don't you get down and come in and stay all night?" Nowhere in the world will you find a more friendly people than our mountain folks, willing to share their food with their friends and neighbors.

When we came to Shade Slone's house, his wife Larcy was standing at the gate with her son Elbert in her arms. We stopped to talk a few words, and one of the older girls made a comment about what a pretty baby she had.

Larcy said, "I wish you could see Willie, he is as pretty as a doll." (She always thought more of Willie than any of her other children, and as strange as it seems, none of the others ever resented this, they just accepted it as a matter of fact.)

"Willie, Willie," she hollered, "come around here and let these girls see how purty you are."

In a few minutes, around the house came a small boy. I know now he was about eight years old, but he wasn't any larger than I was at five. He was riding a stick horse, a piece of rope for a bridle. He had on a long shirt, but no pants (typical clothes for small boys then). He did not stop, just made a circle around the house in a fast lope. All I saw was that long striped shirt and a lot of white hair.

A few miles on up the road Renda said, "What's Verna Mae so quiet about, is she about to go to sleep?"

And Frances, thinking to tease me, said, "No, I guess she is thinking about her feller she seed back there."

I angrily replied, "He is too my feller." And from that day until this one, "he is too my feller." It took me almost twelve years to make him realize it.

CHAPTER 3

When I first awoke that morning I knew it was going to be a Very Special Day. I have always loved those few seconds when I am not quite asleep and yet not fully awake.

I tried to recall why I was so happy about today, as I listened for each one of my family. I never felt quite secure until I knew where they all were.

Renda was getting breakfast, I could smell the coffee. Papa was at the barn, probably feeding Little Beck; I knew he was happy, because I could hear him singing "Amazing Grace." I heard Vada calling "Old Silk." She would soon return with an overflowing bucket of warm fresh milk. Frances was feeding the hens. That accounted for everyone, except Edna. I opened my eyes to see if she was still in bed. And at once I knew why today was going to be the happiest day of my life.

There on the back of a chair hung my new dress, long bloomers to match "with real 'lastic" at the top, and bottom of each leg, just long enough so about one inch showed below the hem line of the dress, new patent leather strapped slippers, and the all-despised white stockings. I had put them there last night. For today was going to be my first day of really and truly school.

I had gone to school with my sisters ever since I could re-member, if Papa wasn't at home. That was the only way they could get to go. The teacher was an old friend, so he allowed this. Often they would take a quilt and make me a pallet in the corner, out of the way, and I would sleep. The teacher would sometimes give me a piece of chalk and I would try to write, all over the place.

Every child in the district big enough to walk was taken to school on the Last Day. It was a well observed custom for the teacher to treat the scholars with stick candy on the Last Day. They also told the ones who would be moved up a grade next year. Only the eighth-graders had a test, and they had to go to Hindman to take it. They might have a Spelling Bee. The braver ones would say "pieces."

But this day was not to be like that. Today my name would be on the roll call. The teacher would call my name and I would shout, "Present!" Just like everyone else.

The week before Papa rode Little Beck to Hindman and got our books for us. Edna had a whole armful. I had only one. I already knew all the pictures in it. I also had a big red-back tablet, and a penny pencil.

I jumped out of bed and began to put my new things on. Renda heard me and called, "No, not until you wash and eat." And I answered, "Oh, well."

I don't think I eat any. I was just too happy.

"Please Renda, can't I take my dinner, like the other kids do? Can I?"

"No, you cannot, we live too close, and anyway, you might get hurt playing at noon."

"All right, but I am going to bring everyone home with me that I can beg to come."

"I don't care, I will have aplenty for everyone. Now later on I might let you take your dinner in a bucket on wash day, because you know I am so busy on wash—"

"Yeah, I know," I sang, "Wash Day, Wash Day, Snack Day, Snack Day."

Soon I was dressed and kissed her goodbye, and was on my way.

Some of the larger boys were raising the flag. We all lined up and repeated "The Allegiance." Then we marched to our seats, and before sitting down we sang "America."

The teacher read one or two chapters from his Bible. Then classes began.

Those teachers must have had the skill of a chess player, to maneuver the classes to include three or four separate subjects for all eight grades.

True, we only had two "privies," marked "Boys" and "Girls." Anyone wanting to be excused raised his hand, and receiving a yes nod from the teacher, placed his book in the door. As long as the book was there, no one else was allowed to leave. Of course, if anyone tried to take advantage of this privilege and stayed too long, the teacher would notice and send someone after them, or go to the door and call his or her name.

There was a "drilled well" in the yard and a bucket and dipper. No one was allowed to drink from the dipper. A lot had those little collapsible tin cups, and some made paper cups by folding a sheet of paper.

We had a large open fireplace, and a coal house filled each year with coal. The teacher usually gave someone a quarter a week to come early and build a fire. I remember the house as always being cozy and warm. The seats were wooden and very hard. The back of each seat made a desk for the one sitting behind. They were placed in long rows the length of the school room, facing the teacher's desk. It was not made of logs and it did have a "double laid" floor, meaning there were no cracks, and there were three glass windows on each side. The back end was painted black, to be used as a blackboard.

I have very pleasant memories of my first year at school, and I was very proud of it.

Do you blame me for crying when thirty-five years later I sat in my own living room and heard over nationwide television a description of Caney? "A wilderness," a "God-forsaken place," with no schools. None of the folks could read or write. Living in small log cabins, with dirt floors and no windows, without sense enough to bathe or wear shoes!

And when the program went on to say that even then (the middle fifties), Caney still had no roads, no mechanics and no cars, I wondered what that was sitting in my garage, that the salesman had sold me the year before, for a new Chevrolet truck.

The first year I went to school was the last year that building was to be used as a schoolhouse. The next year a new, much larger one was built on the hill near the Summer Slone Graveyard at the mouth of Trace.

The old schoolhouse was turned into a dwelling house and wasn't torn down until twenty years later.

The new schoolhouse was much larger. Four large rooms and one small room. A coal furnace was supposed to heat the place, but I remember, when it was so cold, we had to wear our heavy coats inside.

The largest room even had a stage with two dressing rooms, a place to "put on programs." We also had plenty of "cloak rooms," a new thing for us. I did not like the change, for one thing, there was no playground. We still had the two little houses, one marked "Boys," one "Girls," but they were so far away that by the time you got there, you had forgotten what you came for.

We no longer had the close and friendly relationship. We were now among strangers. We were not all kin folks, as before.

My teacher was one of Mrs. Lloyd's "fotched on" teachers. I don't remember her name. I do remember a few things. She had a beautiful white marble paper weight on her desk. It might have been a copy of a classic sculpture. Our parents were scandalized when they learned "the teacher had a naked woman on her desk." Some of them "sent her word" if she wanted to keep it, she had better hide it.

We were all scared to death of her. When asked a question, even if we knew the answer, we would rather murmur a "I don't know" than risk her ridicule, or that blank look on her face, when we used a typical hillbilly word or expression, that she had no way of understanding.

One day we were talking about flags, and we mentioned the Flag Rock (a high rock on top of a hill on Short Fork). It is supposed to be the highest point anywhere in Knott County. We still call it the Flag Rock. A long time ago some man visited Caney and placed a flag on a high pole on top of this rock. It did not stay very long, for an old man climbed up there and took the flag down, and used it to make himself a pair of long-handle underwear. I guess we all have a warm place in our hearts for our flag, but that flag kept that old man warm "all over" for many a cold winter.

Some say the man who left the flag was John Fox, Jr. I have been told that he did visit Caney once, gathering material for one of his books, I guess. He stayed one night with my father, and the next night with Henry C. Short. After he left they found some of the notes he had lost. In describing the night he had spent with Papa, he stated that a snake got into bed with him. My father got very mad when he read this. He said, "Yeah, a snake was in my bed, a two-legged snake. I have my 'pinion of a man that will eat a feller's grub and then tell lies on him. And I fed his horse, too!" That was unusual, because our mountain folks always took feed with them to feed their horses when they went to stay all night.

Anyway, however the flag got there, we were telling our teacher about what had been told, and I said, "Papa told me you could use a spy glass and see this flag from London."

The teacher laughed, "Your father does not know any geography. It would be ridiculous to say you could see so far."

"Papa knows everything," I proudly retorted.

I could hardly wait until I got home to reaffirm my belief in what I thought Papa had told me.

"Didn't you tell me you could see the flag upon Flag Rock from London if you used a spy glass?"

"No honey, I said from Hindman, and you can 'cause I have. It's true I don't know as much geography as your teacher, but I do know that London is in Old England."

"Is London ferder away than Hindman?" I asked.

"Yeah, a whole lot ferder. You see, London is across 'The Waters.' And that's where all our forefathers were from."

"Well, I don't like to be made fun of. Why didn't she explain it to me like you did?"

"I 'spect she ort to, but you can keep from being laughed *at*, always laugh *with* someone. Never laugh *at* anyone or let them laugh at you, always laugh with them, it's much easier. If you can learn to laugh at your ownself, it will help you over many a hard spot in life."

I have always remembered that and have taught my children the same lesson. I agree I am not as perfect as my father was, in laughing at myself, but I am still trying. And it has made life a lot easier and happier.

Another thing our new teacher taught us was drawing. She would have us to copy the outline of leaves, and to color the pictures of apples, grapes, birds, and so on. I loved this very much. I never got to be very good at it, but I sure enjoyed it. The parents objected to this. They said it was a waste of good paper, and they did not send their young'uns to school "fer sich foolishness."

Willie did not go to the same school that I did. His parents lived in another district. I wish we had gone to school together when we were small.

I made that same statement to one of his nieces once, when we were sharing the same ward in the Whitesburg Hospital, and she said:

"You better be glad you did not, for he was one grain the meanest little boy I ever seed. Why, he would tie our hair to the back of our seats; you know how little girls wore them, two long plaits. Will, he would tie them together to the seat, and when we got up, it would pert nigh jerk our heads off. One day he took all our dinner buckets and carried them up to the top of a big sycamore tree, that one in the schoolyard, and he hung them on a limb, away up in the top of that tree," she laughed.

"Well," I said, "I guess he got a whipping about every day."

"No," she mused, "come to think of it, I don't recollect of him ever getting whipped. He was too slick to get caught, for one thing. And then it's funny, but everone liked him, even the teacher. Mean as he was, he just had a nature everbody liked."

She also told me of a dog Willie took to school with him, that he had taught to play ball. When the boys were playing "Round Town" or "Ante Over," the dog would retrieve the ball and bring it to Willie, thus helping them to win the game.

CHAPTER 4

It was real hot that day, my pencil was hard to hold. My hands were so wet with moisture. We had already "took up books" after the afternoon recess. The only break in the routine was when some cows had gathered in the road near the school and the teacher had asked some of the older boys to chase them away.

There were no "stock laws," and cattle and hogs often became a nuisance to the school. Everyone knew the cows, who they belonged to, even what their names were. So it was easy to start them in the right direction toward home. My father said it was a good thing the hogs did run around the schoolhouse sometimes, because they "eat up" the snakes.

I knew something was wrong when one of our close neighbors rode up to the door and got off his mule and asked the teacher to come outside. Although he spoke in a low voice, I heard him say, "Kitteneye wants his kids to come home. Renda got snake bit a while ago." I never waited to hear more, but started running as fast as I could.

Renda was laying on the bed, her eyes were closed, she was breathing so shallow I thought she was dead. I ran to her bedside and "grobbed" her hand.

"Oh Mommy, oh Mommy, don't die, you can't die, not like my other mommy did. Please, God, don't let my mommy die."

Papa came and gathered me up in his arms and said, "Hush, honey, she hain't going to die. She will be all right."

By that time the other girls had got home. Everyone began speaking in a whisper.

"Where did it bite her?" someone asked. Papa pulled the sheet up and showed us her feet. One was swollen twice its normal size and already turning blue. "Here," he said. "Twice just above the ankle. Thank God it was not a rattler, hit was a copperhead, and that's bad enough. We was pickin' berries. Good thing I was with her. I tried to draw all the 'pizen' out, but I was so 'dad blame' mad, I took time to kill the snake before I seed to her."

It wasn't long before all the neighbors began arriving. Everyone brought something: a jar of honey, a homemade pie, some gingerbread, a kettle of chicken and dumplings (still hot from the stove).

All came in and asked how she was. Papa told them, "As well as could be expected."

Each one had a different remedy for curing snake bite. Some said turpentine, some tobacco, some boiled oatmeal, but all agreed on one thing—moonshine whiskey.

My brother asked, "Paw, did you get any whiskey for her?"

Papa answered, "Yes, I used a whole quart."

"What! A whole quart? If you give her that much, why, that could kill her! No wonder she hain't spoke yet."

"No, you fool," he retorted, "I poured some of hit on her leg, I washed my mouth out with some, and drunk the rest myself. How did you think I got strength enough to carry her to the house?"

The neighbors never asked what needed to be done, but went about "doing up the work." One man chopped some wood, someone watered and fed the mule. One of the women got the milk bucket and went to milk the cow, another gathered the eggs.

After supper they all gathered together in the living room, and swapped tales about snakes.

One man told about how he and his brother had chopped a

snake in two while hoeing corn. Thinking it was dead they let it go. When they were pulling fodder, months later, they found it still alive. It had cured up, but had not grown another tail.

A woman told how she had killed one that had swallowed a gourd egg, or "hen fooler," a small round gourd, about the size of an egg. Women raised these and used them for nest eggs. "That one had fooled a snake, instead of a hen."

Some women spoke of how they had "marked" their babies by killing a snake when they were "carrying" them. I remember wondering about that. Why would anyone want to kill a snake with their baby in their arms, and what had they marked the baby with—the blood?

Before I had time to ask Papa about this, some of the neighbors began to gather up their children to go home. As each one left, they would say to Papa, "Kitteneye, if there is anything we can do to help out, just let us know. We'll help out any way we can."

Two or three of the folks were going to stay all night. They would take turns "setting up" with Papa, while he took care of my sister. When Papa saw I was determined to stay up all night too, he asked one of my brothers to take me home with them. They both had children near my own age. I did not want to leave my sister, but after being assured they would take good care of her, and would let me know if she became worse, I was talked into going.

Renda got better, but it was six weeks before she could walk. The neighbors were true to their word. They came each day and helped with the work. Bringing something with them, whatever they had to spare or what they thought we could use. They knew whenever they needed help, Papa would do the same for them.

CHAPTER 5

I remember the first time I came in contact with people — who, to me, were from another world — and bitterly learned we hillbillies had a status rating somewheres between the animals and plants. I had always been, and still am, satisfied with where God placed me on this earth. I lived in a wonderful world where I was a princess, ruler of all my family, with a love shared and enjoyed by all.

Of course, even at that early age, I knew there were people living outside these hills. I knew their ways were different from ours, but I did not envy them. Among our neighbors there were no social differences; we were all equal. Some had more "worldly wealth," but were always willing to share with the less fortunate ones. Did the Good Book not say, "If you have two coats, give one to your neighbor"?

It was summertime and school was out, so I was spending a few weeks with my sister Frances. She could take care of me, and I would help her by playing with her son, Clemons, who was a little over a year old.

Her and her husband, Travis Jacobs, lived about two miles below what is now the Alice Lloyd College.

The day I am writing about was a real hot day. Frances had just given me and Clemons a bath and put us on some clean clothes. She sent me outside to play, so she could get the baby to take a nap. I had pulled my shoes off, and was sitting in a small pile of sand, pouring the sand over my toes, a pastime I always liked.

I heard some horses coming long before I saw them. The squeak, squeak of the saddles and the thump, thump of the hooves caught my attention. I ran to the gate and peeped through the fence to see who they were.

I knew they were strangers. At first I thought it was two men (I had never seen a woman in "riding pants"). I did not know it was impolite to stare at anyone, but I guess I would have anyway, I was so astonished.

The two riders came up to the gate and the man said, "Could you please bring this lady a drink of water?" His voice was strange, and when I did not answer at once, he slowly repeated what he had said, in a much louder voice, speaking as though I was deaf.

I said, "Shore, get down and come in. I'll go get you some water." I had been taught to always invite anyone into your home.

He said, "No, you bring the water out here." It was not a request, but a demand. I did not understand, there was something about his voice that made me feel very uncomfortable, as if I had done something wrong, and needed to be ashamed.

I looked at the lady. She was smiling, not a friendly smile, but more of a smirk, and she said softly, "Please?"

I went into the house and told Frances what I wanted. She filled a glass water pitcher with good cool water, and giving me one of her nice glasses, warned me to be careful and not fall, and while she said, "Be nice," I hurried back.

The horses were stomping and prancing, wanting to get started on their journey. I was scared of them, but I still went up close to the lady's horse and reached the pitcher and glass up to her. I remember the perfume smell, more repellent to me than the odor of leather and horse.

Again the man ordered, "Fill the glass with the water and give it to the lady." After giving her the water I turned to him and asked, "Do you want some, too?" And he angrily answered, "I do not," and then turning to the woman, he began talking about me as if I was not present. "You never know about these people. The water may not be clean. Their toilets may be near their wells, some even use water from the creeks." I knew this was not so, but I had been taught to not tell a "grown-up" that they were lying.

"I guess you want pay for bringing the water?" he said, turning to me.

"Oh no," I answered, shocked that he even suggested such a thing. "My Paw would skin me alive if I was to charge anybody for water. He says water is a free gift from God, and I am pleased to give it to you all."

"Well," he said, and reaching into his pocket he took out a nickel, and tossed it toward me, "you can say I am paying you for bringing the water to us. Here, you can buy you some candy when you go to town."

I burst out in a very loud laugh. "What do you find so funny?" the man asked.

"Why, to think that anyone would go all the way to town, just to spend one little bitty nickel," I laughed. I did not pick the coin up, but left it there on the ground. The man's face turned very red, and I could see the woman was trying to keep from laughing.

He turned to her and said, "Look there in the back yard. How disgusting."

I did not know what the word meant, but there was no mistaking his tone of voice.

"Oh, you mean our chicken coop?"

"No," he said, "it's what you have on the chicken coop. Do you know what that is?"

"Shore," I said, "that's a piece of a old wored out flag."

"You mean you knew that it was the American flag, and still you used it to cover your chickens?"

"Shore, we have a flag at school. We have a tall flagpole, and we give the flag salute every morning. We also have one for the post office. My father is the postmaster," I added proudly.

"Do you know what you are supposed to do with a flag when it becomes worn out, and must be replaced? You must burn it."

"But, Mister," I cried, "that would cause a awful smell, and would do no one any good."

"Folks who care anything about their country would not use a flag as you have." Then he turned to his friend and finished, "That's what you can expect from these backward people."

I did not know that my sister had come out on the porch, until I heard her voice cut through the air, "I guess I love my country as much as anyone. But I don't think any government's going to care if I raise chickens or not. That old flag has kept many a gang of doodles from getting wet when it rains, warm when it's cold, and a shade when it's hot, and God willing, I will raise several more. It's none of your business what I do, and I would take it kindly, sir, if you would go on and attend to your ownself."

My sister Frances sure had a way of cutting the dirt out from under your feet when she was mad. You would never know by looking at her that there was anything wrong.

Little did she know that day, that the little baby she was holding in her arms would serve over thirty-five years of his life defending the American flag, and that his son would one day pay the "Supreme Price" while in the Armed Service.

This same summer that I stayed with my sister Frances, I was to make friends with someone who was to be an influence over my whole life.

Dellie Slone was a close neighbor. She lived in a large, two-story, white house, with her two brothers and two sisters, all grown-up. Their father had died and their mother remarried. Her mother had moved to her new husband's farm. Dellie and her brothers and sisters had remained on their father's farm.

Many times Frances would take Clemons and me, and leave

us with Dellie, when she needed a baby sitter for us. I would take care of Clemons, but I wasn't old enough to be trusted all alone.

I have not got words enough to describe Dellie. She was one of the most kind, unselfish persons I ever knew. She spent her whole life working hard and helping other people, never thinking of herself. I know there are many people who can remember many nice things she did for them—not just her relatives, but anyone who needed help. She was always ready. She was a very small woman in size, but her heart was as big as "all outdoors."

One night her brothers and sisters were going to be away from home, and she asked Frances if I could spend the night with her, as she would be lonesome all alone. I loved her and felt proud she wanted me. After supper, she popped us some corn, and then brought out her quilt pieces and began working on them. I showed so much interest in what she was doing that she got me a needle and thread, cut me a pattern, and started me on a hobby that has continued for a lifetime. That was the first of several hundred quilts I have made.

Dellie Slone never married, but she was a second mother to many kids. Just a few weeks before she died, I went to visit her, and she gave me some house flowers, which I still have.

One evening, Dellie laid down on her bed to rest, and that kind heart gave up and quit beating. She went on to live with Jesus, where the record of her many good deeds had gone on before.

Many people ask me if I remember the first quilt I ever made, and I say, "Sure, I can remember starting it, but I don't know if I ever finished it. A eight-pointed star pieced on paper." When kids ask me to show them how to make quilts, I sometimes hesitate, giving the excuse that I don't have time and don't want to be bothered. Then I remember Dellie and the patience she had teaching me. I get ashamed of myself, and I try to be like her.

CHAPTER 6

Memorial Day does not mean just May 30th to the people of Caney and surrounding hollers and branches. In the past, our ancestors started a tradition, that we faithfully and cheerfully carry on. It probably started in the early days, when we had no preachers, except the circuit rider, who only visited us once a year. So, our dead were buried with no funerals, until this once a year visit. Then everyone met on the graveyard, and a funeral for all our loved ones that had passed on the past year was performed.

Each family that bears the same name, or claims to a common ancestor, has a family graveyard. Ours, the Summer Slone, is at the mouth of Trace Fork on Caney. Here are over ninety graves. All, except three, are directly my relatives, and those three are indirectly attached to us.

The Tripletts have a family graveyard in the head of Hollybush, the Jacobs' are on Ball Point. The Watts' on Watts Fork, the Shorts' on Short Fork, and etc. The Jimmy Graveyard is a combination of three different plots, where a different set of Slones have their final resting place.

So we have a Memorial Service for each graveyard every year, at different dates. Ours, the Summer Slone's, is the first Sunday after the first Saturday in June. This date was chosen because it is close to Grandma Frankie's birthday, which was also the day Jesus called her home.

In my childhood, this day was looked forward to much more than Christmas, and still is a very important day. It's also a family reunion, as all the relatives from far and near come to visit. We also have a dinner, where everyone is invited, plenty to eat and lots of fun. Of course, we now have more conveniences than our grandparents had, such as refrigeration, gas stoves, and paper plates, but we do not have any more to eat, nor more enjoyment. We try to stick to the old traditions as much as we can.

In the old days we would start planning for Memorial (pronounced Morriel Day by us) early in the spring, when we planted our beans and potatoes. We tried to rush our vegetables so they would be ready to eat by the first of June. I remember also, we had a June Apple that was ready for green apple pies. You never eat anything in this world as good as those pies.

All the neighbor men would decide on a given day during the week before, and meet at the graveyard to "clean off" the graves. With axes, hoes, and shovels, they would cut weeds, briars, sprouts around the fence, mend the grave houses putting on new shingles, straightening up the tombstones, and build a "stand." The stand was a platform with a roof, but open sides. Here the preachers and older people would sit. Logs were laid crosswise to form seats for everyone else around this stand. I love to attend these "outside" services. You feel so much closer to God. I have been in some fine, costly churches, but nothing compares with these crude, simple, wooden places of worship. Did Jesus not preach in the open?

Each family rivaled in trying to have the most to eat, trying to have as much work done as they could, before the visitors began arriving. They had to come either by horseback or "jolt wagon." Those that lived far away came Friday or Saturday, and stayed all night. The men folks in our family would have large baskets of corn already "shucked" to feed the mules. They would pick out their largest ears of corn, as a matter of pride.

My cousin, Mary Owens Sparkman, says she can remember her mother filling a large barrel with gingerbread, placing it in the smokehouse, where the spilled salt from the cured meat would keep it damp and moist. She throwed a quilt over the barrel. This way the gingerbread would have kept fresh for weeks. Except, the crowd ate it up long before then. Did you ever eat a "stack cake" made from alternate layers of gingerbread and homemade apple butter? One of the few dishes we still try to have at our Memorial dinners. That and our "shucky beans."

This was also one time of the year when everyone had new clothes. Most all the women folks made their dresses and bonnets. The young girls wanted new hats. I remember how important these new hats were, with their shiny bangles, and bright-colored ribbons and feathers. The owners would slip them into an empty pillow case and hang them from a nail on the wall, when not in use.

It was the buying of my first new hat that caused me to meet my future husband for the second time. Again, I ask you, was it fate or chance?

Father had gone to Uncle Melton Owens' and bought a new hat for each of the older girls, — Renda, Vada and Frances — but he could not find mine and Edna's size. When he saw how disappointed we were, he told us we could go over to Uncle Caney's store and see if he had some. Uncle Caney lived at Hindman, so that meant we would get to stay all night. When I heard this, I did not care if I got a hat or not. I wanted that trip more than anything in the world.

So, early Wednesday morning, we started walking toward Hindman, an eight-mile walk. Too much for a six- or seven-year-old child? Not then, everyone walked and thought nothing of it. If we got hungry, we would stop at someone's house about dinner time and be assured of a welcome invitation to share the family meal.

I don't remember too much about the trip or spending the night. Uncle Caney and Aunt Susie lived in a large, white house, with an "upstairs," close beside his store building. I do remember one thing, his grandson, Jay Patton, was staying with him. It was the first time I had ever seen anyone in a wheel chair. At first,

I was kind of awed at him, but we soon became friends, and he made me know that he did not want me to feel sorry for him. He even let me push his chair for him.

Edna helped with the chores and dishes, but me, I stayed with Uncle Caney in the store, and ate enough candy to stuff a mule. When it came time to buy the hats, I found just the one I wanted. I remember that hat as if it was yesterday: a beautiful, yellow wide brim, a circle of roses and cherries, so real you wanted to eat them, a large ribbon hanging down in the back that bounced when I walked.

My sister Edna's hat was just as pretty, I guess, but I do not remember hers, but I do remember the price. Hers was seventy-five cents and mine was fifty. I did not like this and began to grumble about it. When Uncle Caney learned that I was mad, and wanted a hat that cost as much or more than Edna's, he said he could fix that. He would let her have hers for fifty and I could pay the seventy-five for mine. That satisfied me, but I could not understand why Father laughed so when I told him.

For some reason we decided we would come back up Allum Cave. Allum Cave is so named because of a large deposit of alum under a cave close to the "holler." In old times our folks gathered and used this alum for medicine, and mixed it with their roots and barks to obtain the colors they wanted to dye their yarn.

There is a large, flat rock close to the side of the road. Sam Johnson lived in a house on one side of the road, my future father-in-law on the other. As Edna and I came up this path, Willie and his cousin was sitting on this large rock, fishing for minnows in the holler. They had a bent pin hook and a "sapplin'" pole with a twine line.

We saw them before they saw us. I knew who Willie was at once, although it had been over a year since I had last met him. I wanted to be real friendly, but I sure went at it wrong.

"How fer is it about a mile and a half up this road?" I smart-elicked.

His cousin pulled his hat down over his eyes and never spoke.

Willie waited until he got his fish off the hook, and then looked up with a smile ready to answer me. As the smile slowly changed to a frown, you could tell that it was only then he really paid any attention to the meaning of my words.

"Two measures of a damn fool," he said. "Lay down and measure yourself and see."

His cousin snickered and my sister laughed out loud.

Ever since that day he has never learned to take a joke from me, and I have never had sense enough to quit trying.

As we came on up the road, even Edna began to feel sorry for me.

"Is he still your feller?" she asked, and I slowly answered, "Yeah, I guess so. Anyway it was my fault."

In the hurry and hustle of getting ready for Memorial, I forgot what Willie had said. No, to tell the truth I did not forget, I just pushed it to the back of my mind and the hurt went away, and I could laugh.

We did more house cleaning and cooking preparing for that one day, than we do now in a whole year. We cleaned and cleaned the already clean house.

Of course, I did not do very much, except get in the way. They pushed me out of their way so much that Father made a refrain, "Verna Mae, you're in the way, go and play."

Edna and I went to the creek banks and hunted nice white sand rocks, then taking a hammer, we crushed the rocks into sand. This was sprinkled all over the "puncheon" floors, and with a large, homemade, scrub broom they made that floor shine like new money. I could not understand why we could not just scoop up the sand from the creek, but Renda said it was not clean, and anyway, that's how "we allus done it."

We took all the chairs (bark-bottom chairs my father had made) to the creek bank, and with large rags and the beat-up sand, we scrubbed and rinsed them over and over.

All the quilts and bed clothes were either washed or hung out in the sun to make them smell nice. And, oh boy, is it some job to wash quilts! And how hard it was to wring that water out! We 'most always took them to the creek to "wrinch" them. Father usually helped with this job.

Mary Sparkman's mother, my aunt, took yards and yards of muslin cloth that she sewed together, and tacked each side to the floor of the loft. She then filled this with corn shucks, making a bed about thirteen or fourteen feet long, and about six feet wide. The men and boys would sleep there side by side.

The large fireplace was cleaned of all the cinders, then white-washed with clay gathered from a clay bank found along the creek. The door and window facings were also treated this way, and woe unto anyone that forgot and leaned against them, for the clay would come off on their clothes.

Large bunches of wild flowers and leaves were put in jars, or buckets of water, and placed in the grate and on the hearth.

The walls and ceiling of each room were lined with clean newspapers or pages from magazines, pasted up, one at a time, with paste made from cooked flour. The yard, which was free of any grass, and beaten hard from use, was swept clean. All the many, many flowers surrounding and along the yard fence were weeded and trimmed.

All the silverware (which with us did not have any silver about it) was scoured with wood ashes saved from the cook stove. This was one job I could do all by myself, and I enjoyed doing it.

The stove, and even the stove pipes, were treated to a "blackin'" of soot mixed with butter or lard. Sure, we "made do" with what we had, but I think we deserve praise, not ridicule.

Maybe I should tell here how we washed our clothes. The day before, wood was gathered for a fire to heat the water. The water was either carried from the creek, or drawn from the well or spring. A wash tub or "mink" kettle was placed on two rocks, with a space between them where the fire was "builded." The wash place was sometimes near the creek, or in the yard. In winter we heated our water on the stove and placed our tubs on chairs in the kitchen. The clothes were rubbed on a washboard, after being smeared with homemade lye soap. We washed them through "two waters." That is, washing each piece separately in one tub of water, putting it in another tub and going through the same process again. The "white clothes" were then put in a tub of water, in which a small amount of lye and lots more soap was added, placed on the fire and allowed to boil. They were taken from this water and rinsed through two more tubs of water, "bluing" being added to the last. Then some were starched. The starch was made by cooking flour mixed with water, and straining it through a cloth. The colored clothes were not boiled, just rinsed twice. Then all the clothes were hung one at a time with clothespins on the clothesline to dry. You think this was a lot of work? Remember they yet must be ironed.

The irons — big, heavy, clumsy things — were heated on the stove or fireplace. The handle also got hot, so you must have a rag to hold them with, and one to clean them before smoothing them over your clothes, and we did not have ironing boards, but a folded quilt on the table or floor. I somehow feel guilty with my automatic washer and dryer and drip-dry clothes. I bought my first wringer washer and electric iron in 1950, when my fourth child was six years old. But I am proud to say, my children went to school with very clean clothes. Of course, they did not come back clean.

But, with all this cleaning, cooking, and making new clothes, the corn must be hoed, the vegetables taken care of, and the chores of feeding, milking, etc. Our folks did not feel overburdened, work came as natural to them as breathing. They knew no other life and wanted no other. They were happy and content. I wish with all my heart I could go back to those days. The contentment, the enjoyment of a simple life, the togetherness of family, when the day was not measured by the hours, and a neighbor's worth was not judged by his bank account, and no one envied the other. We had bad times and troubles (like the constant battle against flies and bed bugs), but the good outweighed the bad.

CHAPTER 7

My husband's parents were very different in temperament and personality than my folks, but just as great in their way.

My mother-in-law, Larcy (who was also a Slone before she was married), was the daughter of Isom (at one time there were eight Isom Slones living on Caney) and Pharisee Slone. Her father and mother had separated when she and her brother were very young. Her father remarried. Her mother raised her and her three sisters and two brothers. Ferry, as everyone called her, worked very hard to support her children. She lived to be very old. In fact, she outlived almost all her children.

Larcy, in growing up, had worked as a hired girl for different families. She had stayed a lot with Merland Slone. She had thus learned to be a very good housekeeper, and one of the best cooks in the whole world (I don't except any). Her biscuits were a meal in themselves. As I had stayed at the Community Center for so many years, I did not know how to cook for a family. My mother-in-law taught me how to cook. Of course, I never became the expert she was, but my husband could not use the phrase so many men do, "You don't cook like my mother."

Larcy was one of the few women whose extra pounds added to her appearance, not taking from it. I guess I loved her so much that she would have been pretty to me anyway. I think she filled the place of the mother I never had. She sensed this and accepted me as one of her own, even scolding me along with her own girls. She was so full of love and understanding that she seldom scolded anyone. She so loved to laugh. I have seen her get so tickled over some prank or mischievous doing of the children that she would shake all over, and the tears would stream down her face.

She really used the hillbilly way of talking. I remember one word in particular. She pronounced the word child as "chal." My children loved to get her to repeat this word, and she would pretend to let them trick her into saying it.

She was such a jolly, lovable person that you would never dream she had suffered so many heartaches. The mother of fourteen children, seven of them dying when babies. When two of her sons, Elbert and Ranson, were drafted into the Army during World War II and sent overseas just a few years after her husband's death, the emotional strain was too great for her, and she had to spend a few months in a mental hospital. Although her mind recovered, physically she was never well again. A few years later she died from a kidney infection. One Christmas morning, at about the hour she had so many times in the past awakened to fill the children's stockings with goodies, Jesus called her home.

Larcy did not care to tell anyone that I was her favorite daughter-in-law. But I did not find so much favor in the eyes of my father-in-law. Yet, if he had lived until I became more grownup, I think he would have liked me better.

He was a very conservative, serious person, who seldom smiled, and he took plenty of time to consider the answer to any question (no matter how small), before committing himself. He did not like to do hard work, but he was not at all lazy. He just thought it better to make a living by the way he managed his affairs. He had a real talent for trading, swapping, and bartering. Buying something from one neighbor and selling to another, always with a small profit for himself, seemed a much needed service to the neighborhood.

In the spring of each year he would go to the bank and borrow fifty or sixty dollars (a large amount at that time), and with this loan he would buy the few things that demanded cash money. By making his small deals, by Fall he would have enough to repay the bank, and a few dollars for Winter essentials.

Many of Mrs. Lloyd's friends from up North sent used or second-hand clothing. These were sold in a store called, "The Exchange." It got this name because in the beginning, when Mrs. Lloyd was just establishing her school, the creek people (residents of Caney) exchanged their surplus vegetables and fruit for these clothes. The clothes are now sold for money.

My father-in-law would buy a lot of these clothes and then go from house to house "peddlin'" them, again making a small profit (also being a big help to the people who did not have the time or chance to go to the Exchange themselves, especially mothers with young children).

On his weekly visit to the community he also visited the school library. How that man loved to read! He would sit for hours — on the porch in summer and by the fire in winter — reading, unmindful of the noise around him. He loved novels, but his favorites were autobiographies of the Presidents or great men of history. He was a farseeing man, very seldom speaking his deep thoughts. When Willie was in the CCC Camps his father wrote and told him, "Son, come home. The United States is preparing for war."

He was a very brave man. Once in his younger days, he was out drinking with several men when a dispute developed into gun play. Shade was shot and the men, thinking he was dead, ran off, leaving their hats. When Shade came to he took time to cut up all their hats with his pocket knife, then, following them, he really gave them a run for their money. The men thought they had shot him through the head, but the bullet had only gone through the flesh part of his jaw.

He was one of the few people at that time who had cancer. He first took the flux, a contagious stomach disorder with diarrhea. This kept lingering on until cancer developed.

There was very little that doctors could do for cancer. He lived for almost a year. He gave himself over into the hands of Jesus, joined the church, but never became physically able to be baptized. A few weeks before he died, he refused to take the morphine drugs the doctors had prescribed for him, saying he wanted to know when death came, and he thought it was just for him to suffer if Jesus had suffered for him. I think this took a very brave man to endure that much pain and refuse the morphine.

There was a terrible rainstorm threatening the evening he died, and his last thoughts were of his children. He looked up and asked, "Are all the children in out of the rain?"

I think the grandchildren have ancestors to be very proud of, and I hope they never forget that.

In the mountains visitors are always welcome. No invitation is necessary. It is just taken as a matter of fact that when you go to someone's house you will be welcome, and asked to share dinner or supper—as the case might be—with the family. In fact, it would have been counted as an insult to not be so asked.

Shade and Larcy sure "fed out a lot." I don't remember ever going there but what I would find a house full of folks. Some people would take advantage of this custom, and outwear their welcome. I know many a time Larcy would be so tired and worn out from a day's work in the field, "doing up the work," feeding, milking, getting supper, and washing the dishes, when, just as she would have her children tucked in for the night, here would come a whole family, mother and four or five kids. So, Larcy would go and feed these extra ones, washing the dishes again, then "making beds down," by placing feather beds and quilts on the floor, she would make room for them. She never complained, was always smiling and making them feel welcome. She really enjoyed having them. Myself, I would have thrown a fit.

Watts Fork is, of course, the home of the Watts'. Squire Watts and his wife, Sally, moved here from Lions Fork.

Sally Watts was a midwife, or "Granny Woman" as we called them (in fact, her name is on my birth certificate). Watts Fork is just across the hill from Caney. When Squire divided his land with his boys (a mountain custom), John Watts got the head of the holler, Woleary, next, and Hiram third. The place belonging to Woleary is of most interest to me, for in the early twenties Shade, my father-in-law, bought this farm and moved there.

Up until then Shade had been a renter. In the mountains there is no social distinction made between a landlord and his renters. A good renter is well thought of. The renter was given use of a house, garden patch, and pasture. He could "tend" as much corn as he wanted to, giving the landowner one third of the corn raised. If fortunate enough to have some of the few acres of bottom land, then the price was one half of the corn. The renter usually took pride in the upkeep of his home. Of course, there were some renters "who were not worth their salt." Shade was a well liked renter with a large family that raised plenty of corn for himself and the landowner. But he longed to own his own farm.

Sometime in the early twenties he got his chance. He paid for his farm in a very interesting way.

At that time the people who were sentenced to jail terms had to work for the county while imprisoned, to pay their fine (another good law of the past no longer enforced). I think if some of the folks who go to jail had to work, they would not be so eager to get in. Many prisons today have a higher standard of living than the taxpayers who maintain the prisons.

The county had promised to build a new county road across the hill, connecting Watts Fork and Caney. This was very badly needed by the people of both places. It gave us a wagon road to Hindman, and the residents of Watts Fork a route to the Community Center and school.

So, Shade got the job of overseer. He was sworn in as assistant jailer. He boarded the prisoners for one dollar each, and received two dollars each for each day's work they did on building the road. They were most all friends and neighbors of his, not desperate criminals, so they stayed in his home with his wife and children. Most of the food was grown on the farm, so most all the money could be saved. This way he soon had money enough to pay for his farm.

Lots of times he would let the men go home on the weekends to visit their families, trusting them to return. Of course, this did count on their sentences. Only once did a man betray his trust. When this man failed to return on Monday morning in time to work, Shade waited until dark and, taking some more men with him, he went to get him. They surrounded the cabin. When Shade called to him and asked him to give himself up, he ran out the back door, into the arms of the deputies waiting there. Soon he had handcuffs on him, and he spent the rest of his term in jail.

Ballard, the oldest son of Shade and Larcy, was more of a father to the other children, working whenever he could, after his father became too sick to work. I remember he used to keep bees and always had honey, for their own use and some to sell for extra money. He also raised cattle and pigs to sell. He was married once, but the marriage was annulled. She was a very young girl, and I think he realized his mistake. It sure did not bother him any when she left after a few days.

I remember one day he was trying to kill some rats that were digging in under the cellar. Just a few yards from the main house was a split stone cellar, where the "can stuff"—Mason jars filled with vegetables, berries, and fruits—were kept (along with potatoes, turnips, apples, etc.). On top of this cellar was a frame, wooden smokehouse. Here the meat, shucky beans, smoked apples, onions, popcorn, walnuts, etc., were stored away. Ballard had found a hold dug under the cellar walls, and he decided to "lay away" Mr. Rat. It wasn't long until a bullet from his twenty-two found its mark, and there was one less rodent. He gave the rat to his small brother to bury, and patiently began his watch for another.

Ransome decided he would have some fun at his older brother's expense, so he took the dead rat and, going into the smokehouse, he let it down through a hole on the end of a long string, directly over the rat hole. He just let its nose stick out the hole, then jerked it back. His brother could see the rat, but he could not see Ransome. Soon he shot again, and Ransome let the string drop. "I got him," said Ballard proudly. But I guess he would have spanked his younger brother had he been able to catch him, when he pulled that rat out and found that long string tied to it.

CHAPTER 8

A bean stringing was a social event, as popular in its day as a dance or car race now. Shucky beans or leather britches — as they are called in some localities — is a very delicious dish that has never lost its popularity. Most everyone who has eaten them gets addicted. We all still dry beans, in almost every home on Caney, but we only remember and talk about the bean stringings.

When the beans are still green (some lets them get a little more mature than maybe other folks, but each to his own preference. I like them almost full grown), the beans are picked, and the strings pulled off, then strung on twine like beads, letting the beans cross each other on the string. When full, the twine is looped and hung over a nail on the porch or behind the stove. There they remain until completely dried out. Then they are put away until winter. We now put them in freezers. They are cooked like "soup beans" or navy beans, with a piece of hog's jowl or salt pork. They have a nut-like flavor. We usually serve them with cornbread, pickled beets, or sauerkraut.

But a bean stringing was a social event. Then, families dried bushels of beans. We had no refrigeration, and only a few glass jars (which cost "cash money"), so every bit of food that could be preserved by drying was "put up" like that.

All families helped each other work, but when work and fun

could be combined, so much the better. So, when the beans began to "come in" there was a bean stringing, at first one house then another, all up and down Caney.

The girls would meet and pick the beans. It was a very hot, uncomfortable job, as the beans were planted in the corn, which grew far above our heads, but we laughed and enjoyed ourselves, even when bitten by the worms known as "pack saddlers." Sometimes the boys would come and help us carry the beans to the house, but most always we would rather they did not, because we did not like for them to see us in our old clothes.

The beans were poured in the floor in the middle of the room. After all the work was "done up," and us girls had all "spruced up," then the neighbors began to arrive, bringing their darning needles with them.

At first, everyone would "snout" the beans (pull the strings off). When a good supply was ready, some would begin to put them on the twine. Of course, the boys and girls would pair off in couples and work together. Some boy, or man, would bring a banjo or fiddle and play music, if the home owner allowed it. Many of our folks were "against music," saying it was of the devil and a sin.

After the beans were finished, the mess cleaned up, maybe there would be a dance (again depending on the beliefs of the home owner), but, if not a dance, there would be games: "Hang the Doorknob," "Please or Displease," "Fine or Superfine," "Who's Got the Thimble," and many others. Nice, clean, wholesome fun.

Some of the boys would walk the girls home, others would ride with them on the mules.

I attended many a bean stringing where Willie would also be, with his guitar or banjo, but one I remember in particular.

When I invited him to come to my brother's, where there was to be a bean stringing the coming Saturday, he asked me for a date, and I hope I did not say yes too quickly. But, my dreams were shattered when I rushed to tell my niece that finally, at last, I had a date with my "feller." It seems he had also asked her to be with him that same night. To tell the truth, I did not believe her at first, but it was so. When the night arrived, we were both so angry that neither even spoke to him. I did not know until many years later, when we were married, what had really happened. Willie's cousin wanted a date with my niece, but fearing she would tell him no, he got Willie to make a date with her for himself. They thought when she saw him, Willie with me, that she would be with the cousin for spite. That was kind of a mix-up that backfired in their faces. I don't guess any of this is interesting to anyone but me.

I don't know just where the following should be placed in my story, but I feel I should slip it in somewhere, as it was a part of Caney history. I believe the little, small, unimportant things have their place in the make-up of our lives (and the history of a place), and they tell more than the larger things.

Do any of you remember the Lee or Mason Manufacturing Company? I think they were located in Chicago, Illinois, but I am not sure. Every spring we would receive a small catalog from each or both, full of all the small wonders, rings, pins, dishes, perfumes, pots, pans, silverware, and much more. The last pages were of premiums. By selling an order of the small items, you were allowed to obtain one of the larger for free.

This was of a great help to the women of Caney. Many of them never got away from home to go shopping in Hindman or Wayland. Our small stores did not carry the things found in these sale books.

In 1929, when I was fourteen, I remember "gettin' up an order" for the Lee Company, and I earned a set of dishes with a bluebird pattern, and a wooden porch swing. I took my book and visited each and every home up all the hollers: Orchard Branch, Short Fork, Sparkman Branch, Trace, Bunyun, Onion Blade, Booger Branch, Hemp Patch, Cotton Patch, and Hollybush. Almost everyone ordered something, even if they did not I enjoyed the visit, and they liked to "look in the wish book."

My father had to go to the Lackey depot to pick up the large barrel, which had been sent by freight. Then I delivered the articles to all the homes. Of course, I walked, and enjoyed it.

The pack peddlers were also a very useful part of our lives. Every spring and fall, one or more would make their rounds. They were always welcome, often sharing a meal and staying one night. Oh, the joy of watching them open those packs! I never could understand how they packed so much in such small bundles. They always had foreign accents, and their prices were low. I remember well the last one I ever saw. It was October 31, 1940, the day my second son was born. After that the war began, and the pack peddler came no more to Caney. Some say their supply was cut off, and some folks tried to say they were German spies.

CHAPTER 9

I guess every woman anywhere wants her wedding day to be one to remember, a happiness to share with all her friends and relations. Well, mine was not like that. We were married in secret. It was not even in the day, but at night. One Sunday (May 17, 1936) after dark, we walked around to Preacher Billy's, who lived then on Sparkman Branch, with only the two necessary witnesses, Cora and Victor Sparkman. We were united to be separated no more, except by death.

A mountain wedding was usually a very big affair. A big dinner the first day at the bride's home, another just as large (called the enfair) at the bridegroom's the second day. Everyone was invited. Sometimes the neighbors would "shivaree" the couple (making a lot of noise, singing and shouting as they marched around their house, maybe taking the man for a ride on a rail and the woman in a washtub). All good, simple, wholesome fun. As with everything else, some might get drunk.

A very traditional dish for a wedding dinner was chicken and dumplings. The two were associated so much that it became a joke. You did not ask someone if they were going to get married, but, "When can we expect some chicken and dumplings?" If a boy kept visiting the same girl for a while and they seemed to be getting serious, my father would say that when the old hens saw them coming, they ran and hid.

I remember what happened to our first pig. It was almost fat enough to kill. There wasn't anything wrong when we fed it its supper, but next morning it was dead. It had been such a pet, I don't think I could have eaten any of it anyway. Its name was Sarmol.

My husband asked the neighbors, who owned joining farms to our small lot, permission to bury the dead pig on their land, and both refused. He went and got his father's mule and hauled it to his father's farm. Someone threatened to indict him for taking it along a public road, but there was nothing else he could do. We did not want to burn or bury it that close to our home.

I wish I had words to describe our first home. My children sometimes ask, "Mom, were you not ashamed to live like that?" No, we were lucky. We did have a place of our own. Many of our friends had to live with one or the other's parents when first married.

There had been an old log house, one larger room with a very large chimney. Then another room had been added from sawed lumber. The log house had been torn down, the logs laying in the yard. My husband later built a barn with them. The plank room was the one we lived in. The fireplace had been planned to hold logs for fuel, then later a smaller opening had been made for a grate by walling up the sides with rocks. The one room was about twenty-two feet wide, and at least ten feet to the ceiling, very unusually high. It had a big loft that could be used for storage room. In fact, I think it had been used for a bedroom, beds being made on the floor for extra children. We only used it for a "junk room."

Our furniture consisted of two iron beds (I still have one of them), my sewing machine, his talking machine (record player), his Uncle Billy gave us what had at one time been a wood cookstove known as a "step stove," made to burn wood for fuel. It got the name because the two back "caps" or lids (burners to you) were of a higher level than the front two. It had lost all its legs and most of the doors. One lid was missing, but I solved that by keeping my iron tea kettle there. As long as I remembered to keep water in the kettle everything was fine. Willie solved the problem of the lost legs by sawing four wooden ones from a tree trunk. The only thing wrong with that was, we were always afraid they would get hot and catch a-fire. We always poured water on them before going to bed. He also made me a wall shelf for my dishes and a table from split boards, made smooth with a drawing knife. I had a trunk, the only thing I had that belonged to my mother. As there was only one room, I guess it's a good thing we did not own very much furniture.

With the fifty dollars we saved from our N.Y.A. job, we bought enough lumber to build a "lean to" kitchen and a porch onto our house. Willie and his brothers did all the work. Harlen Watts came and helped to "rive" split boards from white oak, taken from my father-in-law's farm. I guess I was just about the proudest person

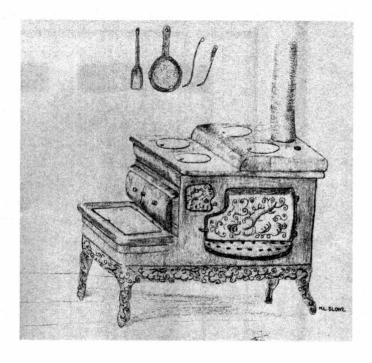

alive then. Not proud in a mean way, just real thankful for what I had. By the time our first son was born we had two rooms to our house, and by the time our second arrived we owned a farm and two houses.

Then why did we keep it a secret? We both were working on the N.Y.A. (National Youth Administration), one of President Roosevelt's programs. It was for single people. We wanted to keep our jobs as long as we could. Maybe this was a little wrong, but mountain folks do not look at it that way. Anything you can get from the government is fair. Most of them really like to outwit the authorities and law enforcers. People who are too honest to take one penny from a neighbor will lie to take hundreds of dollars from Uncle Sam. I guess that's kind of true everywhere, but more so in the mountains.

Willie's job with the N.Y.A. was in a different district. He and the other boys painted and repaired school and church houses. The boys on Caney worked at the school and made chairs for Mrs. Lloyd. We girls made quilts out of the clothes from the Exchange, scrubbed the "homemade chain," and washed windows.

The N.Y. A. program was set up so as to help as many young folks as they could. Each group was allowed only a few months' work. Then different ones were hired. Willie and I had planned on waiting until our jobs were finished to get married, to save as much of our money as we could to buy us some "stuff to set up housekeepin'." A lot of things happened that caused us to change our minds.

I had swapped my part of the old homeplace farm at the mouth of Trace to a horse and garden on Bunyon, in the head of Caney. Here my father and stepmother lived. I stayed with them when I was not at school.

Uncle Sam Sumner had died, and his wife Aunt Cylindea (known by everyone as Aunt Hen) lived near the college with her foster son, Caney. Caney was the real son of Uncle John Sumner and his wife Ethel, who both had died, leaving five orphans. In a case like this the children are always raised by the next of kin. It would have been unthought of for children to be sent to an orphan's home or adopted by strangers. They must be raised by relatives and grow up in the same family.

Aunt Hen had raised a very large family of her own, and they were, at this time, all married. She lived in a large two-story building. She wanted my father and stepmother to move in the lower part of the house. It was lonesome for her and Caney by themselves. I guess my father and Barbara also wanted to be with folks their own age. So it was arranged they would move and let me have my own house.

Also, if we had not married early enough in the spring to plant a garden and some corn, we would have no food for the first winter. We did not like the idea of "staying in the house" with his parents, as many newlyweds did. And there was no way I wanted us to stay with my stepmother. With everything considered, we decided to get married in secret. It was not a secret very long. I was married only nine months and two weeks when our first son was born.

I worked up until a week before his birth. One of my cousins was the boss over our project. No one ever reported on Willie that he was a married man, but it seems as if someone was sending in a report on me every week or so. All my relatives and close friends knew it, but they wanted me to keep my job. When my cousin would get a notice from the government asking him if one of his employees was a married woman, he would have to come to me and ask. I would be standing there so pregnant that I "looked like a cow." I would laugh and say, "No, do I look like I am?"

We worked two days a week and received eight dollars a month. After a few weeks I got a raise to ten dollars, for being "timekeeper." You won't believe we saved fifty dollars that first summer. We also tried to buy something from each check for our home, a sheet, a couple of towels, a few teaspoons, or a fry pan. Did we think of this as being poor or deprived? Far from it. We were happy. We were glad we could do it. When you have no big things, the little ones become important.

We had our health, a place to live. We could grow all the food we needed. I remember canning several hundred quarts of apples, tomatoes, beets, beans, kraut, berries, cucumbers, peppers, peaches, and peas. I made a few dozen pints of apple and berry jelly, blackberry jam, and apple butter. I dried beans, cushaw, pumpkins, and apples. We had a hole of Irish potatoes and a barrel of sweet potatoes, each one wrapped separate in a piece of newspaper. A few bushels of onions were drying in the loft. Squashes and cushaws were rolled under the beds (the smaller ones fed to the hogs). I also had several bags of shelled beans for soup beans. We had enough food to feed an army.

Willie's sister gave us a few hens and my sister gave me a rooster. We did not have a cow. In fact, we bought our first cow three or four years later.

CHAPTER 10

There are so many things I would love to tell about my first home, our jobs with the N.Y.A. program, and all the fun we had. Once, us girls got locked in the Old Science Building, and no one could hear us "holler'n," so I crawled out a window and dropped to the ground, then went for help. One time we got caught in a flash flood and had to stay all night. It was a good thing the boys were on the right side of the creek and let our folks know where we were. I was still taking some classes in high school then. The time I spent in school also counted as work time. I know some of the other N.Y.A. girls resented this, so I tried to make up for it by working harder, bringing the quilts home to hem.

My husband bought some blue wallpaper for our home, the only kind of wallpaper we could get then. It was a heavy grade, known as "ceiling paper." Until then it had always come in a brown color. It was not put up with paste, but with little bright shiny disks, with a tack in the center. Some people saved buying the "buttons" and cut small pieces of cardboard from old shoe boxes, to keep the tacks from pulling through the paper. The ceiling of our house was so high, it was some job to get the paper up. Some of the N.Y.A. co-workers came on their day off and helped me. We had a lot of fun. When finished, one girl said, "It sure is a 'tacky' job, we used several boxes of tacks."

I remember how I solved the problem of keeping my milk and butter fresh. We had a dug well. Many folks would let the bucket or jar of milk down in the well on a rope. I tried this, but then you had to pull up the milk in order to "draw" water. Oh boy, if you happened to spill the milk, then the well had to be cleaned out, all the water bailed out, then someone go down in the well, and with clean water, wash the sides of the walls, which had been made from creek rocks placed one on the other. The uneven sides came in handy as a ladder, but the many foot holes and crevices made the cleaning more difficult.

There was a big Bell Flower apple tree that covered our well. Under this tree I dug a large hole and sank a fifty-pound empty lard can. Each morning I would fill it with fresh cold water from the well. There I could keep my milk, butter, eggs, and leftovers. A lot of trouble? Sure. Now I grumble when I have to clean my automatic defrosting refrigerator. If someone had told me then that I would ever see a refrigerator, let alone own one, I would have said, "Yeah, and the sun is going to come up in the west tomorrow."

There was something that happened about this time, a small thing, but a mystery I never was able to solve. Our chickens I knew by name. Sure we named some of our favorite chickens, some I still remember. There was the Keen Hen, Old Billie Boggs, a large black rooster that was a special pet of Vernon's, then Old Hitler, the mother of a hundred of fryers (my sister Frances owned her). She received the name Hitler because of her disposition. The chickens roosted in some trees back of our house. One morning when they came off the roost, there were two newcomers—a red and white speckled rooster, and a pullet about frying size. They seemed just as much at home as my own chickens. I asked all the neighbors if they were theirs. No one had ever heard of them. I left word at the local country store and told the postmaster to help me. Until this day I don't know where they came from. It was the custom if folks were moving they would take the chickens in the night, because sometimes the heat of the day could cause them to die. Someone moving a long way, who went through here, could have lost them. We had not heard anyone pass during the night nor were there any wagon tracks.

My first son was born March the third. We slept late that morning. I knew I was in labor when I awoke. Willie had been keeping his father's mule, so as to be ready (a mountain expression, "He had been sleeping with his shoes on"). On his way to bring the midwife, he stopped and sent my sister Renda to take care of me until he got back. Dora Belle asked Willie if he would wait until she milked her cow. He waited, but the baby did not. She only had time to wash her hands after arriving. She helped him into the world still wearing her hat and coat.

A lot has been written about our "hillbilly granny women." There was a lot of superstition connected with childbirth, but there was no foolishness about Dora Belle Taylor Gibson. She had taught herself from reading books. She knew as much as a doctor. She had a medical license to practice. She did not believe in using pain-killing drugs. She could understand, because she had been forty-eight hours in hard labor herself when one of hers was born, yet she did not care to call in a man doctor when she saw the need of one. She delivered four of my five boys. If she was alive today I would be willing to risk my grandchildren to her care. Another one of our good common people.

In the old days, when a child was born, they had what was called a "granny frolic." The expectant mother prepared as if for a party, all the neighbor women were asked to come. After the baby was born, someone would ring the dinner bell so everyone would understand everything was alright. Then they would cook themselves a good dinner, no men allowed, it was a day for women only. For some reason I can't understand, they always cut up the Father's hat, if he did not have it hid where they could not find it. Maybe that was supposed to bring good luck.

When my baby was born, many of these traditions were no longer observed, but we still had a nice dinner. When they were all in the kitchen eating, I finally looked at my son. Up until then, he had only been a new toy. I had looked forward to taking care of him, making pretty clothes, and showing him off. There lying in my bed with him soft by my side, it suddenly hit me like a streak of light, "This is another human being, a new soul." It all depended on me, if he ate, if he got hungry, if he stayed warm, if he "faired good or bad," if he was taught not to lie, not to steal, to love his neighbors. Just out of the blue it struck me, what a big responsibility this really was. And I said, "Oh God, I can't do it myself. Will You help me?"

Maybe I did not have all the nice things I wanted for him when he was little, and had to wash his homemade clothes on a washboard, but God answered my prayer. I did just as much for him as the richest mother that ever lived. I did all I could with what I had to do with, and I brought him up the way God told me to, in His Good Book. Now I can say I am very proud of him and his four brothers.

I think that is another thing that made the family so close in the past. The father, grandparents, aunts, and so on, were there when the child was born. Some of my greatest regrets are that I never saw any of my sons get married, nor was I present when any of my grandchildren were born. For the first few hours of their lives, they seem to belong more to the doctors and nurses than to the family.

My father made my first son a very beautiful handmade crib bed from walnut. I kept him in the crib during the day, and at night I let him sleep in bed with me. I don't care what doctors say, I believe it best for the mother and child to be together. I also breast-fed all my children. These new mothers are losing two of the greatest blessings that God gave mothers — the pleasure of sleeping with your child, and letting it nurse. A closeness that cannot be understood unless you have experienced it. How can you expect to hold onto them later in life if you begin their lives by pushing them away?

CHAPTER 11

My husband's next job, after he had finished his N.Y.A. allotment, was with his grandfather, Isom Slone, at Beaver Dam, Kentucky. Isom had remarried after being divorced from his first wife, Willie's grandmother Farry. He had bought a farm at Beaver Dam, which contained a large boundary of trees. He was "loggin' this timber" and wanted Willie to help his son, Isom Jr., cut the logs and get them out of the woods. Willie received one dollar a day and free board. He left home Sunday evening and came back Friday night. I had to stay by myself. I didn't mind staying alone, but now I had the baby to think of. We had no close neighbors and I was scared, afraid he would get sick or something. I sure was glad when the job ended, and Willie got his "slip" saying he was eligible for work on the W.P.A. He was to be one of the men to build the road from Garner to Pippa Passes. This road was built with only picks and shovels. The only other tools were churn drills, to drill the holes for blasting out rocks. Our hills are more rock than anything else.

The other day I heard a man remark that the "W.P.A. workers were given a piece of wood and told to whittle it." That is not the way I remember it. These men, who built that road, worked hard, through one of the coldest winters Caney ever saw. They had little "brush fires" built along the road, but were only allowed to sit around the fire during their lunch break. I have known several times when their dinners would be frozen. My husband had a thermos in which to take hot coffee, but some of the men did not have that comfort.

There was a little wooden shanty built where they kept their tools. Willie got the job of night watchman to guard those tools. We were both pleased with this change. Of course, this meant me being alone at night, but it got him out of the cold weather.

From all these jobs, we had managed to save a few dollars, and with the gift of some from my father, in 1939 we had enough to make the down payment on a small farm that joined our lot. It had a much newer and better house. The new house had only two rooms. We tore down the old house, and with the best of the lumber added two more rooms to our house.

I thought now that we owned a farm, maybe my husband would be willing to stay at home more, but he kept saying, "I must find a 'well paying job.' I have no education, so I must learn some trade. I must have money so I can send my children to college." Mrs. Lloyd was helping a lot of folks through school, and I am almost sure she would have helped us, but we did not want that. We wanted to do it ourselves.

I always say that the reason me and Willie get along so well together is because we both do exactly what I want done. I say this as a joke, but there is a lot of truth in this. He leaves almost all important decisions up to me.

But in one case this was not so, and I am very glad to admit I was wrong and he was right.

One evening about dark, we were sitting on our porch. We had finished "laying by" our corn, our garden was all hoed out. Until everything became ready to harvest, we would have a few weeks' rest.

Talt Watts (one of our neighbors, who had a farm in the head of Watts Fork, tended the farm but had a job in the coal mines) come by. After talking for a while he said, "Willie, I would like for to get you to come and plow my corn tomorrow.

I have several work hands coming to hoe corn; but only have one man to plow."

"Well," Willie began, "I have other plans for tomorrow."

"Other plans?" I asked. "You know we don't have anything that needs doing."

"Well, I sure wish you could see your way to coming. I need you and I have seen you plow. I will give you double wages, two dollars a day. My corn is ruining away in the weeds."

Willie answered, "No, I wish I could help you out, and that's more than a fair price, but I have other things to do."

After Talt had left, with the parting words, "Well, if you change your mind, come on," I demanded, "What are these other all-important plans?" And to my astonishment he said, "I am going with my cousin who's promised to teach me how to run a bulldozer."

"And how much will you get for this?"

"Nothing of course, except to learn how."

"What? You would turn down two dollars a day, and go work for nothing?"

That night when he set the clock to alarm, an hour earlier than usual, I said, "You need not have it to alarm, I won't get you any breakfast, unless you plan on going to plow." And he answered, "Then I will eat with my cousin." That's what he did. I heard him leave next morning, without speaking. For the next few weeks he worked with his cousin. In less than two months he had a job, as helper to the bulldozer driver at the unbelievable rate of fifteen dollars a day. In a few years he had a job with the Kentucky-West Virginia Gas Company, where he remained until he retired in 1974, ten years as a bulldozer driver and twenty-one as a well operator.

A job with one of the gas companies is the most sought-after position by the laboring class of people in eastern Kentucky, and once you are in the union, you have almost a guaranteed job for life. So you see how pleased we were. When his first check came, each one of the boys wanted to get it from the mailbox and bring it into the house. Willie Vernon got mad because Losses outdone him and carried the check to me, so he snatched it and threw it in the fire. Willie had to embarrassingly explain this to his boss and get it replaced.

There was one drawback to this job: Willie had to stay away from home now more than ever. In fact, during the war years, he was sometimes gone for weeks at a time, building roads, wenching pipes up the hill, as the Gas Company drilled more and more wells. He got a deferment from the draft, as his job was classed as essential to the war effort.

I could write a whole book in itself about all the ups and downs that happened to me and the boys, trying to keep house by ourselves. Some funny, some sad, many well worth remembering.

Once, they were playing some kind of a game, where Willie Vernon was a cowboy and his tricycle a horse. When Orbin tried to lasso the horse, Willie Vernon, meaning to cut the rope, slashed Orbin's face. There was no way I could get him to a doctor, the roads were blocked with snow, and there were no telephones, no men folks at any of the neighboring houses. So, with only alcohol, adhesive tape, and prayers, I dressed the wound, which was deep. It cured up with only a very slight scar.

Then there was the time when our pig got out of his pen about midnight. Me and the two older boys went to get it back up. He was determined to outdo us. While one was pushing him through the fence and the other two pulling, he suddenly decided he wanted inside, and threw us all into a muddy, sloppy mess. In the middle of the night we had to heat water for a bath, and leave our clothes on the outside.

The kids will never let me forget the time our cow got into the chicken house, and I demanded she "come out with your hands up," thinking it was someone stealing our hens.

I still keep the old door that we had to replace with a new one, after someone kicked one of the panels out, trying to break in. I sure was scared stiff that time. I had no gun, and would not have wanted to use one if I had. When I said, "Please, God, don't let me have to kill someone," he got the message and ran away.

It was very embarrassing when I had to take my cow to a neighbor who owned a bull. The two older boys driving the cow, me carrying the baby and leading the next oldest, we went up the hill. I was saving having to explain why I had come. The neighbor attended to the animals while I went on with the children and visited his wife. When I was ready to return home, my friend said, "You will have more trouble getting your cow to go home, better leave the little children here and come back after them." This I was glad to do, although it meant climbing the hill again. I can laugh about it all now, but it sure was not so funny then.

When I had to go to the store, I took my kids and left them with my sister, who lived up another holler, Short Fork. After making the two-mile trip to the store and carrying my groceries home, I returned to my sister's after my children. It took all day. I am not complaining, I am only explaining, but I sure was glad when Creps Reynolds opened a store and began delivering his groceries to his customers.

One weekend Willie did not come home. I was disappointed, but did not think anything wrong, because he often had to work through the weekend. He got time-and-a-half for this extra work, but he usually tried to send me word when he was not coming home. Monday evening when his boss, Red Gayheart, came by our house and asked why Willie had not met him to go to work that day, I really began to worry. Red told me Willie had started home Friday, and Red had been told to pick him up Monday morning. It really was just a mix-up in the work orders at the office, but I had no way of knowing this then. The closest telephone was over five miles away, at Will Thacker's. I got some of the neighbors to stay with the children, and getting my brother-in-law to go with me, I went to see if I could locate Willie. To make it worse the rain was coming down in sheets. It was almost midnight when we got the Thackers up and got a call through to the Lloyd Hotel at Pikeville, where I knew my husband stayed when away from home. I asked the night clerk to go check and see if Willie was in his room. When my husband learned who was on the phone, it was his turn to become worried. No one made a phone call at night except in a case of emergency. He did not give me time to explain before he began asking was something wrong, was I sure the kids were all right. After I assured him the children were okay, his folks were okay, my folks were all okay, and yes, as far as I knew everyone on Caney was all right, I told him I was only worried about him because no one seemed to know where he was.

"And you got me out of a good warm bed just for that?" he angrily demanded. Oh boy, did I hit the ceiling then! I said, "You talk about a good warm bed to me. Me and your brother are standing here drenched to the bone, not a dry thread on our bodies, we waded out of Watts Fork to get here, we have to walk back five miles before we can even think about getting in bed! The next time you get lost, you can go hunt your ownself." And with that I hung up the phone.

CHAPTER 12

My friends tell me I live too much in the past. The past does seem so much more beautiful than the present. I don't like the present, I am afraid of the future, so I must relive the past. I am not afraid of the future life after death, only the few more years I have to live here on earth. If I could only recapture the past and share it with my children, as I remember it, but I am handicapped by the lack of an education. I can write of the events, but how can I make them see it as it really was?

How can anyone make another hear the nice musical sounds of the realistic, common everyday things, like the cracklin' of a wood fire, the spatterin' of rain on a board roof, the sharp clangin' of a dinner bell, or the soft tinklin' of a cow bell?

Did you ever awake in the morning to the challenging crow of a rooster? As one crows to be answered by another and then another on and on until it fades away in the distance, only to be begun over and over again.

You can describe the beauty of the autumn trees, but how can you capture the sound of the rustling leaves, and the pattering of scurrying little feet, that tell you "Winter is coming"?

Then you learn the different sounds a mother hen makes as she talks to her small chicks. There is the "squalk squalk" when she is warning them of danger. The "cluck cluck" clucks as she maneuvers them from one place to another. Then the soft "coo-coo-coo" as they settle under her wings at night. She is telling them, "You are safe, I love you, God is watching over us."

If you have heard and loved these sounds as I have, then you know what I mean. Much different from the screaking of car brakes, the grinding bulldozer, or blast of a jet.

The most pleasant sound is the yell of a small boy when he comes home from school, slamming the door with a "Hey Mom, where's supper? I am starving 'tee-totally' to death."

I wanted so to be able to write, but was handicapped by the lack of an education. It must not have been so ordered. Over and over again I have tried, only to be stopped. I am not complaining, only explaining.

The first time I quit school was when my sister's family was in a car accident and needed me. The next time was in the early thirties. People were being given jobs on W.P.A., a work program set up and sponsored by the government, to help poor people. My father and stepmother were much too old to work, so I received the work order. My father cried when I had to quit school again. I tried to not let him know how much it bothered me. There was just no other way, but I planned on going back later.

I was allotted a job with a sewing project located at Hindman with twenty or thirty other women. All the others were much older, mothers whose husbands were dead or disabled. I always loved to sew, and I had been making my own clothes for years. I would also sew for my friends and neighbors. I was paid fifteen cents a dress. Don't laugh, with the price received for three dresses I could pay for enough clothes to make one for myself. Also, being able to sew came in very handy later when I made clothes for my children, often from the best parts of the worn out pants of grownups.

If anyone tells you that people working on W.P.A. had it easy, don't believe them. How would you like to walk eight miles, sometimes through the snow, work all day using a pedal-type sewing machine, and then walk home that night five days a week? Again I am not complaining, only explaining. I have repeated to my children, so many times, when they would want to use the car for a short drive to the store or post office, "I have walked eight miles, worked all day and walked back," that when I began they would say, "Yes, we know!" and then sing-song it back to me.

In a way I liked my job on the W.P.A. I did not like the physical examination by the doctor, required by the government. No mountain woman at that time would accept her privacy being violated this way.

The clothes we made were distributed to the folks who were in need of them. I hated to work with the ugly, sleazy cloth used. And the most awful colors, something that "would not show dirt." The patterns were large, unshaped, sloppy, made so as to be worn by any size person in a certain age group. I wonder why, when something is given to the poor, it's always supposed to be only useful, never pretty. The poor need beauty more than anyone. When you give something to the unfortunate people, don't only give them something you no longer need and want to get rid of. Give them your best, then God will bless you for it. Believe me, I've been on both ends of the stick, and I know.

Even when I got married I did not give up my idea of finishing school. Then, you very seldom heard of anyone going to school after getting married. Mrs. Mattie Pridemore was the only one that I know who did.

In 1939, when my oldest son Milburn was past three, I began to plan on an education for myself. My father, who lived next door to us, would baby-sit. It would mean a two-mile walk and a lot of work. I went to Mrs. Lloyd and asked her if I could return to school, not staying at the Community Center, of course. She said if I passed the college entrance test, I could enter college without finishing high school. I made pretty good on the exams. I bought some white material to make my uniforms, but instead I used it for baby clothes and diapers, for by the last of March I knew I was pregnant again. My new baby meant more to me than an education. I think a baby should be with its own mother for its first years. Before Orbin was two, Losses was born. When Losses was just past two, Willie Vernon made his arrival. So I just put all thoughts of school for myself out of my mind.

You would think after so many times I would have given up, but not so. Willie Vernon was four. By then Willie was making enough money that I could hire someone to help with the house work. My father was gone by then. I began to plan on school again for the next year.

I had gone to dig a "mess" of potatoes for supper. I had almost enough, and I stooped over to pick them up. A pain hit me in under my ribs on my left side, so sharp I thought at first I had jabbed myself with the hoe handle. I don't know how long I lay there in the garden, but I soon made my way to the house and to bed, where the children found me when they come home from school. I remember being so glad that Vernon was taking a nap. It was eighteen months later before I even went outside the house. Doc Duke and Doc Kelly came to see me. One gave me something to make my heart beat faster, one gave me a pill to slow my heartbeat, one said for me to have complete rest, the other said I should be made to get up. They both agreed I had had a nervous breakdown. It was twenty-five years later before I knew for sure what had happened. I was in the Whitesburg Hospital for a hernia operation. Dr. Pigman ordered X-rays and cardiograms. Only then did I know for sure I had had a severe heart attack. It left me so weak that it was years before I could go up stairs or climb a hill, without resting every few steps. Again, not complaining, only explaining. I learned a wonderful lesson in patience. I made a lot of quilts and read many, many books. I had a lot of time to think and understand the Love of God. I think lots of times when we become too engrossed with our ownselves, He makes us stop and begin to realize what life is really all about.

Different people came to keep house for us while I was sick. Ova Jacobs and his wife, Inis, Vernon and Elsia, Willie's Aunt Laura. But I owe more to my sister, Frances, for helping me recover than anyone. I had been sick for so long that I just gave up altogether. She would come and take Willie Vernon home with her. She would bring her family's wash and do it with mine, just so as to be with me more. Sometimes she would beg me to try and walk, again she would scold or shame me. She never gave up trying. I had just lost all desire to want to try and help myself. If it had not been for her help and loving encouragement, I would never have made it. When she finally got me to "stirring around the place," she wanted me to go home and spend the night with her. I was so nervous, I thought I would surely die if I even tried to walk that far, but she never stopped until at last I gave in. I refused to be left alone by myself. Next morning when the kids, except Vernon, had left for school I wanted to return home. I did not know what to think when she said she could not go with me. Surely she did not think I could go by myself. I begged and begged her to not make me go by myself, but to no avail. I carried a cushion with me, and every few steps I would stop to rest. It seemed like hours and hours to make that less than a half-mile journey. Oh, how good my own home looked! When I finally got inside and sat down, I began to cry. I was so hurt because Frances had not come with me, to help me. Suddenly I heard the gate open, and looking out I saw my dear sister entering. Then I understood she had made me come alone, to prove to myself that I could do it. She had been right behind me, out of sight, all the way.

Mrs. Lloyd was not the only one who fought against having roads built on Caney. There were some of our own folks who were not willing to give up some of their land for a road. My children, along with others, had to walk to school, sometimes through the creek, sometimes on a narrow path along the hillside. My oldest son many times took off his shoes and waded across, carrying the younger boys, one at a time, on his back. In 1950, Creps Reynolds sold us his farm close to the college, and we moved. I did not like leaving my home, but the children did need to be closer to school.

In 1953, I again began planning on finishing school. This time I got farther along, and I even attended school for four or five months. Yes, you guessed it, another baby. I hope, by the way I tell this, I am not giving the impression I was not happy with the children God sent me. Far from it. There is nothing, except Jesus, that I love more than my children.

When I was three months pregnant with this baby, I almost lost him. The doctors said I would have an abortion, because my body was still too weak from the heart attack I had had a few years before. I would not agree to that at all. I made Willie promise me that if I did get in so much pain that I might agree, that he would not. I know the prayers of my friends had more to do with saving my baby than the doctors. I had to lay in bed for the last seven months before he was born. I had so much trouble I was afraid the baby might not be healthy, but not so. He weighed in at nine pounds and three ounces.

So I never got to finish school, but I still dreamed of writing. In 1974, with the encouragement of Laurel Anderson, I tried to "scribble" a history of my father's life. I only meant to make a few copies for my grandchildren, but I never dreamed so many people would read it. I take no credit for myself. My father was just such a wonderful person, to know him was to love him. I only wrote what I remembered about him, so others who did not know him could love him. I have received many letters from people from many states, telling me what they thought of the book, "Kitten-eye Slone." The two I treasure most: a woman from New York said, "I wish I had known your father"; a boy, who was once our next door neighbor, came from his home in Indiana to get one, and I said to him, "I guess you want it because it has a picture of your mother and grandparents," and he answered, "No, I want my little girl, Candy, to know about Kitteneye. He was so good to me when I was small." So if I did not get an education, God did let me write, at least so people enjoy what I have to say.

CHAPTER 13

I have had a lot of folks to ask me, "What do you know and think about coal mining in eastern Kentucky?" And I have to truthfully answer, "Very little." I have read a lot of good books on this subject. Some I like, some I disagree with and hate. Again, I will only have my memory to rely on.

Three of my sisters each lost a son in the coal mines. My father nor my husband ever worked in one. True, my father "dug coal" from a small coal bank on his own farm, for his own use. My oldest son had a job with a coal company for a few months (when he was first married), between his school terms as a teacher. I don't think I drew a long breath what time he was "under the hill." Once I almost fainted when I came upon his "work clothes" when I opened a closet door. Just the thought of poor men having to work where their clothes get that "grimy." And that's just the least thing. I sure feel for mothers and wives whose loved ones spend so many hours under the ground, like animals. At last they get good wages, thanks to the union. But they are like the soldiers, getting paid more for "risking their lives," than for the work they do.

There is also the other side. Many men now live in fine homes, have nice new cars, their children in college, because of their work with the coal industry. Some that have no other way to make a living and might otherwise be welfare cases.

I remember on my ninth birthday, in 1923, my father took me with him to visit my uncle, who lived in the Porter mining camps. Everything was so new and different from our home on the farm. All those little houses painted a sickening yellow color. I felt so sorry for those folks, having to live in the same kind of house as other folks. Even then I wanted what was mine to be mine only, and to heck with going along with the crowd. How I hated those rows and rows of houses, and the thought of living in the same building with another family, not knowing or caring who your neighbors were. Even the little outhouses were built together, only a wooden partition separating one from the other. My cousin thought it a great joke, when I kept going into the wrong house, until I memorized the number on the door.

The only thing I enjoyed about my visit, except meeting my kinfolks of course, was going to the "commissary," a large store owned and run by the coal company. This was the largest store I had ever seen—shelves and shelves of canned foods, many I had never heard of before, beautiful clothes, mining tools, even furniture. I could have spent hours and hours just looking. My father said the prices were much higher, the same things could be bought elsewhere for half the same money, but the miners were kind of forced to trade there.

When a miner got a job and moved into one of the company houses, the first month's rent was charged against his first paycheck. There was also a certain amount went to the insurance for a company doctor, the electric bill and gas bill, all and all the miner began working already in debt to the company for sometimes over his first payday. He could also "draw script" against his future wages. Script (sometimes small tin discs) was used at the company store in place of money, and was issued by the company. Thus, the miner—already in debt—must trade at the company store for his food at higher prices. Furniture for his home could also be bought this way. No wonder the poor miner sang of "I owe my soul to the company store." By keeping the miner in debt "head over heels," the company was assured of his not quitting his job.

A lot has been written about the union and how it was formed. I don't know too much about that. One of my brothers-in-law had a very active part, and my sister was one of the women to carry banners and join the picket lines. The union of the gas employees did not have as much trouble as the coal miners. My husband was one of the first union members of his Local 3510. I am a very firm believer in all unions and would back them up with my life. I believe they are the best thing that ever happened for poor hard working men and women.

I would be afraid to express my real feelings on "strip mining," as many of my nephews make their living this way. My heart aches at the sight of a black slug of muck that used to be a clear sparkling brook. Our beautiful mountain tops changed into scarred "tattered hills." So many people prefer "greenback" to green leaves. Our lands were just beginning to recover from the slaughter our grandfathers gave it by repeatedly cutting and destroying the woods to farm our hillsides. They had no other choice, but these strip miners have a lot to answer for. I don't think God would have made our country so beautiful if he had not wanted it to have remained that way. It's not so bad for the ones who have no other way to live, but what about the ones that are destroying something only God can create, just to enlarge their bank account. I want to say, "Money is made by fools like me, but only God can make a tree."

The Black Lung Benefits is a great thing, but it came too late for many who needed it. It's just better late than never. Many of my friends who receive this help have larger incomes now than their paychecks were when they were working to support a large family. They have no breath to enjoy it, and can hardly talk with their friends. It's a very wonderful law, but constructed very unfairly. Many who deserve its help do not receive it. I know a lot of men who are drawing Black Lung Benefits that never were miners. Don't ask me how they do it, I just know they do.

CHAPTER 14

A lot has been written and said about Mrs. Lloyd, the lady who came from Boston and established a school on Caney. She and her mother, June Buchanan, and many others will be remembered. There are a lot of other folks, our mountain people, who in their way did just as much. Without them the school would have died before it was born. Just common folks, and I wish I could tell something about each and every one, make it interesting enough that you would want to read it. I haven't time nor space, but I do want to list a few.

There was Miles, Henry, John and Dan Jacobs, all brothers, and all stonemasons. They built the rock wall, the chimneys, the foundations for some of the houses.

George Tuttle and William Reynolds, who ran the sawmill that cut the lumber to build the houses. Once a week they also ground corn into meal, using the same motor. Part of the corn received for this service gave meal for bread used by the school.

Isom Kitteneye Slone, his son Morrell, and Preacher Billie Slone made the chairs used in the school. Mrs. Lloyd also sold many of these for an extra income.

Bishe Johnson, who built the fires in all the buildings, often carrying the coal on his back in a sack.

Sam Allen, the janitor for many years, and his wife, Rhoda, helped with the laundry for the school.

Dellie Slone, Sara Tuttle, Laura Slone, and Monnie Jones were cooks.

Sara Taylor began as a weaver, and taught weaving, then worked many years as a handywoman, collecting and distributing the laundry.

Vansel Slone, Troy and John Sparkman dug the coal used by the school.

Carew, Ike and Neck Slone, all brothers, ran the first printing machine. Laurance Slone also helped them.

Mr. Gibson — I don't know his first name — ran the Delco generator that supplied electricity.

There was Merlen Reynolds, the night watchman.

Commodore Slone, the architect that drew up all the plans for the buildings, bridges, etc.

Then there were the women who sold the school their fruits, vegetables, milk, and eggs. I remember seeing them go each and every morning, with two large buckets of milk or eggs or whatever.

These people worked for little or no pay. Many months Mrs. Lloyd would not have the money to make good the checks she wrote them. True, when she got a donation or help from some source, she divided it with each and every one she owed. These people did not complain, they shared her dream, and were willing to help. Although their families needed money, they wanted a school more.

The school is slowly changing. Only a few of the first buildings are left. Some of the students are from out of state, many from other countries. It's true, some people are trying to renew the "Old Caney Spirit," but again the outside is taking over. Like "Our Appalachia Day." For the first few years it was just a day for us local people, where we met, showed our handicraft, and played music. The last Day, most of our local folks did not get to take a part. The outsiders had again taken over, playing their music, and selling their handicraft.

Which reminds me of what my father once said to one of Mrs. Lloyd's "brought-on" teachers, who was telling him she disapproved of how his daughters dressed. He said, "We don't like what you all wear either, but we have good manners enough to not tell you to your face."

Mrs. Lloyd helped many boys and girls after they finished their two years of college here, sending them on to other colleges for two or more years. I am almost sure she would have helped with my five sons' education had I asked her, but I did not want to be beholden to anyone. My father always taught me, "Never be too proud to ask for help, but make sure you can't do the job yourself." It was very hard sometimes. My husband and I worked extra hard. The boys also did not have it easy; they would teach "on an emergency certificate," going to school in the summer, taking night classes, often driving many miles. I want to say, their wives helped just as much. They all married in their "teens." You can't blame me if I am proud of a job well done. I think I did just as much for my children as the richest people on earth, because I did all I could with what I had to do, and that's all God asks any of us to do.

CHAPTER 15

When we moved from our home on Bunyun to the new one close to the Center, as the school was then called, it was only a two mile distance. My new neighbors were the same, folks I had known all my life, yet there were many differences. Small things, no better or worse, but took a little getting used to.

It had been so hard, when living up in the head of a hollow, to get in and out that we had always bought our groceries in large quantities. Fifty-pound cans of lard, one-hundred pounds of beans, even sugar and salt by the hundred-pound bags. It seemed so funny to me to know of large families buying a nickel's worth of salt and a dime of sugar, buying only enough for one meal at a time. Many times I was asked to get up after going to bed, and open the store for someone who had forgotten something they needed for breakfast.

We had always, like all people who live "up the hollers," gone to bed "with the chickens" and gotten up with them—an expression meaning we went to bed at the same time that our chickens went to roost (maybe this is where a certain writer got the idea we let the chickens live in the house with us). Our new neighbors were up until all hours, and slept late.

Another thing, while at our old home, children were allowed to visit each other only now and then. When they did go to play with each other, a time limit was set on each visit, and it was understood the visitors were to help with the chores, or "help to do up the work." Feeding the animals, carrying in wood and coal, bringing in water. Now the children of the folks living near the school had none of these chores to do. They were allowed to go from one house to another at will. I tried to keep my children in my own yard, so I ended up with almost all the kids, which was just fine with me. The more, the merrier.

We had spent most of our savings for the new house, so I wanted some way to help out to save more, to have ready for the boys' college education. The folks we bought from had run a small grocery store, and I took the rest of our money and stocked this store.

I could write a whole book on the ups and downs of a country store (and probably will, if I live long enough). In a small community the store is not just a place to buy groceries. It's a meeting place to keep up with all the news. In many ways it took the place of a local newspaper. Someone was always leaving something to be given to someone else—a bushel of apples, a hen, or a book. If anyone had something to sell or buy, they left word with me to pass on. Also, folks came in to use my weights, to learn the weight of everything from a ham of meat, a few ounces of ginseng, or their new baby.

Also, it was a gathering place for young folks. Many a romance that ended in marriage was begun over a Pepsi in my store.

Some of the older folks who had walked out of the hollers to go to the Exchange (a store where Mrs. Lloyd sold second-hand clothes) wished to wait until the mail ran, and would spend the hours waiting with me. I took advantage of this. I kept my quilting frames in one end of the store, and the women folks always were glad to quilt a few rows while they talked.

In some of our mountain country stores, the post office was also in the same building. My father had had a post office at High Rock, in the upstairs of our home, going in by an outside stairway.

When Mrs. Lloyd came, she had a new building and changed the name to Pippapass, later to Pippa Passes. The new post office was first run by Mrs. Geddes, then Mattie Pridemore, followed by Manis Slone. It's still in the same building, very soon to be moved again, maybe by the time this is printed. In Mrs. Geddes' day, the business part of the post office was much smaller. The front was a kind of lobby, furnished with tables and chairs, with such a friendly atmosphere that you wanted to linger and chat.

People seemed to have so much more time then to just be friends, yet they did just as much, if not more, work then we do now. I do so long to go back to those "good old days."

I did not only sell groceries, but feed, a few hardware items (like nails, files, hoes, and tacks), some dry goods, overalls, shirts, yard goods, oil cloth, thread, and cotton batting for quilts.

I made a lot of good friends while running my store. You learn a lot about people by knowing what they buy. When you cash their checks, you can't help but know their income. They also share their joys and sorrows with you. Some cause you to lose faith in human nature, but there are always others who come along to renew it. I think there is no better place to study your fellow man than in a small country store.

When we first moved to our new home, I was to renew an acquaintance with a dear cousin of mine, Carew Slone. My life was certainly made much richer by knowing him and his family. His three youngest boys were waiting to help unload the truck of furniture when we arrived, and were just one of us from then on.

Again, I am handicapped by the lack of an education to help me to picture to you the kind of person Carew was. I am sure he would have been the last person to have wanted to be described with "high falutin'" words. He would have been proud to just be one of my common folks. He was one of the best.

He was not the kind of person you would have picked out in a crowd, small in size, a smile that lighted up his whole face, a small crippled body that housed a soul as large as our hills. He had more courage in his little crooked fingers than a lot of men have in their whole bodies. His beauty was all from the inside. To know him was to love him. I guess of any one person in Knott County, he had more friends than anyone else.

When we bought our first truck in 1952, none of my boys were old enough to drive. Willie's job kept him away from home. Carew did a lot of driving for us. His job as a printer at the college gave him some free time. Sometimes we would go to Pikeville or Prestonsburg to buy my groceries from the wholesale house. I got them cheaper if I picked them up myself. Once we went to Ashland to get the lumber with which he built me some kitchen shelves. Even then his hands had begun to bother him with arthritis.

Once, I remember, he went with Orbin to get his bicycle from a boy who had stolen it. But sometimes we just took the children, his and mine, on pleasure trips. Them, and as many other creek kids that could pile in the back of our pickup, would go to a movie at Hindman. Once we went to hear Bill Monroe. I would like to say I was very disappointed in this bluegrass singer that my husband was so crazy about. We took the kids also, to see Homer Harris and his Wonder Horse. Losses and Vernon were delighted when Homer let them ride the horse. They were the only ones allowed to do this, much to the envy of all the other little boys on Caney.

Margrette, Carew's wife, did not go with us. She was even then sick a lot. She was a very home-loving person, who liked nothing better than to stay at her home with her family, very seldom going anywheres, except to church.

There are so many things I would love to write about Carew. All his children got more education than he had, although he had been a schoolteacher. They all live in very beautiful homes. They have a lot to be proud of, and a great name to live up to.

He had so much determination and will power. He kept coming to church long after many folks would have given up. The last few times he had to be carried in by his son-in-law. The last election he went to, his hands were so crippled that he could not use the voting machine, and rather than let someone help him, he made a hook from a clothes hanger, so he could move the pully with it.

Once, on his birthday, his children gave him a surprise party by having a church service in one of their homes. Having church, or a religious gathering, in the homes is a traditional thing carried on by the Old Regular Baptists, a custom that begun when our folks first settled here, before they built church houses.

Carew always had a kind word for everyone. He was a deputy clerk, and wrote many deeds for folks, never wanting any pay for it. He loved to joke. He always called me "old ugly" in fun. The last time I went to visit him before he died, I asked him if he knew who I was, because he had been so sick for a while that he had not known anyone. He looked up at me and grinned, "No," he said very slowly, "I don't believe I do, Verna Mae." Then he turned to the crowd and asked, "Why did she think I would not know that old ugly face, it's the same one she has had all her life?"

People outside of the family, or outside of the mountains, would not have understood what he meant, and thought I should have taken offence. We are not people who easily express our emotions in words, but I knew what he meant. It was, "You are my cousin, I like you and I know you like me, so I can call you old ugly." And he may have known he was telling me good-bye.

Carew was not the only good neighbor we had. There was Manis Slone, the postmaster, who came and carried Losses in his arms to and from his car, taking him to the hospital at Lackey when Losses had pneumonia. Willie and Orbin were in the Hazard Hospital at the same time, Willie for a nasal operation and Orbin was having his tonsils removed.

Commodore Slone and his wife, Jeannette, were good neighbors. Jeannette was such a pal to the young folks on Caney that they nicknamed her Jim Netta, much to her delight. All my boys, as well as several of their friends, learned to drive a car by taking her where she needed to go, in her own car. She always owned one, but never learned to drive. I think she did it more for the boys' sake than her own. She also kept them in spending money by paying them to mow her lawn, to tend her flowers and vegetables, to pick apples and wash windows, always giving them more than they earned. I had stayed a lot with her when I went to school. I guess there are hundreds of folks she helped this way. Seems as if there was always someone there to help eat her delicious meals. She was an artist cook, loving to cook more than anyone I ever knew.

Ethel Jacobs was my next-door neighbor, up the creek. We became very good friends. We would go with the kids to take care of them when they went trick or treating, go together to pick "salet greens," go walk the television line. The antenna for a television was set on top of the hill and a line run from it to the house. It was always getting broken by a fallen limb or heavy snow. We would go and repair this line. Work? No, a lot of laughs and fun.

If someone was to ask me, "What was the most embarrassing moment of your life?" I would have to tell the following story. When we moved from our home on Bunyun to our new home, which was only new to us, we also had to move our farm animals. The new place had the usual barn, pig pens, chicken house, and cow shed. Merion Jacobs hauled our furniture in his pickup truck. Vernon Slone took the pigs in a sled. We waited until after dark to get the chickens (they are easy caught off the roost). But the cow was another problem altogether. Her young calf was about six weeks old. We had promised to sell the calf to one of the neighbors, so we thought it best to just leave it in the barn for him to get that evening. The cow did not like the idea of leaving her baby behind, and even after being safe in the new barn, she kept wanting to return to where she thought her baby still was.

I kept hoping she would soon forget, but the longer, the worse, and every chance she got she would try to return. One morning, after everyone was gone except myself, I took the cow to the creek for a drink of water. Suddenly she jerked the rope from my hands and got away. Up and down, first in the road then the creek, I kept chasing. Our dog, Old Ranger, began helping, his barking called all the other neighboring dogs to the rescue. The poor cow became so confused, she did not know what to do. We ended up with me in front of the high school building, and her going on through the college. I was desperate, I knew if she got on the highway she could be hit by a car. I thought as I was already there I would just go into the school and get my two oldest boys to help. I had not been there before, so I did not know which room to go to. I thought I would knock on the first door I came to, and ask if my boys were there. I have always been a person that, when excited or confused, would say something off the top of my head. When I timidly gave a soft knock, there must have been something wrong with the catch or hinges on the door, and it began to open by itself. I gave a grab for the knob, missed, and went stumbling into the room. As I looked at those rows and rows of silent faces, with questioning eyes, I heard myself stuttering, "Is — Is — Is my cow in here?" Can you just imagine what those students thought? There I stood, splattered with mud, my husband's big overshoes on, my hair stringing, my apron tied over my head. Well, if the teacher had not been a cousin of mine, he would probably have sent after the men in white coats and a straitjacket for me.

CHAPTER 16

I guess my scribblings are like my crazy quilts, without any form or unity. The more I write, the more I remember. There are just so many things I want to say, maybe some are interesting only to me. Our young folks have lost so much without ever knowing they never had it to lose.

It's also true that sometimes truth seems more strange than fiction. God must have a certain purpose for my fourth son, Willie Vernon. He has come so near death, and yet lived. I will not write of all these near escapes, but only three.

On Christmas Day in 1947, when Vernon was just past three, his grandmother died. I believe that was one of the coldest spells I ever remember. A deep snow, creeks froze over from bank to bank, temperatures away below zero. Willie had been staying with his mother for two weeks or over. He sent me word to not try and bring the children to the funeral. My oldest son loved his grandmother so much that he wanted to go, so we bundled up and started. It's not over two miles' distance from our house to where she was at another one of her sons'. As I have said before, we did not think anything about walking, even children. We knew of no other way. It wasn't so cold as long as we were between the hills. We had to walk very slow, because the children were small and the snow deep. When we got to the top of the hill, the road ran for a long way around the ridge, and here there was no shelter. I knew we should go faster, so I asked Milburn to carry Vernon on his back, and I would lead the other two. Vernon was small to his age (he only weighed 68 pounds when he was eleven), so Milburn could easily carry him. We had walked on for some time. It was so cold we were not trying to talk, when Milburn said, "Mom, I think something's wrong with Vernon, he has just all slumped down and quit holding onto my neck." I looked and, although his eyes were open, I knew he was not seeing. I quickly felt for his heart, and found it warm. When I took him from Milburn, his arms and legs did not relax, but remained in the same position. I pulled my coat off and wrapped it around him, and started running on, shouting back for Milburn to bring the other two as fast as he could. I remember running, stumbling, falling, praying, the cold air like knives in my lungs. I kicked on the back door and stumbled into the kitchen. When the warm air hit me I passed out, as someone took Vernon from my arms. Later I was told that some went to find the other boys, others took care of Vernon and me. Too late I remembered what my father had always told me, to never quit moving when out in the cold. It would have been better to have had Vernon to keep walking, or better still to have kept them all at home.

In the summer of 1949 we decided to put water in our house. I guess we were one of the first few people on Caney to do this. Some folks used springs, some dug wells, only the county schools had drilled wells. Even the college got their water from a large tank sitting on top of the hill above the school. We had a real good dug well, still have it, and keep it cleaned out and covered even yet, so as to have it to use in case of emergency, although we have two drilled wells with electric pumps. But our first attempt at indoor plumbing was different. High on the hill above our house is a natural water spring. Someone in the past had tried to make an opening to a coal bank. Usually, water from a coal seam is sulphury, but not this. It's very clear, sparkling and good. We hired Ernest Slone to make a basement from cement around this spring, then we laid pipes from there into our house. I remember the government was not allowing pipes to be sold for private use. The company Willie worked for let us have them, the man brought them after dark and charged us triple what they should have been. We had to have these pipes buried very deep so the water would not freeze. Our hills are very steep, and the ditch was deep enough to not be washed out by rain run-off. Vansel Slone and his boys dug this ditch for us. It was this ditch that was to save Vernon's life the second time. But in order to tell my story, I must go back and bring up the rest, like turning the heel when you are knitting a sock.

The year before, one of our cows had died, leaving a very young calf. Usually, in a case like this, the calf was just killed, because it was not worth the trouble and expense to feed one that small. My boys always loved animals, so they wanted to try and raise the calf. When it was still small, they would hold its ears and butt heads with it. Finally it was too strong. Its strength grew faster than theirs. I honestly don't believe they were cruel, but for some reason the calf learned to hate children. It would chase them and try to kill them. This wasn't so bad until it became grown. Well, as the men were finishing the ditch for our water line, it ran through the pasture where Blackie was kept, safe behind a high fence. Vernon decided he wanted to go talk with Vansel and the other ditch diggers. They looked and saw Blackie and him at the same time. She was coming with lowered head and running fast, straight toward Vernon. He would not have had time to get out of the pasture, and the men were too far away to help. Vansel began to yell, "Hurry, Vernon, get in the ditch and lay down." Scared as he was, he did as he was told. The cow jumped over the ditch where Vernon was, with no more damage except kicking dirt in his face.

When Willie learned of this he sold the cow to a neighbor. The neighbor said he thought he could break Blackie from wanting to fight. After a losing battle between the man armed with a pitchfork and the cow, she was taken to the Rock House sale. I heard that later she had to be killed when she broke loose from the stockyard, when some children passed the pen where she was.

Willie Vernon was some older when the third accident happened. I guess he was about seven, because we moved from Bunyun in 1950 when he was six. Our new home was built close to the creek and back against the hill. We had no front or back yard at all. In fact, the bridge across the creek to the road was attached to the front porch. The back was so near the hill that once, when we were working in the garden on the hill above, a rock came unlodged and rolled straight through the window and landed on the dining room table, splashing into our dinner. You may think I did not like this home, and you are right, I did not, I hated everything about it. All the time I lived there I felt as if I was in jail, and longed for the day when I could move back to my home on Bunyun, where I now live. I only lived there because it was close to school. There were people who would not have a road built over their land, and my children would have had to walk two miles to school through the creek. Thank God we now have a road, and my grandchildren ride the school bus. So do the grandchildren of the people who had to be forced to give us a road.

I am afraid I have gone off on a tangent again, so back to my story. Although we had no front or back yard, there was a small space on each side of the house where the kids could play. The older boys had put up a goal where they could play ball. Time and again the ball would go into the creek, and someone would have to chase after it. They had lost several basketballs this way. I finally got tired, and when I bought another one, I told them if they let it float off, it was the last one I intended to buy. Next day Losses and Vernon were playing, and sure enough, into the creek went the ball. There had been a rain and the creek was up to the flood level. Losses said, "You know what Mommie said, Vernon," and before I could stop him, in he went. The waters were over his head and very swift. Milburn ran across the bridge and down the road meaning to try and get ahead of him. There were some low willows bending over the creek far below the house. Milburn shouted to Vernon, "Try to catch hold of those trees and hang on." I don't see how he had the presence of mind to do this, or even to hear over the loud noise of the waters. Again, I think it was God's will, an answer to my prayer. He held onto the branches, and Milburn waded in, also using the tree limbs for support, and got him out, and would you believe it, he had got the ball and had it clutched under one arm.

I was just about as scared over Milburn as I was over Vernon, because at that time he was just recovering from rheumatic fever, and was under doctor's orders to not even get out of bed. I made them both change clothes, put them in bed, and made both some catnip tea, and asked the Lord to take care of them. Of course, it did not hurt either.

CHAPTER 17

As I tell the story of my family I think I represent most of the folks on Caney. We were a typical family. On a hundred percent scale we would have rated about eighty in regards to wealth. Here in the mountains there is very little social status rating. People are not judged by their bank account. In our church we have a millionaire and we have people on welfare. The rich man may dress different, but he is just as friendly and common.

In writing I have tried to use some of the words and expressions that belong only to us, and yet to not use so many that other people with different backgrounds could not understand. I do not like to be called "culturally deprived." Different, yes. Simpler, yes. A fiddle in place of a violin. Why should a man, who lies and cheats but knows what spoon or fork to use, be counted worth more than an honest, hard-working Christian man that drinks his coffee from a saucer? Our folks are poor, but do not think of themselves as poor. They have a hardiness and a love of fundamental goodness that surpasses understanding, a family closeness found nowhere else. Many have more than we do, but none has better. The outside is slowly coming into the mountains, bringing improvements, but destroying more. Soon our mountain way of life will only be a memory, distorted by the writers, who have written only for money. Most that has been written was by outsiders, with an outsider's viewpoint. Many of our own have turned traitor, and written what they thought people wanted to read, or what would sell.

I have lived through four wars. I was too young to remember very much about World War I. It did not touch the people on Caney very much. Many of our boys were drafted, it's true, and some did not return. The thought of their buddies being left so far from home hurt. Even in death our mountain families want to still be together.

All I remember is Father being away from home. He worked as a planer in a carpenter's shop at Wheelwright, making the small shanties furnished by the coal barons for the miners to live in. He always counseled us to be sure and lock the doors, never go any-wheres alone, be sure and fasten up the animals. He said he knew there were "scouters," boys that had deserted the Army or were hiding from the draft. I remember once when he and I were hunting our cow, we came across a campfire and a long-handle fry pan. He told me to be sure and not mention it to any of my friends.

I can't forget the flu epidemics that followed the war. My father took me with him to help dig so many graves, that I still cannot look at yellow dirt without feeling gloomy. Why did he take me with him? I had no mother, and my sisters were sick. I don't think the flu hurt me very much. We did not lose any of our immediate family, but a very dear cousin, Henry C. Hughes, and many others died, nineteen in all.

The Second World War was different. Two of my brothers-in-law were in Europe, and many of my nephews were in active duty. Again, none of my close relatives were lost. Several boys, sons and grandsons of my cousins lost their lives, but this time the government did return their bodies.

My husband was exempted from the draft, because his job as a bulldozer driver was classed as essential to the war effort. Here in the mountains, where we grew most of our food, the ration was not so bad. We were allowed only two pair of shoes each year, and that's about as many as we could afford anyway. We learned to adjust to our allowance of coffee and tobacco, but we needed the sugar for canning our fruits. I remember how we used some salt in our apples so as to use less sugar. We could spare only a small amount for jelly and jam. The biggest jolt was when the government confiscated the only truck on Caney. It was our only means of getting in and out of Caney, except to ride the mail truck. Many times we needed to take someone to the doctor at night.

A funny thing happened when we went to sign up for our ration cards. With us, off-color words were not used in mixed company. I was taught that the word "sex" was a "four-letter word." Even in all our record books, it's "boys" or "girls," "men" or "women," even the word "female" was not used. When I began giving the man at the desk the name and age of each child, the first two he knew were boys by their names. Then I said "Losses," and he looked up and asked, "Sex?" Oh boy, you could have knocked me over with a feather. When I did not answer he thought I did not understand and said, "I mean is it a male or female?" "Oh, I knew what you meant," I replied, "I just hain't used to having a word like that thrown at me." A lot different from what television has brought to us now.

It was a long hard struggle, but we all did our part. I mean most everyone did. Lard and meat was another thing that became scarce. We raised and killed our hogs. We had always been a people that used a lot of pork and pork grease. To use any other shortening was to us just a "make out." Once during the war years, lard went to a dollar a pound. Some man came to Caney with a truck load of fifty-pound wooden tubs of lard, selling them for thirty dollars a tub. I did not buy any. Many of my friends and neighbors did, and when they began to use the lard they found the tubs had been filled with mashed potatoes with just a little lard on top.

When we bought a new tube of toothpaste we had to return

the old empty tube. The government bought up all the scrap aluminum, and even bacon drippings and table scraps that were meat. There are so many things I would love to tell about these times, but I know old folks would get bored and the younger ones would not believe or understand.

In the Korean War, my sons were too young, but I worried and wept with my sisters, whose sons fought. Again, none of our close family was killed. Then in the Vietnam War we were not so lucky. Phylip Jacobs, my sister's grandson, was killed. I had only seen him twice in his life. His father had been in the Army, and was stationed in California, but he was one of mine and I loved him. My sister was never well, and I think the news of his death hastened her death. I agree with many others, I think this war was such a waste.

During World War II my father had an income of eight dollars a month, old-age pension. He supplemented this by whittling hammer and ax handles, and repairing chairs. He was still very active for a man past eighty. He cut down on his tobacco and coffee, so as to have money to buy newspapers and keep up with the war news. I don't pay any attention to news. Oh, I listen, but I don't believe half of what they say. I have heard so much that I knew was lies, or half truths, that I question it all.

We didn't have a radio then, so it was September the third, 1945, before I knew the war was over. My husband went to work that morning and returned about ten o'clock. The company had given them the day off to celebrate. I remember I killed two fryers and used the last of my sugar to make some "half-moon apple pies." There was no one except the family to help me eat, but I had to do something, I was so happy.

In January 1959, one of my sons volunteered for the draft. He spent most of his two years in El Paso, Texas. After his eight weeks of boot training at Fort Knox, Kentucky, he got married and took his wife with him. We all visited him once, while he was still in Kentucky, and one of his brothers spent a whole summer with him in Texas. It was the first time I had ever stayed away from any of my children, and I don't have to tell you it was very hard. We are, like all mountain people, a very close family.

CHAPTER 18

As I have said before, there were many folks who will not be remembered for their good deeds, but have the label of "Bad Men." Seems as if every family clan had at least one "Bad Man," but I think many had more fame than their just due. The only one that had any connection with my life was Bad Amos Fugate, or Little Amos as he was called by his friends, and he had many more friends than enemies. The story goes that his sister had a fight with some neighbor woman, and the other woman was killed. Amos confessed to the crime to save his sister and was sentenced to prison. Before his sentence was up, he dressed in women's clothes and walked out with some visitors. A price was placed on his head, to be brought in "dead or alive." Whenever he saw one of these posters he would mark out the word "alive," saying that he would have to be killed before captured.

He was a cousin to my brother-in-law, Sam Fugate, and a very good friend. My sister and their children really loved Amos. They helped him by giving him food while he was hiding from the law.

My father was going to visit his daughter, Flora Fugate. As he was going across the hill to Ball, where she then lived, he came upon a group of men sitting by the narrow bridle path. The men were drinking and playing cards. My father said he was upon them before he knew who they were. He said he was really scared when he recognized one of them as Amos Fugate. At first he considered the idea of turning back, but then thought better of that. The men moved back out of the path and let him ride on by. Just as he thought he was getting out of sight and all was well, Amos called and said, "Hey, are you Kitteneye?"

My father turned back and said, "Yes." Amos said, "Come back here a minute." Father really got scared then, but he turned his mule around and went back.

"Did you want a drink of good corn likker?"

"Shore would." And Amos handed him his bottle.

"Do you know who I am?" Amos asked.

"Yeah, I think I do," Father replied.

"Well, you are Flora's paw, so go on, and don't tell a livin' soul you saw us here." And Father promised.

That night after supper at Flora's house, and after Father had gone to bed, Amos came to the door. Sam let him in and gave him his supper. Amos asked Flora had my father told them about seeing him, and he laughed when she said, "No." "Well, I didn't mean for him to not tell you, but I guess when I said to tell no one, he sure meant to keep his promise."

A few days later, Amos was coming back to visit Sam again, and some men "lay waid" him and riddled his body with bullets from a machine gun. His own folks kept the killers from getting his body, then they guarded his grave for one year, keeping a lighted lantern setting on his tombstone at night, with a "round the clock" guard. The bounty hunters received no reward.

The next story I am going to tell is true also, but I will change the names. One of the men is dead, the other gave me permission to tell the story and use his name, but I think it better to not.

Bill was a nice enough fellow, young with a few wild oats to sow. His girl friend was staying at the Community Center, and Mrs. Lloyd had very strict rules about letting girls and boys have dates. He only got to see her once in a while. Meantimes, he would spend his weekends by visiting a place on Long Fork (also a made-up name), where they made and sold whiskey, and the home of some good looking girls. One day Mr. Long's brother shot Bill. It was supposed to have been an accident, but the Longs paid all the doctor's bills. Just as soon as Bill got so he could walk without his crutches, he went back again. He said he wasn't mad and did not "carry a grudge," but I guess they did not believe him, because this time one of the Long cousins, Roy, beat him almost to death.

It was days before Bill could even see to walk, but this time he was really mad. He went and bought him a gun, and knowing where Roy Long went across the hill to his W.P.A. job, he "lay waid" him with the intention of killing him. Somehow Roy got word and went home by a different route. That night Roy packed his furniture and, taking his wife and children, he moved to West Virginia, only his kinfolks knew where.

Twenty years passed before Roy and Bill were to meet again. By this time Bill had married and settled down. He had a job at Prestonsburg, and each weekend he rode the bus from there to Wayland.

This Friday the bus was full, only one empty place, in the seat where Bill was, when the bus stopped at Allen to pick up a passenger. Though time had changed him, Bill knew Roy as soon as he came aboard, but Roy did not recognize Bill until he was almost ready to sit down by him.

His face turned a deadly white, and he almost turned to run, when Bill said, "Hello, Roy."

"Please, Bill," Roy began, "I know you should hate me, but believe me, I have been punished a lot, having to stay away from my folks. Never hearing from them all this time, I just had to come back. I would not blame you if you beat me up, but I don't have a gun, not even a knife."

"Hush, I don't want to hurt you, I forgave you long ago. Come sit down here and let's talk about old times. I am a different man now, I don't want to hurt you."

So they finished the bus ride, laughing and talking.

Bill did not know until a few weeks ago that my father was

responsible for getting word to Roy that Bill had bought a gun and was "lay waying" him, thus probably saving us from having another "Bad Man."

I don't think any of our "bad men" really started out to be bad. They usually were kind and gentle, loved by their folks. Something just happened and one thing led to another, and people expected them to be bad. Many had folk songs written about them, thus causing their fame to grow and be remembered.

You may think, after reading this, that I approve of "Bad Men." Far from that, I don't like any wrong doing, but they were a part of our past, and I want to give a true picture of mountain life.

Also, I think there were not as many of these "Bad Men" as have been told about, and those few were credited with more bad deeds than they really had done. But it's all true that their family and friends "looked up to them" and helped in every way they could to protect and hide them from the law.

If one man "turned another man in" (whether wanted for moonshining or murder), he most always had a "grudge" against him and did it for spite, and not for the reward or civic duty. The "tattle tale" was thought of as a lesser man by his neighbors than the lawbreaker.

CHAPTER 19

In the late sixties Dr. Grady Stumbo and Benny Bailey started the East Kentucky Health Services Center, in less than three miles of my home. Just last week I went there to get my dental plate repaired. They had been patched so many times they had more seams than one of my crazy quilts, so I ended up just having a new set made. The upper plate only cost $200.00. The whole set in the early thirties cost $84.00. But how I came by that $84.00 is the story I want to tell.

My father's generation most all had good teeth. He himself had never had a cavity when he died at eighty-four, and I have seen him crack nuts with his teeth, not often, just sometimes to show us that he could. There were a lot of our old folks who had no teeth. I remember watching them scrape apples with a spoon so as to eat them raw. The only cleaner they used was salt and baking soda, some used a raw potato. For a brush they used the fuzzy end of a broken twig. There was always someone in each neighborhood that owned a pair of "tooth pullers," a tool not much different from a pair of wire pliers. Father had some, and they were kept in the sewing machine drawer. Many an evening someone would come to him with an aching tooth which he would pull for them, no medication except a "slug of moonshine" for both my father and the person who lost the tooth. A real good mouthwash was made from "yeller root." My brother-in-law pulled my stepmother's teeth all at one time, one after another, without her ever getting up from her chair. She had some "new teeth" made but never wore them. Four of my sisters had dental plates, which they kept in their purses, not in their mouths.

I can remember having "toothache" even as a child. By the time my third child was born, I did not have a "sound tooth in my head." A mountain saying is, "A mother loses a tooth for each child."

My husband was driving a bulldozer and working for the county. C. B. Thornsberry was magistrate then, and he and Willie were repairing the county roads. Willie received four dollars a day, and sometimes had to wait for months to get that. We were still paying on our home, there was just not enough spare money for me to spend for teeth, and anyway I had always paid for everything which I use for myself, with money that I made extra. I have never let my husband buy my clothes, not that he would have minded, I just don't want to be beholden to anyone for anything.

Lots of mountain women, when wanting to buy something extra, will raise a gang of chickens, or a mule, cow, and etc., and sell to pay for whatever they want. This money is theirs, and not to be used for household expense. My sister had just sold a cow and bought a sewing machine. I decided I would do the same way, only I would have my teeth pulled and get some new ones. As luck would have it the next calf our cow had was a heifer, and my husband said I could have it for my own. At two months old, when weaned from the cow, it would probably have sold for five dollars. I kept it until it was a year and a half old and was "with calf" itself, and sold it for eighty-five dollars, and my teeth cost me eighty-four.

Can you imagine how many times I fed that animal? Night and morning, come rain or snow or heat. And that was not all, I had to grow that feed myself, enough over and beyond what we needed to feed the milk cow, fatten two or three pigs, feed the chickens, and make bread for the table. I did not think of it as hard work, I was glad that God had given me a way, and thankful we owned a farm of our own on which to grow corn.

Maybe I should tell you just how we raised our corn. A new ground (pronounced as one word) was best. This meant ground that had been cleared of all the trees and underbrush, and now was ready to be planted. The trees were cut down and let lay for a few months, so as to dry out. If any of the logs were to be used for a building or fuel, then they were "trimmed up," all the excess limbs removed, the logs "skidded" to the desired place, and the remaining smaller stuff placed in piles to be burned. We pronounce the word brush, meaning these limbs and twigs, as "brash." It was a lot of fun to go at nightfall and "burn brash piles." The whole neighborhood joined in, many staying until away into the night, keeping the fire under control, so the hills would not get caught on fire. "Letting the fire out" often occurred. If this happened, again everyone joined in and helped. The thing they feared most about a forest fire was losing their split rail fences. Many times the men (and women) would go and pitch the rails down the hill out of range of an advancing fire, only later to have to go carry the rails back and rebuild their fences.

If you were lucky enough to have a "new ground" in which to grow your corn, you would be assured of a good crop (pronounced "crap" by us), but a lot more work. It had to be all done by hand, using only hoes. Although most of the larger roots and stumps were removed — either by burning or dynamite, sometimes pulled out by oxen — there were still too many small roots and sprouts to make plowing possible.

So, early in the spring, sometimes as early as January or February, we would begin "grubbin," digging the young sprouts that were beginning to grow around where the trees had grown. After these were all dug, they were raked into piles and burned. Then we took hoes and shaved off the weeds. Each one working would take a "swith," a distance as much as could be reached with a hoe, and one above the other, each one just a little ahead of the one above, around the hill they would go, raking a very small layer of the topsoil along with the weeds onto the row below him. After this was finished, they would "dig in" the corn, about every three feet, in rows about four feet apart. A small loose hole was dug, here was dropped from three to five grains of corn, and the dirt drug over it. My father always said to plant five,

> "One for the ground squirrel,
>   One for the crow,
>   One to rot,
>   And two to grow."

When the corn was about a foot high, you begun to hoe it, cutting all the weeds, and thinning it to two stalks to a hill. Someone would always joke and say, "Pull up the large ones and give the little ones room to grow." We replanted any missing hills and a few weeks later we hoed it again. This second hoeing was called "laying it by," because this finished all the work with the corn until time to save the fodder and gather the corn. The fodder in September and the corn brought to the barns in November. When we "layed by our corn" it called for a wild celebration. Folks on joining farms were always in friendly competition. Each would rush to beat the others. The way our hills are so close, many different family groups could see and hear each other. When the last "hill of corn" was hoed they would begin to yell, beating their hoes together or against rocks, thumping on the dinner bucket, anything to make a noise. Someone at the house would ring the dinner bell, telling all their friends that they were through with their corn. An extra good dinner or supper, as the case might be, would be cooked, and everyone had at least one whole day's rest. Even the mules got this one day without working.

I would love to tell here another little saying of my father's that he used to help us remember what happened when you waited too long to plant your corn.

In July, corn knee-high,
In August, he layed it by,
In September there came a big frost.
Now you see what corn this young man lost.

Now that I have told you how the feed was grown, fodder also must be saved. All the blades from where the ear of corn grew down were stripped from the stalk, leaving the one on which the corn grew. Every few handfuls was placed between two stalks close to the ground, here they would cure out. After a few days, these would be tied into bundles, and stacked in a shock, or hauled to the barn. The remaining stalk was cut off just above the ear of corn, and tied into bundles and placed together in smaller "shocks." These were called "tops" and were not as valuable as the blade fodder. The "tops" were usually fed to the cows, and the rest kept for the horses. Taking care of fodder was one work I could never do. I know now I was allergic to the smell. I did not know what was wrong then, I just knew I always got sick when I pulled fodder or cut "tops," but it never seemed to bother me once it was cured out, and I could help put it away.

We had no dentist in Knott County at that time, so I went to Dr. Messer's at Garrett in Floyd County, about thirty miles away. I got one of my nieces to come the night before I was planning on going. She stayed with the children for me. I walked two miles to the post office and caught a ride on the mail truck over to the Garner post office, there I got a taxi. After seeing the dentist, I got another taxi back to Garner, hoping I would be in time to connect with the mail truck on its return to Caney. Sometimes I missed. If I was lucky I might hitch a ride with someone coming my way. If not, then I had six miles to walk. I had eight teeth pulled each trip, then three or four more trips for the "fitting." But of all this, what I remember that I "dreaded" most was having to endure the smell of that awful old cigar that Dr. Messer kept in his mouth. I have always thought, "Does anyone who smokes realize how much they are causing the non-smokers to endure?" I have seen and heard so many say, "Is it all right if I smoke?" And all the time they are preparing to do just that, knowing good and well no one is going to say, "Please don't." The one who smokes has a choice, he can smoke or not, but the rest of us have to put up with foul-smelling air, and there is nothing we can do about it.

I have always laughed when I remember what a friend of mine said to me when I told him, "I am raising that calf to buy me some new teeth." I said, "I am going to put that calf in my mouth." And he replied, "You will look awful funny, with its tail a-hanging out."

CHAPTER 20

This is not intended to be used as a cookbook. Our mountain folks did not use recipes in written form. They learned from each other, mother teaching daughter. I only want to tell as much as I can about the different foods we grew, and how we prepared and "put them up" for winter use; also some of the superstitions concerning food.

Apples were the most used fruit. Almost every home had several apple trees growing in the yard. They furnished shade as well as food, also a place for the chickens to roost. Apples were dried. Some folks had a "kil" made of rocks and clay, where, by using fire, several bushels of apples could be dried each year, while some folks, who only wanted a few, dried them in the sun, or strung them like beads on twine, after they were peeled and cut into slices. There was a small worm that sometimes got into our dried apples and ruined them. I now put mine in the freezer to prevent this, but then we had no freezers. My father's generation had no glass jars, so they did not can fruits or vegetables. They filled large crocks or churns with apple butter; when boiled down very stiff and sweetened with molasses it would keep fresh for many weeks. Big barrels were filled with "smoked" apples; a few holes were made in the bottom of the barrel so the juice would run out, then filled up a few inches with apples which had been pared, sliced, and the core removed. On top of these was placed a dish in which a small amount of sulphur was slowly burned, by placing a heated piece of iron into the dish. A quilt over the top kept the smoke from escaping. Next day, another layer of apples and another amount of sulphur was burned and so on, until the barrel was full. The sulphur gave the apples a little "off" flavor that took a little getting used to, but was supposed to be good for you. I loved the taste myself, and always served them topped with blackberry jelly.

And then the late apples could be "holed away." A hole was dug in the ground (often the floor of the house was removed and the hole dug there), lined with straw, the apples poured in, more straw and the dirt mounded over. You must be very careful that none of these apples were bruised or rotten. Some were kept in barrels, each wrapped separate in a piece of paper. Sweet potatoes were also kept this way. Many times these barrels were left all winter in a corner of the bedroom, hid from view by a curtain or quilt. Apples were fried, made into pies and dumplings.

Peaches were canned in syrup. We had a small peach, which was called a "cling stone," meaning the stone could not be removed as the others could. Often we would peel these and can them whole, the stone gave them a very nice flavor; sometimes using sugar, and some in sugar, vinegar, and spice. We had a few pears, and I remember my sister, Frances, had a quince tree. Some folks, not many, had cherries and plums, but almost everyone had a gooseberry patch, and strawberries were found wild in many places. We picked and canned huckleberries and raspberries, but the most used were the blackberries; from these we made jelly and jam. Dumplings were made by bringing the sweetened, cooked berries to a boil and dropping in fist-sized balls of biscuit dough. Berry sass (sauce) was a breakfast dish. The boiling berries were thickened with a little flour and water, not quite as heavy as for a pie filling, sweetened and served like a pudding. I always loved to pick berries. No one ever went alone, because of snakes. The huckleberries grew on tops of the ridges. Every year, when they began to get ripe, someone would start a rumor that there was a bear or wildcat seen up on such or such a holler, or maybe the story would be some crazy man or desperate criminal was loose. Moonshiners started these tales so as to scare the women. They were afraid the women would find the moonshine stills while hunting huckleberries.

No one picks berries anymore; most all the old orchards are gone. Of the fourteen apple trees that grew in my yard when I moved here, only four remain, too old for fruit, very little shade, and almost dangerous to let stand. In fact, during the severe cold weather this past winter we reopened our fireplace, and chopped one of our apple trees into firewood. I almost felt like I was forsaking an old friend.

All fruits and berries were eaten raw, or cooked in syrup, made into jelly and jam, but most were used for dumplings or pies. Peach cobbler, where the slices were baked with layers of biscuit dough. Apples were used in fried pies, apples or apple butter folded into small thin sheets of dough and fried in deep fat. I have also heard these called half-moon pies or moccasin pies. We also used vinegar as a substitute for fruit, making pies or dumplings flavored with vinegar, sugar, and spice. A "barefoot dumpling" was when the balls of dough were cooked in boiling water, containing only salt and lard. Of course, they were better in chicken broth or fresh meat "sop."

We grew corn for feed and bread, but we also used it as a vegetable, canning it and pickling it in brine salt water for winter use, while the kernels were still young enough to be soft. Pickled corn is good fried in a little sugar, but best of all is to eat it as a snack, sitting around the fire at night and biting it directly off the cob. "Gritted bread" (probably from the word grater) was made from young corn; a gritter was made by driving holes in a piece of tin, maybe an empty peach can, with a nail, then fastening the tin to a board. The ears of corn were rubbed over the sharp edges made by the nail holes, to make meal. If the corn was young enough, there was no water needed to be added, just a little salt and baking soda, baked in a greased pan. Eaten with sweet milk, it was a meal in itself. You can use corn to grit until it gets old enough to shell from the cob. After the juice or "milk" on the inside of the grains begins to dry, the meal requires water added, to make a soft dough before baking. Mush is made by adding meal to boiling salt water; drop by spoonful into a bowl of milk, and eat while still hot. Let it get cold, slice it, and fry in fat, and eat as pancakes.

I still have a "gritter." I use it every year. I now put up several packs of "gritted" meal in my deep freezer. In the past our folks would use up all their old meal before the new crop came in, then they must "grit." Now we just do, because it tastes good and helps us to remember.

I guess of all vegetables, beans were the most used. There were many kinds of seeds, from the "bunch" beans grown in the garden, to field beans, planted along with the corn. The stalks of corn make a place for the bean vines to grow. I have already told about "bean stringings" and how beans were dried. Beans were also pickled in brine salt water; large wooden barrels full. We also canned them. Many times, we placed the filled, closed glass jars of beans in a wash tub, filled with water, on a fire outside, and allowed them to cook for several hours.

Then there was a "tough" bean. The hull was too hard to eat. These were used for "soup" beans, cooked by themselves or mixed with the dried beans. When cooking, salt pork or hog's jowl was added. A friend once told me how his mother had him and his brothers and sisters shell these beans. Every night, before being allowed to go to bed, each had to shell enough beans to fill a large cup.

We always raised two crops of cabbage. The later one was planted in early July; planted in the hill and not transplanted. These were "holed away" for winter use. A long trench, or "fur," was made with the plow. The fully grown cabbages were pulled up "by the roots," a few of the bottom leaves broken off. The remaining excess leaves were wrapped around the "head," and placed side by side with the roots turned up, in the hole made by the plow; then dirt was thrown up around the cabbages, leaving part of the stalk and the roots exposed. This way they were easily found and removed. They would stay all winter and keep fresh. Cabbages kept this way have a sweet wholesome flavor that you can get no other way, and far exceeds anything you can get in the supermarket.

And then, of course, there was sauerkraut, cabbage pickled in salt. I also use a little sugar and vinegar. We now put kraut in glass jars, but "back then" we used large churns or crocks or wooden barrels. Our folks would sometimes put the cabbages in the barrel whole, a layer at a time, and cut them up with a shovel. I don't see how our folks ever ate all these many barrels, holes, cans, and sacks full of beans, corn, cabbage, and many other fruits and vegetables that they called "sass"; but they did. And still they were labeled as "poor and starving," by people who did not know what or who they were talking about.

I have known of people that dried cabbage. I remember watching an old man, when I lived at Dwarf, drying cabbage leaves on his housetop. I never did eat any.

Beets were cooked and canned in sugar, spice, water, and vinegar; they were eaten no other way. We served them with "shucky beans" or as a snack. I love to pickle boiled eggs in the liquid where the beets were cooked; the bright red color makes the eggs pretty and gives them a nice flavor. This is a must at Easter for my family.

Tomatoes were thought to be poison by our grandmothers, and were raised only as a flower. We canned the ripe ones to be used in vegetable soup; some added sugar and used it for a dessert. Of course, during the summer they were sliced and served with green beans, or added to slaw. Green tomatoes are good sliced, rolled in meal, to which a little salt and pepper is added, and fried in deep fat. My husband likes them sweetened, I don't. There is a small variety which we call "tommy toes." Green tomatoes were also canned in sugar, spice, and vinegar, sometimes by themselves, sometimes with peppers, cabbage, and other vegetables. We also mixed green tomatoes, green pepper, green cabbage, and etc., and pickled in brine salt water; we called this "pickle Lilly" or "chow chow." No matter what you called it, it was good, fried in grease and eaten with beans and cornbread. We ate cornbread for at least two meals each day. Very few people do this anymore. It's easier to use the toaster, I guess.

Next to the beans, I guess more potatoes were used. They were "kelp over" by holing them away. They were "fried, baked, cooked, roasted in the ashes under the grate, added to soup, and boiled with their jackets on." Sometimes we would take them to school with us and boil them in an empty lard bucket, on the coal heating stove. The teacher would help us eat them at recess.

We "bedded" our sweet potatoes in a "hot bed" made from shucks, manure, and dirt, and covered with fodder and an old quilt. After they began sprouting, the fodder and quilt were removed. When large enough, the plants were then transplanted to "hills" or ridges. Sweet potatoes were baked, roasted, fried in sugar and lard, or cooked with some salt and sugar added. We canned them by cooking them in jars, like the beans. We kept them through the winter in barrels or boxes, each wrapped separate in a piece of paper.

Sweet peppers were eaten raw; stuffed with meat, sausage, and etc.; canned in sugar, spice, water, and vinegar; mixed with other vegetables to make "pickle Lilly" or mixed pickles. Hot pepper or "strong" pepper was eaten as an additive to other vegetables. We also canned it in vinegar, or strung it up on twine, and allowed it to dry for winter use. Some folks like it added to "fresh meat," when cooked. We put a few pods of hot pepper on the top of our barrels or churns of salt pickles. It kept the gnats from bothering them, and also give a good flavor. We added red hot pepper to our paste when we were lining our houses with newspaper and magazines. This kept the mice from eating the paste and ruining the paper. I remember once I had a large kettle of paste, which I had made from flour and water, and had added a large amount of pepper. I had set it on the back of the stove to cool. One of my boys come in from school, took a large spoonful, thinking it was his supper. It really give him a hot mouth; I was sorry for him, but I had to laugh. He said he knew why the mice refused to eat it.

Cushaw and "punkins" were planted in the corn, every fourth hill, every fourth row. The small ones were fed to the hogs or cows. The hard-shell cushaws were chopped into small chunks and cooked, then placed in a pan, covered with sugar and spice, and baked. The soft-shell ones were peeled, sliced, cooked, and mashed, sugar and spice added and called "cushaw butter." Some folks added cooked cushaw or pumpkin to their cornmeal dough, and baked it. "Molassie bread" was made this way, also. Cushaws are better if molasses is substituted for sugar. And, of course, there were "punkin pies." Many cushaws and pumpkins, along with squashes, were dried. A "green" pole was hung by strings over the open fireplace. The cushaws and etc. were sliced into large circles or rings, then hung on this pole. In a few days these were dried, then more were hung up. This way they could be preserved for winter use, cooked with sugar and lard added; again, maybe salt pork or hog's jowl—very good. I have seen bushels of dried cushaws and "punkins" hung up in the smokehouse in the winter. In the spring, it would have all been eaten.

Asparagus was only grown as a shrub in the yard, never eaten. The full-grown bush, with the green fern-like leaves and bright seed pod, is very beautiful. I have heard the old folks say, "You know, there are folks who eat 'spar' grass' when the sprouts are little." Yet, I never knew of anyone trying it.

Artichokes to us is the potato-like roots of a tall plant, which has beautiful yellow flowers that resemble daisies. It was only eaten raw, as a snack.

Cucumbers were sweet-pickled and canned; used with other vegetables for "mixed pickles"; also pickled in brine salt; eaten raw, sliced, and served with green beans, or in slaw.

Peas were one of the earliest seeds to be planted, sometimes as early as February. We grew a tender-hull kind, that can be cooked like string beans, hull and all. We very seldom shelled them. Peas are delicious cooked together with very small young potatoes.

We grew two crops of turnips, a few planted in ridges for summer use. Then in the fall a larger crop, "broadcasting" the seed over maybe the now empty garden. The tops were cooked for greens, or as we say "salet"; the roots were holed away or put in the cellar. The cold weather does not hurt turnips; they keep growing almost all winter. I like to cook them together, the tops and roots, when the turnips are small.

I don't think our folks used carrots until the early twenties, and very few people liked them. My boys loved them raw. Often, when they returned from school hungry as all kids are, they would come through the garden and pull up a handful of carrots.

Rhubarb we called "pie plants." Every garden had a long row, used for pies or dumplings, fried as apples, mixed with strawberries to make jelly. It "came in" just as most of the winter food was used up, and the new garden was still too young to use. It was supposed to be good for you; help to cure "spring fever."

Some of us grow a few gourds just for the fun of it, but our forefathers grew them to be used. The larger ones would hold lard, salt, soft soap, meal, molasses, or whatever. The small long-handled ones were water dippers. A small round egg-shaped kind, we called "hen foolers" because we used them for nest eggs.

There were many different kinds of onions. Fall and winter onions grew through the winter, and could be eaten green. "Tater onions" got its name for the way the new ones grew in a cluster around the old one; they were kept for the roots. "Spring shell-lots" were very early and very small.

Onions were eaten as a dish, not an additive; fried either while green or after grown, not as "onion rings" as now used. To keep for winter, they were pulled while there was still some top remaining, tied in bunches, and hung from nails in the barn or smokehouse. They become better after being allowed to freeze. Onions were used as a medicine, roasted, mashed, and made into a poltice placed on the chest, to help "break up" a cold. Onion soup was also used for a cold or tonsillitis.

Then there were wild greens or "salet." There are many different kinds, sometimes the same plant was known by a different name by different people. "Plantin" is the one used most, a small thick leaf with a very distinct flavor, a little like cabbage. Then there was "sheep's leg," "groundhog ear," and "speckled dock," to be cooked. Poke salet had to be used very carefully, because it could be poison; it was cooked in one water, washed and cooked again, then fried in a lot of lard. If eaten too often, it can become a laxative. The stalks were also good peeled, rolled in meal, and fried. "Crow's foot," "shoestring," "chicken salet," and "creases" were eaten raw, cut up, salt added, and then "killed" by pouring real hot grease over them.

In my father's time hogs were allowed to run wild. There were no stock laws. The gardens and corn fields were fenced in; all the "stock" ran loose. Each man had a "mark" so as to tell his own. The pig's ear was either notched or split, some used both; some the left ear, someone else the right, maybe both, but no two exactly alike. When a sow mothered a "gang" of pigs, if the owner did not catch the small ones and mark them in his own mark before they were weaned, and they had quit running with the mother, they were then accepted as "wild pigs"; anyone who caught them was the owner. He could put his mark on them or butcher them for food. Wild hogs grew very fat on "mast," nuts and roots they found in the woods. I thought this gave the meat a good flavor, but I have talked with some folks that said this was not so; they were better if brought in and fed corn a few weeks before butchering them.

More beef and sheep were used for meat by the older generations than we did, but chicken and dumplings was counted the best dish of any. I have seen my folks cook as many as sixteen grown hens at one time, in an old-fashioned iron "mink" kettle, when there was a big crowd at a wedding, funeral, or family "get-together."

No, our folks on Caney, in the past, had plenty of good wholesome food. Maybe they knew nothing about vitamins or a balanced diet, but they do not deserve to be called "poor and starving." They worked hard to grow and put away food, and were not "lazy and shiftless."

OUR PETS

It seems as if my children had more interesting pets than most mountain children. Last night one of my sons said, "Mom, be sure and write about our animal friends." I always let them have all the pets they wanted; many times I would have to do the taking care of them, but I thought it would teach them love and consideration for others.

Besides the dogs and cats, there were rabbits, groundhogs, turtles, and believe it or not, a fox, fish, hoot owl, and a gang of chicken hawks.

I think Trexie was the most interesting pet of all times. The day that Milburn and his friend, Paul Jacobs, were supposed to be attending their eighth-grade graduation, they went hunting. As me and Paul's mother watched and waited, they still had not returned. Then when it was too late for them to go to school, they came in, with three little gray foxes, so small they had not even opened their eyes. The boys were so proud of themselves, and had forgotten all about their graduation. They told how they had found the mother fox, dead at the mouth of the den. Someone had shot her, but she managed to return to her babies before dying. The boys had heard the whimpering and crying of the young foxes, and dug them out.

Paul took one fox home with him. It lived for several months, but never did become tame.

Common Folks

I took care of the other two. I made them a warm bed, with a towel and hot water bag. I fed them with a medicine dropper, warm milk, and water. One died, but the other lived for almost five years.

We named her Trexie. She thought she was a person. After getting too large for her box, she had the run of the house. I always shut the door, not that she would have gone out, but I could not trust the neighbor's dogs.

She learned to climb up on the backs of our chairs and sleep. If she found someone not of the family sitting in the chair, she would run down, quick as a wink, and hide under the bed.

If she got up in my lap and I was reading a book or magazine, she would "guile" up on the book, and look so innocent, as if she knew what she was doing. If I was sewing, she would drag my cloth out of her way and lay down. If I happened to drop my dish cloth or towel, she would snatch it up and go back under the bed with it.

My husband fixed a collar for her neck and ran a chain through it, so she could be fastened to the clothes line, thus giving her room to run. When she got after the chickens, her natural instinct told her to kill them, but we only had to scold her and she stopped.

I also had a strap made, one end fitting around her neck and the other around my wrist. This way I could feel safe to take her with me wherever I went. I loved to watch the astonishment on people's faces when I went to Hazard or Prestonsburg with Trexie on my shoulder, or peeping out of the truck window.

The boys also taught her to drink from a bottle (she loved soda pop), holding the bottle with her front paws. We had a small grocery store, and all the kids saved the last of their pop for Trexie just to see her drink it. This may have been what caused her death, for it was not the natural food for a fox.

The kids also liked to give her balloons to play with. She would roll them over the floor and toss them in the air. When they burst she would run and hide.

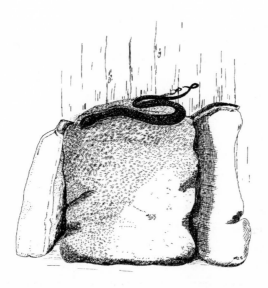

One evening, real late, we all returned from Hindman, where we had gone to a movie, to find Trexie had gotten out of her cage and was nowhere to be found. We called and called. We just gave up and knew some dogs had killed her. Milburn went to milk. He had his bucket full of milk, and turned to pick it up, and there sat Trexie, quietly drinking the nice warm foamy milk. No one cared that the rest of the milk had to be given to the pigs and we did without the next day.

Next there was Pete, a large blacksnake. We sold a lot of feed in our small grocery store, hundreds of sacks of corn chop, meddlins, and dairy feed. The rats and mice were a problem, until Pete moved in. Many times we would have to take a broom handle and gently remove him from the top of a bag of feed. He got where he was not afraid of humans. He became very fat and large on his diet of rats and mice. Every winter he must have had a hole under the building or beneath the roots of the large beech trees just back of the store.

Every spring, when Pete came back out of his winter retreat, we counted it as a privilege to be the first ones to greet him. He lived for many years, coming and going his own way. I had always taught my children the difference between poison snakes and friendly ones, and to not kill or be afraid of the good ones. But someone must not have felt that way. One Sunday we came home from church to find Old Pete dead, surrounded by rocks, showing how he had been beaten to death. I hope he did not think it was us who betrayed his friendship. He had learned to trust humans, and so did not know to try to get away from the rocks being thrown at him.

The children were always so hurt when their pets died, that I sometimes wonder if it was worth it all. But death is a part of life. And so we must learn to meet it, even at a young age.

When Len was about five he had a small turtle that he kept in my washtubs, between wash days, and in a jar then. He fed it lettuce and cabbage leaves. Once, we were going on a visit to my sister's in Virginia, and were going to be gone for a few weeks. Len was very concerned about leaving his turtle. Vernon and his cousin, Miles, were going to keep house while we were gone, and repair our fence for us. Len kept repeating instructions on how to take care of his turtle. Over and over again, he made Vernon to promise to not forget to feed it. The day before we returned, Miles and Vernon found one of the largest tarpins I ever saw in my life. Thinking to have some fun out of Len, they removed his turtle to a safe place, and placed the monster one in the washtub. As soon as Len got home he ran to the tub. "Oh brother," he screamed, "I did not mean for you to feed it that much."

When we first moved from our farm to our home close to the college, someone gave Losses three little ducks. These three soon became a flock of over thirty. I ended up with several feather beds, which I still have, and many big fluffy feather pillows.

The college had started a building, and for several years, did not get farther along with it than the rock walls of the foundation.

This made a fine roosting place for my ducks. It also was a secret meeting place for the boys and girls at the college. Mrs. Lloyd had a very strict rule that her students did not have dates. This did not keep them from getting together, it only caused them to hide. Ducks are better than dogs to give warning when someone comes around after dark. Before I knew what was happening, the girls had killed most of my ducks. I sold what few I had left. Yes, I know it's hard to believe, seeing the college as it is today, that less than twenty-five years ago, ducks could find a home on its premises.

Of the many dogs that came and went, I think I should mention a few. Koley was a little black terrier that became a part of our family the same week Orbin was born, and was always considered as being his dog. He lived to be fifteen years old. I taught him to not eat anything unless I told him it was his. Once, when I spent a week in the hospital, my sister kept putting his food in his dish, but did not say, "This is for you," and hungry as he must have been, he refused to eat it. I wonder if he would have starved to death if I had not learned in time and explained to her.

Ruff was Len's dog. Never were there two more close friends. He went to school with Len, like Mary's Little Lamb, every day for three years, lying under his seat, following him to the blackboard. My oldest son was the teacher. In order to please Len, he made out a report card for Ruff, much to the amusement of all the school. I had to pack a lunch for the dog also, and if I did not, Len gave him his. All the children saved their crusts and bones for Ruff. He entered into all their games at recess. He really thought he was a person. And so did we.

John D. is a rabbit, a large pink stuffed rabbit, long floppy ears, two large black buttons for eyes. No, he does not have the breath of life, but he nor any of our family realized this, for he was immortalized by the love Len had for him. He was given to Len on his second Easter by Joleen Cornett, now Joleen Pridemore. I don't know where Len got the name John D. I had never heard the name then. Later, Willie was to work for a man by that name.

I always say God sent me a family of four boys, and He must have been satisfied with the way I was bringing them up, because He sent me Len as an extra bonus when the others were almost grown up. As Len had no playmates his age, John D. was a real live person to him. He watched T.V. with him, slept with him, went everywhere he went, even to the hospital. The nurses had to give John D. a shot every time Len had one, and if John D. did not cry, then Len would not.

He fed his rabbit everything he ate, except ice cream. He said John D. did not like ice cream.

He pulled him around by one ear, until poor old John D. became almost a total wreck. He began to look so ragged, we became ashamed for folks to see him. I went to Hindman and bought another one almost like John D., thinking I could get him to swap. Len would not even give the new rabbit a name, just called him John D.'s brother. One day he took the pretty new rabbit out to the creek bank and threw him in, then marched back into the house and told me, "John D.'s brother got drowned."

A few months ago I was rambling around up in the attic and found John D. I brought him down, sewed up his wounds, replaced his eyes, gave him a bath, dressed him in some of Len's baby clothes, and hung him on my living room wall. I called on the daughters-in-law and asked them did they remember John D. And they all answered, "Yes, who could forget him?" When I asked Vernon, he said, "As many times as I had to go out in the yard and hunt him, before Len would go to sleep? Sure, I remember him."

All this may not be of any interest to anyone except my own family, but I wanted to write it, to prove we are just "common folks."